God and the Self in Hegel

SUNY series in Contemporary Continental Philosophy

Dennis J. Schmidt, editor

# God and the Self in Hegel

Beyond Subjectivism

Paolo Diego Bubbio

Published by State University of New York Press, Albany

© 2017 State University of New York

All rights reserved

Printed in the United States of America

No part of this book may be used or reproduced in any manner whatsoever without written permission. No part of this book may be stored in a retrieval system or transmitted in any form or by any means including electronic, electrostatic, magnetic tape, mechanical, photocopying, recording, or otherwise without the prior permission in writing of the publisher.

For information, contact State University of New York Press, Albany, NY
www.sunypress.edu

Production, Eileen Nizer
Marketing, Kate R. Seburyamo

### Library of Congress Cataloging-in-Publication Data

Names: Bubbio, Paolo Diego, 1974– author.
Title: God and the self in Hegel : beyond subjectivism / by Paolo Diego Bubbio.
Description: Albany, NY : State University of New York, 2017. | Series: SUNY series in contemporary Continental philosophy | Includes bibliographical references and index.
Identifiers: LCCN 2016031501 (print) | LCCN 2017020478 (ebook) | ISBN 9781438465258 (hardcover : alk. paper) | ISBN 9781438465241 (pbk. : alk. paper) | ISBN 9781438465265 (ebook)
Subjects: LCSH: Hegel, Georg Wilhelm Friedrich, 1770–1831. | Religion—Philosophy. | Theology.
Classification: LCC B2949.R3 (ebook) | LCC B2949.R3 B83 2017 (print) | DDC 210.92—dc23
LC record available at https://lccn.loc.gov/2016031501

10 9 8 7 6 5 4 3 2 1

# Contents

| | |
|---|---|
| Abbreviations for Hegel's Primary Texts | vii |
| Acknowledgments | xi |
| Introduction | 1 |
| Chapter 1  Christ as Symbol in Kant's Religion | 13 |
| Chapter 2  Hegel's Conception of God | 31 |
| Chapter 3  The Reality of Religion in Hegel's Idealist Metaphysics | 55 |
| Chapter 4  Hegel's Version of the Ontological Argument for the Existence of God | 85 |
| Chapter 5  The Trinity and the "I" | 105 |
| Chapter 6  The Death of God and Recognition of the Self | 125 |
| Chapter 7  Beyond Subjectivism | 147 |
| Chapter 8  The Relevance of Hegel's Philosophy of Religion Today | 161 |
| Notes | 177 |
| Bibliography | 213 |
| Index | 225 |

# Abbreviations for Hegel's Primary Texts

## Hegel's Main Works

For these works, I give the volume and page number from the German *Werke in zwanzig Bänden* (W), edited by E. Moldenhauer and K. M. Michel (Frankfurt: Suhrkamp, 1969–1971), followed by the page number of the equivalent publication in English translation. These works are signified as follows:

E I  *Enzyklopädie der philosophischen Wissenschaften I* (W 8). Translated by K. Brinkmann and D. O. Dahlstrom as *The Encyclopedia of Logic* (Cambridge: Cambridge University Press, 2010).

E III  *Enzyklopädie der philosophischen Wissenschaften III* (W 10). Translated by W. Wallace and A. V. Miller, revised by Michael Inwood, as *Philosophy of Mind*. Part III of the *Encyclopedia of the Philosophical Sciences* (New York: Oxford University Press, 2007).

FS  *Frühe Schriften* (W 1).

GP  *Vorlesungen über die Geschichte der Philosophie* (W 18–20).

  LHP  Translated by H. S. Haldane as *Lectures on the History of Philosophy* (Lincoln: University of Nebraska Press, 1995).

  ILHP  Partially translated by T. M. Knox and A. V. Miller as *Introduction to the Lectures on the History of Philosophy* (Oxford: Clarendon, 1987).

GW	*Glauben und Wissen.* In *Jenaer Schriften* (W 2). Translated by Walter Cerf and H. S. Harris as *Faith and Knowledge* (Albany: State University of New York Press, 1977).

L	*Wissenschaft der Logik* (W 5–6). Translated by George di Giovanni as *Science of Logic* (Cambridge: Cambridge University Press, 2010).

PG	*Phänomenologie des Geistes* (W 3). Translated by A. V. Miller as *Phenomenology of Spirit* (Oxford: Oxford University Press, 1977).

R	*Grundlinien der Philosophie des Rechts* (W 7). Translated by H. B. Nisbet, edited by Allen W. Wood, as *Elements of the Philosophy of Right* (Cambridge: Cambridge University Press, 1991).

VSF	*Vergleichung des Schellingschen Prinzips der Philosophie mit dem Fichteschen.* In *Jenaer Schriften* (W 2). Translated by H. S. Harris and Walter Cerf as *The Difference between Fichte's and Schelling's System of Philosophy* (Albany: State University of New York Press, 1977).

## Hegel's Lectures

For these works in general (including the *Lectures on the Philosophy of Religion*), I refer to the more recent German edition of Hegel's works, *Gesammelte Werke* (GeW) (Hamburg: Felix Meiner, 1968–), and to *Vorlesungen: Ausgewählte Nachschriften und Manuskripte* (V) (Hamburg: Felix Meiner, 1968–). The page number from the German edition is followed by the page number from the corresponding English translation. These works are signified as follows:

JS-III	*Jenaer Systementwürfe III* (GeW 8), edited by R. P. Horstmann. Translated and edited by Leo Rauch as *Hegel and the Human Spirit: A Translation of the Jena Lectures on the Philosophy of Spirit (1805–6) with Commentary* (Detroit: Wayne State University Press, 1983).

Rel I, II, III	*Vorlesungen über die Philosophie der Religion* (V 3–5), edited by Walter Jaeschke. Hamburg: Felix Meiner, 1984. Translated by R. F. Brown, P. C. Hodgson, and J. M. Stewart, with the assistance of J. P. Fitzer and H. S. Harris, edited by P. C. Hodgson, as *Lectures on the Philosophy of Religion*, 3 vols. (Berkeley: University of California Press, 1984–1985).

VBD  *Vorlesungen über die Beweise vom Dasein Gottes*, in *Vorlesungsmanuskripte II (1816–1831)* (GeW 18), edited by Walter Jaeschke. Translated by Peter C. Hodgson as *Lectures on the Proofs of the Existence of God* (Oxford: Oxford University Press, 2007).

VPG  *Vorlesungen über die Philosophie des Geistes 1827–8* (V 13), edited by B. Tuschling. Hamburg: Felix Meiner, 1994. Translated by R. R. Williams as *Lectures on the Philosophy of Spirit 1827* (Oxford: Oxford University Press, 2007).

For the *Lectures on the History of Philosophy*, I refer, when possible, to the more recent and accurate German edition by Pierre Garniron and Walter Jaeschke (VGP), and to the corresponding English translation. This edition, however, is limited to the 1825–1826 lectures. For the material not included in this edition, I refer to the Moldenhauer-Michel edition (GP; see p. vii) for the German text and to the corresponding English translation (LHP). I refer to Knox's partial translation (ILHP; see p. vii) when I find it more appropriate. Abbreviation is as follows:

VGP  *Vorlesungen über die Geschichte der Philosophie 1825–1826* (V 6–9), edited by Pierre Garniron and Walter Jaeschke. Translated by R. F. Brown as *Lectures on the History of Philosophy 1825–1826*, 3 vols. (Oxford: Oxford University Press, 2009).

For the *Lectures on the Philosophy of World History*, I refer, when possible, to the recent German edition edited by Dring, Brehmer, and Seelmann, and to its corresponding translation by Robert F. Brown and Peter C. Hodgson. For the material not yet included in GeW, I refer to the Lasson edition (Hamburg: Felix Meiner Verlag, 1968) for the German text, and to its corresponding English translation, *Lectures on the Philosophy of History*, translated by J. Sibree (New York: Dover 1962). These works are signified as follows:

VPW  *Vorlesungen über die Philosophie der Weltgeschichte* (V 12), edited by Karl Heinz Dring, Karl Brehmer, and Hoo Nam Seelmann

(Hamburg: Felix Meiner, 1996). Translated and edited by Robert F. Brown and Peter C. Hodgson as *Lectures on the Philosophy of World History* (Oxford: Clarendon Press, 2011).

VPW Lasson   *Vorlesungen über die Philosophie der Weltgeschichte*, edited by Georg Lasson (Hamburg: Felix Meiner, 1968). Translated by J. Sibree as *Lectures on the Philosophy of History* (New York: Dover 1962).

## Hegel's Other Writings

B I–IV   *Briefe von und an Hegel*, edited by Johannes Hoffmeister, 4 vols. (Hamburg: Felix Meiner, 1969). Translated by Clark Butler and Christiane Seiler as *Hegel: The Letters* (Bloomington: Indiana University Press, 1984).

If I have altered an English translation sourced from the previous works or provided a translation that better renders the German text than any of these works, I provide details of the alteration or alternative in an endnote. When a single page or page range is given in a citation, this is the German page number or page range and there is no published English translation available for the passage quoted. In those few cases, the translation is mine.

# Acknowledgments

I wish to thank a number of people for their help and encouragement during the preparation of this book.

While I had acquired a textbook-based knowledge of Hegel's philosophy during my undergraduate years, I was properly introduced to Hegel by Maurizio Pagano in a series of conversations that started in 2003—conversations that have continued and intensified over the years. I'm grateful to Maurizio for his ongoing willingness to engage in such conversations, even when my approach was somehow diverging from his own.

My encounter with Paul Redding in 2006, when I joined the Department of Philosophy at The University of Sydney, has been seminal for my understanding of the Anglo-American interpretations of Hegel's philosophy. I am grateful to Paul for his mentorship and for many years of fruitful collaboration.

Proper research for this book commenced by way of a Discovery Project grant that Paul Redding and I secured from the Australian Research Council in 2009 (DP0984296, "The God of Hegel's Post-Kantian Idealism"). I enjoyed our collaborative work between 2009 and 2012, and while this book is the outcome of my engagement with that project, it is also the result of the development of my research interests in a slightly different direction, which I took when I became convinced that the question of the "I" was also central for Hegel's account of religion and God. Research for this book continued, therefore, by way of an Australian Research Council Future Fellowship Project (FT110100418, "The Quest for the 'I': Reaching a Better Understanding of the Self through Hegel and Heidegger," 2012–2016).

In 2012 I moved to Western Sydney University. I wish to thank all my colleagues in the Philosophy Research Initiative for their support, enthusiasm, and for their collective capacity to build a collegial and friendly environment. I am particularly grateful to my colleague and friend Dimitris Vardoulakis, who has never ceased to contrast my pessimistic attitude with his determination and resilience.

Special thanks are also due to Terry Pinkard, who read the manuscript of my book during my Visiting Scholarship at Georgetown University in September 2015, and to Stephen Houlgate, who did the same during his visit to Western Sydney University in March 2016. From both I received many invaluable comments.

I have also been helped by a number of other individuals who offered suggestions about specific sections of the book along the way. I cannot thank them all, but let me at least mention Damion Buterin, Alfredo Ferrarin, Sebastian Gardner, Heikki Ikaheimo, Luca Illetterati, Simon Lumsden, Douglas Moggach, Dalia Nassar, Stephen Palmquist, and Robert Williams. A special thank-you is also due to the colleagues of the Hegel Studies Lab hosted at the University of Eastern Piedmont: their annual conferences have always represented a wonderful opportunity to obtain valuable feedback.

I am also very grateful to Dennis Schmidt, series editor, and Andrew Kenyon, acquiring editor, at State University of New York Press, and to the three anonymous scholars who acted as manuscript readers for the press.

During the long engagement with this project, I have also received important emotional support from a number of friends: Stephen Buckle, Damian Byers, Luigi Dentis, Fabrizio Gallino, Andrea Lasagna, Daniele Limerutti, Emanuele Miroglio, and Alessandro Rodani. If Hegel is right that a "true friend" is "someone whose way of acting conforms to the concept of friendship," they are definitely true friends!

Finally, I wish to thank my family. My children, Sofia and Alex, filled my life with positivity and fun; I should be grateful for their patience, most notably to Sofia, who never ceased to tell me that "it will be a great book," despite the fact that my engagement with it inevitably subtracted time that would otherwise have been devoted to playing with her and her brother. And I thank my wife, Silvia, for her help, support, and understanding throughout the time of this book's preparation.

Some of the chapters that follow recast material that had appeared earlier, often in a different form, in other settings. I thank the following journals and publishers for allowing me to draw on that material:

The first and second sections of chapter 3 are an extended version of "The Reality of Religion in Hegel's Idealist Metaphysics," *Hegel Bulletin*

37, no. 2 (2016): 232–257, with kind permission from Cambridge Journals. The third section draws on ideas already included in the final section of "God, Incarnation, and Metaphysics in Hegel's Philosophy of Religion," *Sophia: International Journal of Philosophy and Traditions* 53, no. 4 (2014): 515–33 (with kind permission from Springer Science+Business Media).

The first section of chapter 4 is an altered and expanded version of the first section that I wrote for a paper I coauthored with Paul Redding: "Hegel and the Ontological Argument on the Existence of God," *Religious Studies: An International Journal for the Philosophy of Religion* 50, no. 4 (2014): 465–86 (with kind permission from Paul Redding and Cambridge Journals). The other sections of chapter 4 then develop the topic in a different direction.

A version of chapter 5 appeared as "Hegel, the Trinity, and the 'I,'" *International Journal for Philosophy of Religion* 76, no. 2 (2014): 129–50 (with kind permission from Springer Science+Business Media).

Chapter 6 is an extended version of "Hegel: Death of God and Recognition of the Self," *International Journal of Philosophical Studies* 23, no. 5 (2015): 689–706.

Chapter 7 draws on the first half of "Hegel, Heidegger, and the 'I': Preliminary Reflections for a New Paradigm of the Self," *Philosophy Today* 59, no. 1 (2015): 73–90.

The second section of chapter 8 includes some ideas that were already included in "Metaphilosophical Reflections on Theism and Atheism in the Current Debate," in *Politics and Religion in the New Century: Philosophical Perspectives*, ed. P. Quadrio and C. Besseling (Sydney: Sydney University Press, 2009), 354–81.

# Introduction

Hegel famously begins the preface to the *Phenomenology of Spirit* by saying that, although "it is customary to preface a work with an explanation of the author's aim, why he wrote the book, and the relationship in which he believes it to stand to other earlier or contemporary treatises on the same subject," in the case of a philosophical work, however, "such an explanation seems not only superfluous but, in view of the nature of the subject-matter, even inappropriate and misleading." In fact, Hegel explains, "whatever might appropriately be said about philosophy in a preface—say a historical statement of the main drift and the point of view, the general content and results, a string of random assertions and assurances about truth—none of this can be accepted as the way in which to expound philosophical truth." Even more importantly, Hegel continues, in philosophy "more than in any of the other sciences," that which is salient about its subject matter is expressed "in the aim and the final results, the execution being by contrast really the unessential factor" (PG, 3:11/1). In this introduction, I will mostly follow Hegel's lead in this respect, especially in relation to his claim that what is salient about a book is expressed "in the aim"—but I will not be entirely consistent with Hegel's suggestions, and I will also provide some "inappropriate" (according to Hegel's definition) explanations, hoping that they will not be too "misleading" (after all, Hegel *himself* does something of that sort in the remaining part of his preface to the *Phenomenology*).

This is a book about *Hegel's philosophy*; more specifically, it is about some aspects of his *philosophy of religion*. Clearly, it would be out of line to claim that this is an original topic. A quick look at the shelves of a university library or a specialized (or even semi-specialized) bookshop will make clear that there is no shortage of volumes addressing this or that specific aspect of Hegel's philosophy; and if it is true that religion is probably not one of the most popular subjects of investigation in Hegel scholarship, even under this respect the corpus of secondary literature is solid. Indeed, as O'Regan puts it in the introduction to his influential *The Heterodox Hegel*, "the museum of interpretive shapes [. . .] is showing signs of overcrowding."[1] And since O'Regan wrote these words in 1994, the "overcrowding" of interpretations has continued. In this context, one might legitimately wonder whether it is appropriate to contribute to that "overcrowding" by writing a book that not only addresses some of the most central themes of Hegel's philosophical project but also does that from an angle—that of religion—which is sometimes regarded "marginal" for a consideration of Hegel that aims to go beyond the disciplinary field of the history of philosophy.

The only possible answer to this skeptical consideration is, I believe, the open admission that a book such as this one may be written only by someone who thinks that some aspects of Hegel's philosophy may contribute to the current philosophical debate, and that a philosophical work that strives to clarify those elements of Hegel's projects that have hitherto remained opaque or not completely "unpacked" would enable the identification of such contribution. Specifically, I think that Hegel's philosophy of religion effectively represents an important perspective on the nature of religion, one that has been excluded from consideration for more than a century, because of misunderstandings. Several of these misunderstandings have already been clarified by other scholarly works; from this point of view, the intent of the present book is to provide a contribution to such an enterprise. Also, and perhaps less modestly, this book has the ambition to show to what extent Hegel's philosophical project on religion is still relevant today.

My last disclosing statement is already indicative of the kind of methodological approach that I adopt in this study. The question of method deserves to be addressed, not least because recently there has been a flurry of statements either endorsing or criticizing various methodological approaches to Hegel's philosophy. A good, albeit not neutral, survey of the most prominent positions in the context of such a debate can be found in Robert Williams's recent book, *Tragedy, Recognition, and the Death of God*.[2] Williams addresses Beiser's criticism of those Anglophone scholars whose concern is "to emasculate, domesticate, and sanitize" German idealism, "to make it weak, safe, and clean for home consumption":[3] methodologically, these scholars are regarded as providing "text-free" reconstructions of Hegel's thought that fit their own philosophical agenda. To this criticism, Pippin has replied that "there is nothing to be gained by mere pious paraphrase of Hegel's texts in his own or in even more obscure terms."[4] Pippin has also pointed out that "submissive textualism/historicism" or a "text-free" interpretation are not the only alternatives[5]—and Williams agrees with Pippin on this point; however, Williams argues, "this observation scarcely disposes of Beiser's question: whether, in view of the stubborn irreducibility of metaphysical elements in Hegel—*including religion and theology*—non-metaphysical interpretations of Hegel are tenable."[6] Moreover, according to Williams, not even Beiser does justice to the role of religion and theology in Hegel's philosophy, because "Beiser excludes theology from the list of metaphysical topics he deems essential for a proper understanding of Hegel."[7]

Here at stake are two questions that, much as they are interrelated, are, at least in principle, distinct. The first is the properly *methodological* question, that is, which method or approach is more appropriate to deal with Hegel's philosophy? The other question is the broader *interpretative* one, that is, are the specific interpretations of Hegel (those that Williams refers to as "non-metaphysical") tenable, sustainable, and ultimately legitimate, once Hegel's view on religion is adequately appreciated and taken into consideration? How does the present study stand in relation to these two questions?

Regarding the *former* (the properly methodological question), I have tried to avoid that which Kristeller called the "ventriloquist approach," in which the interpreter reads her own views into a thinker and "discovers" them there.[8] On the other hand, however, I remain deeply convinced of the validity of Gadamer's hermeneutic principle of the "fusion of horizons" (*Horizontverschmelzung*):[9] in interpreting a text, one can never completely "step out" of one's own horizon or background, and this inevitably influences one's interpretation of the text; at the same time, nevertheless, the interpreter's horizon is inevitably modified by the encounter with the text. The outcome of this encounter is precisely a *fusion of horizons*, and the formation of a new context of meaning. Understanding always implies a process of mediation, and as such, it can never achieve a final completion or direct transparency. The adoption of this principle is also consistent, I think, with the spirit of Hegel's philosophy (despite Gadamer's claims to the contrary).[10] Therefore, the outcome of my encounter with Hegel's reflection on religion is not, and does not aim to be, an exhaustive reconstruction of Hegel's philosophy of religion. Rather, my aim has been to identify a movement, as it were, within Hegel's philosophy of religion, and while I have analyzed such movement in its own right and in its own historical and philosophical context, I have also become convinced that it could be very relevant for *our own* historical and philosophical context.

The methodological approach is clearly important, but once the two extremes (that is, "submissive textualism/historicism" and "text-free" interpretation) are excluded, one is left with a (still wide) range of approaches that cannot be easily dismissed as illegitimate. Therefore, when the *latter* question mentioned earlier (the broader *interpretative* question) is considered, one is led to admit that, while the chosen methodological approach influences, to some extent, the outcome of one's interpretative enterprise (that is, what one takes Hegel's fundamental philosophical project to be), ultimately it is precisely *this* outcome that matters: its historical appropriateness, as well as its internal consistency. The range of interpretative outcomes of Hegel scholarship is impressively diverse. Without venturing into a detailed discussion of the various positions—something that I do later in the book, in relation to the question of the status of religious claims and notions in Hegel's philosophy (especially in chapter 3)—here I refer, for the sake of brevity, to the informative taxonomy provided by Redding.[11]

Redding identifies three main streams in contemporary Hegel scholarship: the *traditional* metaphysical, the "revisionist" *non*-metaphysical (or "post-Kantian"), and the *revised* metaphysical view. In the traditional metaphysical view, Hegel is seen as offering a metaphysico-religious view of Absolute Spirit "as the ultimate reality that we can come to know through pure thought processes alone" and "as an advocate of an idea concerning the logically necessitated teleological course" of the history of the objective world, which, in turn, "had to be understood as conceptually informed." Redding mentions Charles Taylor as an example of this interpretative attitude, and he adds that "aspects of it can be seen reflected in the contemporary approaches of Frederick Beiser and Rolf-Peter Horstmann."[12] The revisionist or "post-Kantian" view regards Hegel "as both accepting and *extending* Kant's critique, ultimately turning it against the residual 'dogmatically metaphysical' aspects of Kant's own philosophy."[13] This interpretation has been pioneered by North American Hegel scholars such as Robert Pippin[14] and Terry Pinkard,[15] but Redding argues that a broadly similar view has also been put forward, from an analytic perspective, by Robert Brandom.[16] Despite the differences among these interpreters, the characteristic feature of this interpretation seems to be a conception of Hegel's philosophy as extending Kant's transcendental program to include historical and social forms in the condition of human "mindedness." Therefore, the subject of Hegel's philosophical investigation is regarded to be such mindedness, rather than supposedly fundamental "structures" of the world.

The revisionist/post-Kantian view has often been criticized on two fronts: first, by proponents of a *revised* metaphysical (or "conceptual realist") view, who usually appeal to the conceptual instruments of contemporary analytic metaphysics to argue for Hegel's philosophical inquiry into fundamental "structures" of the world itself;[17] and second, by defenders of a more traditional approach, who consider the revisionist/post-Kantian view as "deflationary,"[18] that is, as presenting a version of Hegel that Desmond suggestively calls "Hegel Lite": "Hegel Lite is a watered down version of Hegel, suitably drained of the headier religious and metaphysical intoxicants, just about palatable to the middling tastes of the last professors."[19] And while there is, among the large majority of Hegel's interpreters, an across-the-board agreement about the importance of Kant's critique of dogmatic metaphysics for Hegel, the advocates of the revisionist/post-Kantian interpretation are often considered guilty (to use another suggestive expression, offered this time by Beiser) of having "thrown the baby of metaphysics out with the bathwater of pre-Kantian dogmatism."[20] Insofar as a philosophically interpreted religion is traditionally regarded as advancing metaphysical claims, the impact of this interpretative debate on the role of theology within Hegel's system is clear, and Williams expresses it as follows: "Beiser agrees with Hegel (and with me) when he asserts that if theology is as central to Hegel's project as it appears to be and as he claims it is, non-metaphysical interpretations of Hegel are untenable."[21]

I also agree with Williams (and with Beiser, and with Hegel) on this issue: non-metaphysical interpretations of Hegel are untenable, because Hegel is indeed committed to a metaphysical project. But I also agree, and even more so, with Redding, when he points out that it is not clear which issues dividing the two interpretative trends "are substantive and which are ultimately verbal."[22] After all, even Pippin explicitly rejects an "anti-metaphysical" interpretation of Hegel. As early as 1989, in fact, Pippin openly critiqued Hartmann's "non-metaphysical" view[23]—effectively a "category theory" considered in isolation from any account of reality—and wrote: "the evidence is overwhelming that he [Hegel] would reject any construal of it [Absolute Idealism] as a particular way of uncovering and analyzing our 'thought game.'" Thus, Pippin continues, a non-metaphysical approach "leaves too much of Hegel's problem with 'objectivity,' or the epistemological status of the Notion, unexplained."[24] There is, of course, a *broader* sense in which Pippin has always denied that Hegel has a metaphysics—effectively denying that he has what Kant calls *dogmatic* metaphysics.

In other words, the question here is what we mean by "metaphysics." Once it is assumed that Hegel is not merely reiterating a pre-Kantian *dogmatic* form of metaphysics, the point of contention becomes either one concerned with terminology (that is, whether it is appropriate to use the term "metaphysis" to refer to Hegel's distinctive philosophical project in general, and to do so without adding further qualifications), or one concerned more specifically with the meaning of Hegel's particular claims and how they fit within Hegel's general project (regardless of the name with which we define it).

In this light, whether the position of a *specific* "revisionist/post-Kantian" interpreter is effectively "non-metaphysical" is open to debate, but investigating this matter would take us too far from the main question that this work is meant to address. An analysis of some of Hegel's tenets and their relevance within Hegel's overall project (including the central question of the possibility of a post-Kantian metaphysics) is occasionally pursued in the book. In general, I incline toward a *qualified revisionist* interpretation of Hegel's project. The term "qualified revisionist" was coined by Redding[25] to refer to Longuenesse's tenet that Hegel's metaphysics is "an investigation of the universal determinations of thought at work in any attempt to think what is." In short, "metaphysics after Kant is a science of being as being thought."[26] The definition of "qualified revisionist" can be extended to Redding himself: in fact, Redding sees Hegel as preserving the empirical realism of Kant's account, while yet denying that thinking allows us to access a mind-independent reality. Within the (still broad) interpretative framework of a qualified revisionist interpretation, however, I introduce a *further* qualification: this qualification is an interpretation of the objective reality that Hegel wants for metaphysical objects in general, and for religious ideas in particular (most prominently, the idea of God) as *mediated* objectivity.[27] With the notion of mediated objectivity of metaphysical knowledge, I refer to an objectivity that does *not* reflect the reality of an object *distinct from* and *opposed to* human consciousness, but an objectivity that takes into account the contribution of our self-conscious mind for the establishment of the content of that metaphysical object and thus reflects the relational unity between subject and object.

I contend that this qualification is important to clarify what is God for Hegel, and what is the status of religious notions in Hegel's philosophy of religion. The main focus of this book, in fact, is not Hegel's metaphysics per se, but the status of religion in Hegel's thought, and the relation in which religion stands with respect to metaphysical knowledge. In this context, it would be inconsiderate not to take into account the contributions of other scholars (regardless of the "interpretative stream" to which they belong) who have previously addressed and elucidated aspects of Hegel's philosophy of religion. Therefore, in the development of this work, I constantly refer to such contributions insofar as they provide arguments convincing enough not to be in need of further demonstration (consistent with a conception of philosophy as a collective enterprise).

It is against such a background that I develop the central thesis of this book: in Hegel's view, subjectivism can be avoided, and content can be restored to religion, only to the extent that God is understood in God's relation to human beings and human beings are understood in their relation to God. I will address the question of subjectivism at length in chapter 2; here, it is sufficient to define subjectivism, in very broad terms, as the tenet that there is no underlying "true" reality that exists independently of the activity of the cognitive agent. Hegel saw subjectivism as a danger implied in some interpretations of Kant's critical philosophy; the problem of subjectivism, however, lies for Hegel not in factoring the cognizer's activity in the cognitive process but rather in the misleading assumption that it is indeed possible to distinguish a priori an underlying "true" reality from the activity of the cognitive agent. Such an assumption has serious implications for an understanding of God. In fact, if God can be understood only in God's relation to human beings, and human beings can only be understood in their relation to God, it follows that we cannot know God without knowing ourselves, but at the same time we cannot know ourselves without knowing God, and this knowledge is possible only in the context of an epistemological openness (perspectivism) and practical openness (recognition). It is this openness that made God human in the incarnation, and it is this openness that makes us human: I take this to be Hegel's fundamental speculative intuition. The treatment of particular aspects of Hegel's philosophy of religion thus enables the development of this thesis; therefore, I make no claim for completeness in my treatment.

For the development of my central thesis, Redding's qualified revisionist interpretation is particularly relevant because of the attention devoted in his work to Hegel's perspectivism, and to the dynamic of recognition considered beyond its standard fields of application (such as social and political philosophy) to include important cognitive and epistemological aspects.[28] More recently, Redding's work has been seminal in clarifying the consequences that an account of Hegel's metaphysics (interpreted according to the qualified revisionist interpretation, that is, as the discipline in which reason is concerned with its own products) has for the interpretation of Hegel's philosophy of religion.[29] In this book, I move in a *reverse* but *complementary* direction, to examine the consequences that Hegel's idea of God as elaborated in his philosophy of religion has for his understanding of an idealistically conceived metaphysics.

I am aware that such work departs quite substantially from Hegel's manner of organizing the material, and I consider the current structure of my work as being consistent with the hermeneutic nature of my methodology previously outlined, that is, a methodology that takes into consideration the historical situation both for Hegel *and* for us as interpreters. In other words, I have chosen the current strategy (the examination of the consequences of the idea of God for Hegel's metaphysics) not because I think that it illuminates the issues at stake more clearly than Hegel's own, but because I am convinced that it is always fruitful to approach a philosophical thought from a different angle—one that inevitably mirrors *our own* historical and theoretical perspective. This strategy also implies that one start from Hegel's conception of God and from other religious representations (*Vorstellungen*) and *then* clarify their transformation into philosophical concepts (rather than start from the concepts and then consider their related representations). In this way, I aim to show that religion is an essential component of Hegel's idealist project to develop a *post*-critical metaphysics.

I am also aware that, in pursuing such an aim, I am relying on two streams of interpretation that have been seen so far as scarcely compatible: in fact, while the argument that religion is an essential component of Hegel's thought has been put forward by interpreters such as Robert Williams and Peter Hodgson, the analysis of Hegel as a post-Kantian philosopher has been carried forward particularly by revisionist interpreters such as Terry Pinkard and Paul Redding. Given the suspicion expressed by readers such as Williams and Hodgson of nontraditional readings of Hegel, one might wonder whether it is possible to rely simultaneously on both lines of interpretation. It is indeed one of my central arguments that these two interpretative lines are not necessarily incompatible when it comes to Hegel's religion. Without underestimating the distinctive standpoint of each interpreter, I think that some of the difference between the "religious" interpretation of Williams/Hodgson and the "post-Kantian" interpretation of Pinkard/Redding (I use such expressions for the sake of brevity) is, as already mentioned, somewhat terminological. An instance of this is the variation in interpretation of Hegel's use of representations (*Vorstellungen*). That Hegel's use of *Vorstellungen* is not restricted to his writings on religion is not a matter of dispute, and many of the analyses Hegel pursues in the *Science of Logic* are also expressed through, or make use of, *Vorstellungen*. It seems to me that the point of divergence relies on the fact that, on one hand, the "religious" interpreters tend to consider such material as making up Hegel's metaphysics and thus recognize a type of seamless continuity between Hegel's theology and his metaphysics; on the other hand, the "post-Kantian" interpreters tend to stick to the idea that metaphysics is conceptual, and thus they do not consider such material as "metaphysical"—or at least they are skeptical about taking it in some sort of representationalist way, as if it were advancing some general claims about *what is*. Once again, the question is what we mean by "metaphysics."

The nature of my thesis, according to which Hegel is committed to a conception of metaphysical knowledge as *mediately objective*, is inseparable from the conception of Hegel's philosophy as *extending* Kant's critique, and therefore it should shed some light on the somewhat unusual choice to begin a book on Hegel's religion with an entire chapter devoted to Kant and, specifically, to an aspect of Kant's philosophy of religion that is often considered marginal, that is, his theory of grace and conversion. However, I think that Kant's theory of grace is precisely the point where Kant gets as close as possible (given his theoretical premises) to providing content for religion, and significantly, this happens via a (problematic and not ambiguity-free) account of the relationship between the human subject and Christ. Here my contention is that Kant's approach to Christ paves the way for similar (albeit more sophisticated) philosophical moves in Hegel's philosophy of religion.

With chapter 2, a proper investigation into Hegel's philosophy of religion begins. Specifically, I argue that the idea of *kenosis* plays a fundamental role both in Hegel's philosophy of religion (via the incarnation of Christ) *and* in Hegel's metaphysics. In my book *Sacrifice in the Post-Kantian Tradition*,[30] I argued for the relevance of the notion of kenotic sacrifice (a withdrawal, a "making room" for the other) for the entire tradition of post-Kantian philosophy from Kant to Nietzsche, whereas in chapter 2 of the present book I focus on the consequences that Hegel's conception of the incarnation (God renouncing God's own divinity) has for an idealistically conceived metaphysics.

Chapter 3 is a crucial step in the development of my thesis; there I argue for the interpretation of the objective reality that Hegel wants for God as *mediated* objectivity. I then analyze how Hegel's "mediated objectivity" applies to religious representations, suggesting that a *figural* reading should be adopted. On such grounds, I reconstruct Hegel's distinction between the image (*Bild*) of God, the concept (*Begriff*) of God, and the Idea (*Idee*) of God, and I argue that it is in the process that transforms the concept into the Idea that the answer to the question of the objective reality of God in Hegel's philosophy of religion can be retrieved.

The (mediated) objectivity of the concept of God needs a philosophical justification. In chapter 4, I argue that such justification can be found in Hegel's "infamous" defense of the ontological argument for the existence of God. Actually, rather than defending previous formulations of the ontological proof, Hegel *criticizes* them and reformulates the argument in his own terms, with the aim of showing that the Idea of God (the full actualization of the concept) involves its existence. This is, I maintain, an important strategic move against subjectivism, and a crucial step in understanding how Hegel wants to restore *content* to religion.

The ontological argument, as reconstructed by Hegel, shows not only the possibility of the knowledge of God but also tells us something about the *content* of that knowledge. In fact, God as "absolute Idea" is shown to be in an intrinsic relation with human subjects. The *relationality* of God (both God's outward and God's inward relationality) is the subject of chapter 5, which is devoted to Hegel's account of the Trinity, conceived as a relational structure—another step in Hegel's strategy for restoring content to religion.

Chapter 6 then narrows the focus to the crucial notion of the death of God, which represents, I contend, the overcoming of the subject/object opposition in the human–divine relationship. The death of God is a central aspect of Hegel's critique of modernity, both religiously and philosophically. In fact, the realization of the death of the abstract God of traditional theism and ancient metaphysics exposes the human subject to the establishment of a normativity apart from the relation with God and the world. This risk finds historical realization in the Enlightenment and in the thought of Fichte—and, later on, in left Hegelianism. This is the reason why Hegel's struggle against theological subjectivism is not complete without a corresponding critique of *philosophical* subjectivism, which reduces the world and God to a reflection of the "I," which alone is regarded as real.

The overcoming of the subjectivism of the concept of God always implies, therefore, a corresponding overcoming of the subjectivism of the "I," so that content can be restored to both God and the "I" in their mutual relationship. In this context, an explanation of the proper function of the concept of God for the "I" will be needed—and this will show how Hegel's reconceptualization of God has consequences for an understanding of idealist metaphysics in its overcoming of subjectivism. In the course of this investigation, one comes to realize, I suggest, that the overcoming of religious subjectivism is possible if not only God but also the human "I" is reconceptualized beyond the subject/object opposition. Such conception of the "I" stands as groundbreakingly original in relation to other philosophical accounts of the self (including contemporary accounts) and would fruitfully be the subject of further research.

Against this background, the very idea of a "philosophy of religion" needs to be reconsidered in light of the overcoming of (religious and philosophical) subjectivism. Even more importantly, philosophy of religion can no longer be conceived as a secondary form of philosophy, because it addresses questions and problems that are crucial for the way we think of ourselves as cognitive and moral agents and therefore has practical implications for a variety of contemporary issues. In chapter 8, therefore, I briefly consider the Hegelian legacy vis-à-vis contemporary philosophy of religion and its potential contribution to contemporary problems, and going (admittedly) beyond Hegel, I explore the consequences of a revaluation of Hegel's idealist approach to religion for contemporary philosophy.

If, as Hegel maintains in the preface to the *Phenomenology of Spirit*, what is "salient" in a philosophical work is expressed in its "aim," then what is meant to be salient in this book is showing that Hegel's idealist approach is an underestimated alternative in the conception of religion and God, and that it can represent an alternative to today's theist and atheist philosophies. Within the limits of the hermeneutic principle of the "fusion of horizons" mentioned earlier, I argue that such an interpretation does not force things by reading my own view into Hegel: rather, I suggest, this philosophical perspective is still relevant today because Hegel's thought can be regarded as an attempt to think through the complex relation between philosophy and the modern world, and to think through everything such a relation entails. In this respect, we are not beyond modernity but rather in its critical phase, and phenomena such as (religious and philosophical) subjectivism, the inquiry into the source of normativity, and the overcoming of the subject-object relation are the same problems for which Hegel attempted to provide not only a diagnosis but also a possible cure.

It could be objected that there are other philosophical ways to deal with such problems—ways that are meant to avoid Hegel by either opposing or ignoring his approach. Indeed, as Foucault said in his Inaugural Lecture at the College de France in 1972, our age has constantly attempted to flee Hegel, "whether through logic or epistemology, whether through Marx or through Nietzsche" (or whether, we might add, through an array of other "postmodern" approaches); however, "truly to escape Hegel involves an exact appreciation of the price we have to pay to detach ourselves from him." Even in thinking about religion and God, one cannot easily be anti-Hegelian without wondering, as Foucault does in this oft-quoted, and yet always suggestive, passage, whether anti-Hegelianism is possibly one of Hegel's "tricks," at the end of which "he stands, motionless, waiting for us."[31]

# 1

# Christ as Symbol in Kant's Religion

Kant's philosophy of religion has often been considered marginal in the context of his broad philosophical enterprise. Even when Kant's philosophy of religion is taken seriously, some of the arguments adopted by Kant in his writings on religion are sometimes treated as little more than oddities, and as having little (if any) relevance to the way Kant's legacy has been received and elaborated by post-Kantian thinkers. From this angle, focusing on Christ as symbol in Kantian religion, as I do in this chapter, might seem relevant merely in exegetical terms. However, I contend that, if properly reconstructed, the Kantian conception of Christ as symbol of sacrifice is indicative of the innovations and limits of the Kantian philosophical project in the context of religion, and it paves the way for similar (albeit more sophisticated) philosophical moves in Hegel's philosophy of religion.

Religious notions, for Kant, have to be understood as symbolic presentations (*Darstellungen*) to be used to apply the moral law to the world. As such, they can be used properly or improperly. For instance, Kant rejects the sacrificial symbol of the *Akedah* and Abraham's willingness to sacrifice his son Isaac because of a direct command by God.[1] In the case of the sacrifice of Christ, however, the question is more complex. Kant gives no shortage of warnings regarding improper ways of interpreting (Christ's) sacrifice, but in one place, he seems to suggest that we must ourselves *participate* in Christ's sacrifice. This place is in *Religion within the Bounds of Bare Reason*, Second Piece, Section One, Subsection C, when Kant addresses the third of the three ethical difficulties that arise out of any belief in divine assistance, or grace. Kant's conception of grace, traditionally underplayed in favor of a reading that supports Kant's emphasis on salvation by works, has recently been the subject of a set of studies that has debated and clarified this issue, showing the relevance of grace in the context of Kant's view on religion.[2] Although Kant's conception of grace inevitably enters into the analysis carried on here, the primary goal of this chapter is not to offer a contribution to the debate on the notion of grace but rather to focus on Kant's conception of Christ as symbol, to clarify its relevance in the context of Kant's philosophy, and to point toward significant philosophical issues that are implied in this conception and that were inherited and transformed in the idealist tradition, particularly in Hegel's philosophy of religion.

First, I address Kant's notion of conversion, which provides the framework within which Kant advances his idea of the "new man" being a symbolic Christ on behalf of the "old man," or "former self." In this context, Kant's conception of proper sacrifice emerges in connection with a representation of Christ conceived as the model for that sacrifice. Then, I analyze the two ways in which Christ should be considered as a model for sacrifice: acceptance of vicarious punishment and openness to forgiveness. I also underline how this openness can be related to the Kantian idea of truthfulness. Finally, in the conclusion, I outline both the limits and the relevance of Kant's conception of Christ as symbol and its implications. In the next chapter, I will argue that, among the post-Kantians, Hegel built on Kant's account in such a way that allows a possible solution to the unsolved aspects of Kant's conception.

## Conversion and Christ as Exemplar

In *Religion within the Bounds of Bare Reason*, Kant argues that the human being is *originally* good but *radically* evil. In order to become a morally good subject—that is, in Kant's own words, a subject "who, when he cognizes something as a duty, requires no other incentive beyond this presentation of duty itself"[3]—the human being must transform her underlying disposition from evil to good. To refer to this transformation, Kant also uses the terms "revolution" (*Revolution*),[4] "conversion" (*Übergang*),[5] "change of mentality" (*Sinnesänderung*),[6] and "change of heart" (*Änderung des Herzens*).[7] The latter two expressions are probably those that best capture Kant's conception of conversion as a "change of disposition" (*Gesinnung*)—a conception that is consistent with the original meaning of the Greek expression μετανοεῖτε used in the Gospels (Mark 1:15), which properly means "change your mind" or "change your way of thinking." The idea implied here is that the "revolution" in one's way of thinking, and the consequent adoption of a different perspective and underlying disposition, represents a turn to a new principle of *action*.

*Religion within the Bounds of Bare Reason* is not the only work in which Kant addresses the notion of conversion. The notion is also discussed in *Anthropology from a Pragmatic Point of View*. In this work, sometimes underestimated, which originated from Kant's lectures on anthropology, Kant is mainly concerned with knowledge from a pragmatic perspective—that is, knowledge of humans as "freely acting beings." In the *Anthropology*, Kant refers to conversion as "revolution" and "rebirth" and emphasizes its "instantaneousness": the "firmness and persistence in principles," he claims, cannot be affected "gradually," but only "by an explosion [*Explosion*] which happens one time."[8]

The idea of a moral "revolution" that happens in a specific moment in time, and yet radically changes the subject, can seem surprising and perhaps not sufficiently grounded. Kant, however, has very good reasons to think this way. As explained by Frierson, "a change in moral status cannot be gradual but must be an absolute transformation from good to evil."[9] In fact evil is, in Kant's view, the subordination of the moral law to the inclinations of the senses. A less frequent subordination of the moral law, or its subordination to very strong temptations, does not make a moral subject less evil. "Only a complete shift, such that the moral law assumes absolute priority," Frierson continues, "constitutes genuine moral improvement on Kant's account." Frierson, however, believes that the moral revolution described in the *Anthropology* "is not *identical* to the moral revolution described in the *Religion*."[10] As evidence for this claim, he stresses the temporal and conscious[11] nature of the *Anthropology*'s revolution, as opposed to the atemporal and intelligible[12] nature of the *Religion*'s revolution.[13] In emphasizing the difference between the two revolutions, however, Frierson fails, in my view, to take into consideration Kant's *perspectival* attitude, which is here applied on both a logical and a theological level. On the logical level, the "change of heart"—a noumenal event that happens outside of the temporal chain of phenomenal events—determines a corresponding event in time, which initiates a gradual process of moral development; in other words, the change of heart is the condition of the possibility of the "gradual moral progress of man in time."[14] On the theological level, Kant is indeed talking about the same conversion, but from two different points of view: the point of view of God in the *Religion* and the point of view of the moral subject in the *Anthropology*. As Hare puts it, "What God sees (by intellectual intuition) is revolution; what we experience is reform."[15] I will come back to the implications of Kant's perspective view of conversion at the end of the next section. For now, it is sufficient to underline here two aspects of Kant's account of conversion. First, conversion is initiated by a single, "revolutionary" act, but this act then requires an ongoing lifelong commitment: "Virtue in this sense is acquired little by little, and means to some a long habituation (in observing the law), whereby the human being, through gradual reforms of his conduct and stabilization of his maxims, has passed over from the propensity to vice to an opposite propensity."[16] This is an important remark, which is meant to respond to the concern about whether conversion would not create "a disturbing discontinuity in someone's empirical character"[17]—a concern that becomes more evident through the analysis of the former self / new self dynamics that Kant carries on in that context (more on this soon). Second, as an implication of the previous point, precisely because the moral conversion is a lifelong commitment, we can only *hope*[18] to have changed our underlying disposition from evil to good, but we can never be completely sure that we have actually changed it.[19]

Thus, in Kant's account, the innate propensity to evil can only be overcome through a "revolution" in one's way of thinking (*Revolution für die Denkungsart*): this is a single event, which is, however, the necessary condition for a (gradual) reform of character (*für die Sinnesart*). The revolution is, therefore, the opening moment of a new life characterized by an ongoing progress toward goodness. As such, it is not merely an intellectual happening, as it involves a practical and unending process of reformation. There are substantial claims about anthropology and about the nature of morality operating here. Anthropology is conceived by Kant as the systematic doctrine containing our knowledge of man, and in contrast with the general optimism of his age, Kant puts at the center of his anthropology the idea of the innate propensity to evil. At the same time, the nature of morality is defined for Kant by the categorical imperative, which is the reason why—as I anticipated earlier—in order to become a morally good subject, the human being must transform her disposition (from evil to good). These issues also bear on discussions of Kant's notion of virtue, given that virtue is acquired little by little. However, in the context of such discussions, the role of the "revolution" (which then leads to conversion) is often downplayed, in the name of a more "secularized" conception of Kant's moral philosophy.

Also, there is undoubtedly an issue of coherence. First, there clearly is some tension between the "revolutionary" aspect and the "reform of character." Second, to some, Kant's motif of a "rebirth," that is, the description of moral conversion in terms of the birth of a "new man," can appear as a mere "pictorial filler for a conceptual lacuna"[20]—as if Kant has to resort to religious notions because of a lack of convincing arguments. However, as others have remarked,[21] Kant's move is far from a "retreat into the irrational." On the contrary, Kant's argument is very rigorous. If humans are radically evil, that is, if they have an underlying disposition to evil, a change toward the good would not be possible without a *supersensible* help—which, in theological language, is called "grace."[22] The charge of irrationality might be acceptable only if Kant had considered religious notions and narratives as idle and superfluous, but this is not the case: on the contrary, Kant maintains that the content of revealed religion is useful "in making up the theoretical deficiency which our pure rational belief admits it has (in the questions, for example, of the origin of evil, *the conversion from evil to good*, man's assurance that he has become good, etc.) and helps—more or less, depending on the times and the person concerned—to satisfy a rational need."[23] Clearly, Kant is very well aware that his move—that is, the attribution of the possibility of conversion to some sort of supersensible intervention—generates further questions: "how is rebirth (resulting from a conversion by which one becomes an other, new man) possible by God's direct influence, and what must man do to bring it about?"[24]

The answer to the first half of the question resides in the presence in us of a moral archetype, symbolized by Christ; the answer to the second half resides in the possibility of "activating" the archetype so that the "old man" (the former self) dies and the new self can come to birth. Therefore, the remaining part of this section will be devoted to an analysis of Christ, and then to the former self / new self transition process. In the context of this analysis, the notion of Christ as symbol and its relevance in the context of Kantian religion will start to emerge.

An analysis of Christ as an archetype should appropriately start from the pure idea of moral perfection, an idea that—as Kant maintains in *The Metaphysics of Morals*—"reason frames a priori."[25] However, the pure idea of moral perfection needs to be applied to the world and, as Kant remarks in the *Critique of Practical Reason*, "nothing corresponding to it can be found in any sensible intuition."[26] We need transitional forms to apply the pure principle of moral perfection to experience;[27] in other words, the pure idea of moral perfection is to be *symbolized* in an *archetype* (*Urbild*). The archetype is a discursive, image-dependent understanding (*intellectus ectypus*)[28] and "an object of intuition, insofar as it is the ground of imitation."[29] The archetype should not be confused with a related idea, that of the "prototype" (*Vorbild*): the archetype is the original notion that makes something what it is, whereas the prototype is the first model that is adopted from that notion.[30]

In the *Critique of Pure Reason*, Kant identifies the prototype of pure moral disposition in the wise man of the Stoics (the "sage"), claiming that "we have in us no other standard for our actions than the conduct of this divine human being, with which we can compare ourselves, judging ourselves and thereby improving ourselves, even though we can never reach the standard."[31] Later on, however, in the *Religion*, Kant rejects the Stoic sage as the prototype: in the new picture dominated by the idea of radical evil, the wise man representing the ancient ideals of *ataraxia* (absence of worries) and *aponia* (absence of passions) is clearly too abstract and does not fit with the corruption of human nature.[32] Another prototype is to be adopted: Christ.

It should be stressed that in this identification of Christ as the prototype, Kant's attitude remains strictly philosophical. Christ, being the prototype of pure moral disposition (that is, the first symbolic model that fully represents this notion), confirms the reality of the archetype (*Urbild*). The archetype is always already present in a human being, although its presence cannot be explained rationally: it is "a God-shaped hole in the heart of human reason."[33] The presence of the archetype is, in other words, independent of faith in the historical Jesus (the prototype). Previous scholarship has already remarked that Kant was unconcerned about the historicity or "veracity" of the events of Christ's life as they are narrated in the Gospels.[34] The idea of moral perfection is an idea of pure reason; being its symbolic representation, the archetype makes possible the application of that moral perfection in the world, but as such, it is not concerned with phenomenal reality. However, this remark, which is correct in itself, might easily lead one to conclude that Kant's choice of Christ is arbitrary or *merely* culturally driven and that therefore Christ can in principle be substituted by some other figure. This is not the case:[35] there are at least two fundamental reasons why Kant identifies the prototype with Christ. First, Kant maintains that only God (whose idea is for Kant indissolubly connected to another idea, that of moral perfection, which reason frames a priori) should properly be considered the archetype of the good:[36] being divine and human at the same time—God incarnate—Christ is the perfect symbol of pure moral perfection.[37] Second, as an implication of the previous point, Christ is thought of as "fraught with the very same needs and thus also the same sufferings, with the very same natural inclinations, and thus also the same kind of temptations to transgression as we are."[38] The emphasis that Kant puts on this conception of Christ can perhaps be considered to be Kant's answer to a potential objection, that is, that Christ is an unreachable model because, being "superhuman," he was immune from natural inclinations and temptations; but if Christ was *not* immune from human limitations, then the objection no longer stands, and his role as model should be taken seriously. The remark by Kant surely has the nature of a counter-objection; at the same time, however, its philosophical value is well beyond that of a specific counter-objection and touches the very strong connection that links, for Kant, Christianity and morality. In fact, the idea of a god becoming human and, as such, being exposed to the limitations and constraints connected with a finite nature, is clearly grasped by Kant as the novelty of Christianity, a novelty that allows Christ to be regarded as the *bodily exhibition*, or *incarnation*, of the good.[39]

Kant's attitude toward the use of a moral example might be regarded as ambiguous. Although in the *Critique of Practical Reason* he briefly emphasizes the positive role of examples, especially in the context of moral education,[40] in the *Groundwork* he expresses strong doubts about the fruitfulness of empirical examples for the establishment or adoption of moral principles,[41] claiming, "Nor could one give worse advice to morality than by wanting to derive it from examples,"[42] and "[i]mitation has no place at all in matters of morality, and examples serve only for encouragement."[43] Why then does Kant speak so highly of the role of Christ as a symbol in the *Religion*? Is Kant merely inconsistent? Not at all. Kant always maintains a negative attitude toward the use of empirical examples, precisely because they are *empirical*. As a symbol, Christ is different:[44] he should not be regarded as an example on which we are to model this or that particular moral action, but as an embodied *ideal (das Letztere)*. The ideal component of this symbol resides in its divine nature (Christ is God), while at the same time Christ's human nature makes it accessible. Moreover, Christ evokes the adoption of a different "way of thinking," whose possibility is already *in us* (as Kant claims, "in order to regard something as an archetype, we must first have an idea according to which we can cognize the archetype"[45]), but which requires a revolutionary act of will[46] (which initiates the conversion) in order to be, as it were, "activated." Since this act cannot be properly conceptualized or schematized (we are not in the realm of theoretical reason), it can only be *symbolized*, and there is, according to Kant, only *one* symbol suitable for the purpose: Christ. As Kant explains: "If we have an idea of something, e.g., of the highest morality, and now an object of intuition is given, someone is represented to us as *being congruent with this idea*, then we can say: this is the archetype, follow it!"[47] It is important to understand that, in Kant's view, the role of Christ is not meant to be that of a *passive example*; in the *Religion*, he claims that the archetype "can give us power [*Kraft*]" to "elevate ourselves to this ideal of moral perfection."[48] Kant is still arguing within a philosophical framework here, and he is careful not to trespass into a theological realm; therefore, he acknowledges that we cannot say whether the archetype in us has supernatural origins; he does claim, however, that "we are not the idea's originators" and that this idea "has taken its place in the human being without our comprehending how human nature could have been so much as receptive to it."[49]

Now, we need to clarify what this different "way of thinking" is, and why Christ is the only symbol able to help us in the process of conversion. The answer to these questions resides precisely in the specific sacrificial dynamics that Christ symbolizes—that is, Kant's emphasis on Christ's willingness "to take upon himself all sufferings."[50]

Before proceeding to the unpacking of the way of thinking of the converted man, we should first clarify the context in which Kant regards this sacrifice as happening: the death of the "old man" (the former self) and the birth of the moral "new man." Kant provides such a context when he addresses the third of the three "Difficulties Opposing the Reality of This Idea," that is, difficulties threatening the reality of the archetype.[51] The third difficulty wonders how a just God can overlook pre-conversion evil. Given that conversion, as we have seen, marks a turning point in the moral status of a human being, Kant refers to the pre-conversion subject as "the old man" and to the post-conversion subject as "the new man." The argument that follows from here is, in itself, fairly simple. The sins of the former self have not been punished, but justice *requires* such a punishment, because the good deeds of the "new man" are not enough to compensate for the evil done by the former self. Who is going to pay for those sins? The former self is, morally speaking, "dead"; at the same time, the "new self" is innocent and deserves no punishment. Therefore, the punishment cannot occur *before* the conversion (in that case, there would be no need for conversion in the first place), but it cannot occur *after* the conversion either (precisely because the post-conversion subject is a "new man," and holding him responsible for the sins of the former self would imply that no radical change has occurred). Therefore, Kant maintains that the punishment must happen *during* the conversion—or, better, *in* the act of conversion itself. Thus, the new man indeed takes upon himself the punishment, but only as a spontaneous (that is, not externally required, but freely accepted) and yet necessary (because without it no conversion is possible) sacrifice, *modeled* on Christ's sacrifice. Kant summarizes these dynamics in a passage that is worth quoting in full:

> The exit from the corrupted into the good attitude (as "the dying of the old human being," "crucifying of the flesh") is in itself already a sacrifice and an entrance upon a long series of life's ills that the new human being takes upon himself in the attitude of the Son of God—in other words, merely for the sake of the good—but that yet were properly deserved by a different human being, namely the old one, as punishment (for, the old one is morally a different human being).[52]

If the argument in itself is simple, understanding its various implications is difficult. First of all, let us clear the air about what Kant does *not* mean with this argument. First, this is not a classic theory of salvation for vicarious or substitutionary atonement—that is, a theory according to which the historical Christ bore our sins, was punished, and died as a substitute for all humankind.[53] Kant does not argue that the crucifixion of Christ *in itself* has a salvific power that redeems us. Second, Kant is not merely suggesting that the punishment is a sacrificial offering, in the form of suffering and troubles, that satisfies an angry God who can now look at our moral debt as discharged.[54] Such an account would suggest that there is a way to please God other than by pure moral conduct—not with prayers or praises, but with sufferings and struggles; but Kant always strongly rejects any way to influence God's benevolence. It is true that Kant argues that, because of this sacrifice, humans "can hope to appear before their judge as justified";[55] but first, this is only a hope, not a knowledge; and second (and even more importantly), the justification evoked here is something more than a mere discharge. I will come back to the issue of justification in the next section.

Thus, in Kant's account, Christ is neither a vicarious victim nor a model for the discharge of our moral debt through suffering and struggles. In which sense then is Christ an embodied ideal? First, Christ symbolizes moral purity, and the new man is indeed pure. Second, Christ is the *redeemer* (*Erlöser*) and the *advocate* (*Sachverwalter*),[56] and the new man is called to play the same role in redeeming the former self and in advancing hope for salvation. Kant's "earlier denial of transmissible liability" is not "revised"[57] with the introduction of the idea of punishment as sacrifice: here Kant is proposing a brand new conception that, while it does not admit traditional transmissible liability, introduces important innovative elements.

To grasp the novelty of Kant's conception, consider two issues that, at first, might even appear to be problematic aspects of Kant's account: how the moral subject can really take upon herself the "long series of life's ills," if this sacrifice is supposed to happen *during* the conversion (and not *after* it); and how Kant can appeal to the former self / new self distinction without generating a lack of personal identity in the moral subject.

Regarding the former issue, we have already noted that, although the "change of heart" is supposed to be an instantaneous act of the will, Kant elsewhere stresses that a pure moral status is the objective of a lifelong, gradual improvement. This apparent contradiction can be explained only by appealing to Kant's perspectivism, which clearly appears in the context of the *Religion*, when Kant discusses the first difficulty. Two perspectives need to be taken into consideration: the temporal and finite point of view of the human subject, and the timeless and infinite point of view of God. With conversion, and the birth of the new man, our moral status appears as changed to God, who grasps the entirety of our moral life and can therefore see "the stable disposition of the heart";[58] but we live in time, and therefore we experience a gradual improvement, which never comes to an end. As Hare puts it: "What God sees (by intellectual intuition) is revolution; what we experience is reform."[59] Considered as such, sacrifice is "the culmination of the conversion itself":[60] the new man's willingness to sacrifice himself is really the object of the imitation of Christ, or, even better, the fulfillment of the "Christic disposition."[61] However, we must remember that the archetype is always already (mysteriously) in us, and it is the idea that gives us the power to initiate the process of conversion; thus, what is required of us is, as Kant explicitly states in the *Conflict of the Faculties*, "to make room for it [*ihm Raum zu verschaffen*]."[62]

Now, consider the problem of the lack of personal identity in the moral subject.[63] Although *physically* the same, the post-conversion subject is *morally* "a new man." This is just an implication of Kant's conception of conversion as a revolutionary act of the will: if the change of heart is as radical as to imply a complete change of one's way of thinking, a split in moral identity is unavoidable. However, Kant's conception includes the solution to this danger. The death of the former self coincides with the birth of the new self, and in turn, the willingness of the new self to pay for the old self's sins bridges the gap in moral identity. It would be misleading to regard this lack of moral identity as "merely figurative," as suggested by Frierson.[64] The gap is, on the contrary, indubitably there; and yet, a sacrifice modeled on Christ is able to bridge it.[65] To regard the lack of moral identity as merely figurative means to downplay the status of Christ as a symbol of sacrifice; conversely, such status is essential precisely in order to avoid a risk of loss of moral identity that would otherwise present itself.[66]

To summarize: a revolutionary act of the will causes the death of the old self, and the transformation of the underlying disposition from evil to good creates the condition for the birth of a new self. The process of conversion, however, is not completed without the willingness of the new self to take upon itself the evil of the earlier self, and this willingness can derive only from the archetype of pure moral perfection, which is always already in us, but which needs a symbol in order to be activated through imitation; this symbol is Christ. The process of conversion, therefore, culminates in the adoption of a new way of thinking and acting. Subjectively experienced, post-conversion life is therefore a continuous sacrifice, not only (and not primarily) in the sense of a quasi-legal retribution for pre-conversion evil. From this angle, the definition of the suffering of Christ (on which the sacrifice of the new man is meant to be based) as "no more than a symbol for the remorse and misery of the repentant sinner consequent upon his former misdeeds" is reductive at best.[67] The meaning of Christ's sacrifice goes far beyond that for Kant. Therefore, the next section will be entirely devoted to a clarification of the meaning of Christ's sacrifice, and to a discussion of what it means in Kant's view for one to participate in (to become one with) that sacrifice.

## Vicarious Punishment and Openness to Forgiveness

Christ, who is the symbol of the sacrifice that the new self performs on behalf of the former self, is not merely an appended metaphor but plays an essential role in Kant's account of conversion. In fact, this sacrifice has to be performed if justification (forgiveness of pre-conversion evil) is to be rationally justifiable.[68] The sacrifice modeled on Christ is the pivotal point of the entire process of conversion, as Kant clearly states.[69] But recall that the relevance of Christ as symbol consists in the capacity of this symbol to "activate" the archetype and, consequently, to make the ideal of pure moral perfection applicable to the world. Therefore, the question is: what is the *meaning* of this sacrifice, and what consequences and implications does it have for the life and conduct of the post-conversion moral subject?

There are two meanings of this sacrifice, coexisting in Kant's account; although it is possible to regard them as mutually compatible and even complementary, there is a tension between them, with Kant emphasizing now one, now the other, thus retaining some degree of unresolved ambiguity.

The first meaning of this sacrifice is *vicarious punishment*. The "third difficulty" properly wonders how a just God can overlook pre-conversion evil; from this angle, the answer is simply that God *cannot* overlook that evil, and therefore, someone has to be punished for that evil: the sacrifice of the "new man" makes atonement possible. This is the way in which Michalson interprets the new man's Christic sacrifice: it is "the locus of the punishment,"[70] with the "long series of life's ills" referring to the "ongoing process of moral struggle,"[71] an "atoning sacrifice [. . .] mandated by the moral economy of Kant's universe, a universe requiring symmetry and correct proportion."[72] According to this interpretative angle, Christ is the symbol of sacrifice because the "punishment for the old self is thus analogous to Christ's death on the cross."[73] There is no doubt that this is *one* aspect of Kant's account of the sacrifice of Christ as a model; to Michalson's account, one might add that the expiative punishment extends across the whole life of the converted man,[74] but the punitive and retributive aspect of this sacrifice is clearly there. However, and this is the point, this is only *one* aspect of Christ's sacrifice. As already noted by Wood, Kant "does not in fact restrict himself to the (essentially irrelevant) question of punishment for man's guilt. [. . .] Alongside Kant's statements that the 'new man' (the disposition to progress) takes upon himself the sufferings and punishments due to the former self (the propensity to evil) and bears his guilt vicariously, we find also the statement that this disposition 'takes the place of the deed in its perfection (*vertritt . . . die Stelle der That in ihrer Vollendung*),' and that the 'new man' as advocate makes it possible for men to hope to appear before their judge as justified (*gerechtfertigt*)."[75] Wood does not, however, unpack the implications of the Kantian conception of sacrifice as a "disposition"—which effectively represents the second (and most important) meaning of sacrifice.

In order to understand sacrifice as a disposition, we first have to underline an aspect of the Christic sacrifice that was not properly addressed during our previous analysis—*forgiveness*.[76] It has already been said that the sacrifice performed by the new man is a spontaneous and free act of the will (because the new man, insofar as he is innocent, is under no obligation to suffer for the evil made by the former self);[77] but the new self, as already stressed, is not only the "redeemer"; he is also the "advocate" for the former self. As such, the new (post-conversion) self *forgives* the earlier (pre-conversion) self; without this act of forgiveness, no justification can be possible, and the process of conversion cannot be completed. Christ is the symbol for this sacrifice, and this should not come as a surprise: when Kant refers to the redeemer and the advocate, he might well have in mind Christ dying on the cross saying, "Father, forgive them, for they do not know what they are doing" (Luke 23:34). As stressed by Palmquist, conversion for Kant is not a mere intellectual acknowledgment of radical evil; it is a "radical conversion of one's disposition"[78] modeled on Christ's incarnation. Consistent with the kenotic tradition, Christ's first sacrifice is the incarnation itself: God renouncing his absoluteness to become human, accepting all the limitations and constraints that come attached to our finite condition.[79] Analogously, the self (the new, post-conversion person) changes her underlying disposition from a dedication to her own self-interest to "a recognition that she is not in herself any more valuable than anyone else."[80] Only if we follow the archetype in adopting this attitude can we indeed fully participate in Christ's sacrifice and become one with it.

In this sense, the sacrifice of the former self is not only punishment; it is primarily a lifelong attitude, and because of this (as I have already stressed), we can never be completely *sure* to appear as justified before God (the condition that, in theological language, is called "the state of grace"), but we can only *hope* to be so.[81] This is what Kant calls "practical faith in this Son of God":[82] an attitude that is, at the same time, a lack of absolute certainty and *truthfulness*. Only the person who adopts this attitude is, Kant claims, "entitled to regard himself as the human being who is an object not unworthy of divine pleasure."[83] This is important, because it shows how Kant's account of religion in general, and of Christ in particular, is not severed from Kant's epistemological preoccupations.[84]

To clarify the relevance of the notion of truthfulness in relation to the connection between Kant's religious *and* epistemological concerns, it is useful to refer to another of Kant's works, the 1791 essay *On the Miscarriage of All Philosophical Trials in Theodicy*. Here Kant addresses the book of Job and, commenting on the "debate" that opposes Job and his not-so-friendly "friends," he shows a clear disregard for the "subtle or hypersubtle reasonings of the two sides," while—he claims—"the spirit in which they carry them out merits all the more attention." Job, in fact, "speaks as he thinks," whereas—Kant continues—his friends "speak as if they were being secretly listened to by the mighty one."[85] A few paragraphs later, Kant draws the important distinction between truth (*Wahrheit*) and truthfulness (*Wahrhaftigkeit*):

> One cannot always stand by the truth of what one says to oneself or to another (for one can be mistaken); however, one can and must stand by the truthfulness of one's declaration or confession, because one has immediate consciousness of this. [. . .] I can indeed err in the judgment *in which I believe* to be right, for this belongs to the understanding which alone judges objectively (rightly or wrongly); but in the judgment *whether I in fact believe* to be right (or merely pretend it) I absolutely cannot be mistaken, for this judgment—or rather this proposition—merely says that I judge the object in such-and-such a way.[86]

There is no doubt that the notion of truthfulness plays an important role in the context of Kant's practical philosophy. Kant defines truthfulness as "the greatest virtue in the world"[87] and as "the supreme *principium formale* of morality."[88] Kant's treatment of truthfulness has a very large set of ethical implications, which cannot be taken into consideration here. What really matters for our purposes is the distinction between truth and truthfulness. As Zupančič puts it, truth is about "the relation between our statements and the 'facts' to which they refer," whereas truthfulness is about "the agreement between our statements and our beliefs"—in other words, it is about the *will* to tell the truth.[89] In the 1797 essay *On a Supposed Right to Lie Because of Philanthropic Concerns*, Kant points out that the expression "to have a right to the truth" is "meaningless," and that "one must instead say one has a right to his own truthfulness (*veracitas*)."[90] Now, there are two ways of reading such a position with respect to the story of Job. On one hand, one can read it as meaning that Job's view is honest but not necessarily correct: as one commentator puts it, "Truthfulness, while better than mendacity, is no guarantee of truth."[91] On the other hand, one can emphasize the inappropriateness (on an epistemological level) and arrogance (on a practical level) of a position that claims to have *direct* access to truth. Kant's conclusive statement about the story of Job mentioned earlier seems to go in the latter rather than in the former direction. The pretension of having a direct access to truth implies a naïve standpoint of self-certainty that, even when considered from a strictly epistemological point of view, does not serve the cause of truth and knowledge well; from this angle, it can be argued, as Hanna does, that "practical truthfulness is the enabling presupposition of all propositional truth"[92]: "It is rather that we must be truthful, that is, non-cognitively aimed at truth (so this is truth-conation, or 'the love of truth'), because this is a necessary condition of all the other intellectual and moral virtues that together constitute an ideally successful rational human life."[93] On a practical level, the danger of confusing one's account of truth with *truth itself* (thus demanding a right to truth rather than to truthfulness) is also very dangerous, because hypocrisy toward others can be grounded on an inner self-deception.[94] Untruthfulness, the sin of which the so-called "friends" of Job are so evidently guilty in their arrogance to "speak the truth" and to see the world "from the point of view of God," is nothing other than the "radical evil" of *Religion within the Bounds of Bare Reason*.[95]

It is precisely at this point, however, that things take a surprising turn. For, at the end of the book of Job, God shows up, as God's voice is heard coming from a "cloud" showing God's power, proclaiming God's absolute freedom over God's creation, and eventually condemning Job's friends for their arrogance while, at the same time, commending Job for his truthful words. As one commentator has noted, this is one of the few places in Kant's works where God speaks;[96] and it is striking that Kant introduces God here, precisely in the context of one of his most powerful attacks against a pretension of embracing a God's-eye view. This performative contradiction is really meaningful in order to understand Kant's (philosophical) predicament. On one hand, Job is presented as the rightful man, one who has adopted the good as the underlying principle of his disposition and truthfulness as his ongoing conduct of action, to the point of defending his right to truthfulness even in the face of his pious "friends" who pretend to speak "from the point of view of God." On the other hand, Kant *needs God* to intervene as a guarantor and to clarify that no one is entitled to offer an authentic interpretation of the world, *except God Godself*.[97] This state of affairs mirrors the role that Kant attributes to God in the context of his analysis of divine grace. Recall that Kant says that the act of will can indeed activate the archetype and thus initiate the process of conversion, but that the sacrifice of which Christ is the symbol, which is expressed in a lifelong commitment to virtue and truthfulness, would not grant us redemption, unless God, who is able (through his intellectual intuition) to grasp the entirety of our moral efforts, makes that conversion real. In other words, "a God's-eye view of our state is needed."[98] Here one can recall Kant's repeated insistence that the moral subject must listen to moral commands as if they were spoken by the voice of God.[99] The new man's sacrifice, which signals the "entrance upon a long series of life's ills that the new human being takes upon himself in the attitude of the Son of God," is the path to moral perfection; but the very possibility of this moral perfection in the Kantian religion depends, both epistemologically and practically, on a conception of a God's-eye view, unattainable by humans, that is yet required.

## The Limits and Relevance of Kant's Conception of Christ

We are now in a position to appreciate the philosophical meaning of the Kantian conception of Christ as symbol in the context of Kant's theory of conversion. Therefore, we can now briefly examine the strengths and limits of this move.

Although occasionally referred to as "opaque" by some interpreters,[100] Kant's solution to the question of conversion presents several aspects of philosophical innovation, organized in a coherent way. First, Kant relies on the idea of an internal archetype of moral perfection that needs to be "activated" by adopting a unique embodied ideal on which we model a sacrificial attitude: Christ thus becomes the symbol of a sacrifice that is conceived in an unorthodox manner, not only and not primarily as a punitive retribution but also, and more importantly, as the will to forgive. With this account, Kant succeeds in avoiding any irrationalist drift in conceiving the process of conversion (via the notion of the internal archetype), while at the same time he takes into consideration the religious element represented by Christ, treated not as an accidental metaphor but as a symbol that has a conceptual connection with the internal archetype. As Kant puts it in the *Conflict of the Faculties*: "Even the Bible seems to have nothing else in view: it seems to refer, not to supernatural experiences and fantastic feelings which should take reason's place in bringing about this revolution, but to the spirit of Christ, which he manifested in teachings and examples so that we might make it our own—or rather, since it is already present in us by our moral predisposition, so that we might simply make room for it [*ihm Raum zu verschaffen*]."[101] Consider that here Kant adopts, once again, a kenotic language: the archetype is already in us, and what we should do when we encounter the triggering symbol of Christ is to "withdraw" and make room for it.

This is for Kant the path to conversion and to moral perfection. However, moral perfection is still an ethical notion; is this also the path to (religious) *redemption*? In Christian theology, in fact, redemption, as the deliverance from sin, is an essential element of salvation. Is the activation of the archetype through the encounter with Christ enough to deliver us from sin and *redeem* us?

Kantian scholarship is split on this point. Firestone and Jacobs argue that "[r]edemption is not brought about by a historical Christ-figure"; therefore, in their view, there is room for redemption in Kantian religion, but only for a redemption considered as "self-redemption worked out in our mirroring of the symbol that is Christ."[102] Conversely, Reardon argues that Kant's moral theology "cannot admit the idea of redemption," pointing out that "the word itself occurs but once in his book [the *Religion*], and then only in a context which depreciates its meaning."[103] In fact, Kant uses the word "redemption" (*Erlösung*) only once in the *Religion*, in the context of a criticism toward those who pretend to know the precise mechanism whereby God brings salvation about.[104]

There is a sense in which both positions are accurate, insofar as each captures different aspects of Kant's theory. On one hand, Firestone and Jacobs are correct in their claim that the imitation of Christ's attitude is *as close as it can be* to the idea of (self-)redemption: the converted person somehow redeems herself through the adoption of a sacrificial attitude. On the other hand, Reardon is right insofar as there is no room for *proper* (religious) redemption in Kantian religion. In fact, redemption implies, properly speaking, forgiveness for past sins: a forgiveness that is not meant to be merely a legal absolution. Kant's God is a judge who provides legal absolution to the moral subject, so that the subject can appear justified in front of God (thanks to the subject's sacrifice), but who does not grant proper forgiveness. This can be considered the major weakness of Kant's theory of conversion. It has already been noted that Kant's theory requires a God's-eye view: sacrifice makes sense because there is a God who recognizes this sacrifice, and conversion is possible because God, grasping our struggle toward moral perfection through God's intellectual intuition, makes us justified.[105] This God is, at the same time, the "supreme legislator" and the judge: as such, God is commanding "not mercifully," Kant says, and "not forbearingly (indulgently) toward the weakness of human beings."[106] As Wood correctly points out, Kant remarks in several places that "a 'pardoning' or 'beneficent' judge, one who judges leniently and not according to the law, is a contradiction in terms."[107] In other words, in order to work properly, Kant's theory needs a God's-eye view, that is, an external, judging standpoint from which the moral subject can be either condemned or absolved (and thus justified)—but not forgiven.

There is therefore, in Kant's theory of conversion, an emphasis on the need of the subject's participation in Christ's sacrifice, so that—to use Hare's words—"[w]hen God looks at us, he sees his Son, because he is imputing to us his Son's righteousness,"[108] but Christ is still treated as an external symbol, and this symbol's conceptual relation to the internal archetype is not fully pursued by Kant, thus resulting in the underdevelopment of an aspect that remains only suggested: a full participation in Christ's sacrifice, to the point of becoming one with it. The post-Kantians, and especially Hegel, subsequently provided alternative theories of (moral and/or religious) conversion, thus addressing various issues that appeared in Kant's philosophy and that have been briefly sketched here, such as the question of radical evil, the possibility of a kenotic sacrifice, the meaning and use of religious symbol, and the question of moral identity; but it is important to recall that it is upon Kant's theory of conversion that these theories have been built.

# 2

# Hegel's Conception of God

## From Kant to Hegel

Kant published the first edition of *Religion within the Bounds of Bare Reason* in 1793 and subsequently followed it with a second edition in 1794. In order to appreciate the peculiarity of this work, as well as the influence it has had on the post-Kantians, it is appropriate to briefly address the "lay of the land" in the philosophy of religion and philosophical theology in this period. This is a huge topic in itself; therefore, here I will only focus on a few influential figures.

When Kant's *Religion* first appeared, a small group of German theologians still held a conservative approach to the Bible, endorsing a substantially literal reading of it and a dogmatic conception of authority, and hence they strongly opposed any theoretical proposal advanced by the Enlightenment. One of the most representative figures of this conservative trend was the pastor and prominent Lutheran theologian Johann Melchior Goeze (who often went by "Hauppastor Goeze," as he was the senior pastor of all the Lutheran churches in Hamburg from 1760 to 1770). Goeze saw himself as an apologist, and hence he published a number of works denouncing the Enlightenment developments in both theology and philosophy. In his works, he often engaged in direct polemics with several Enlightenment thinkers, particularly with Johann Salomo Semler, the founder of the historical critical method (who rejected the conception that all parts of the Bible had equal authority and, in general, the identification of the Scriptures with revelation), and, a few years later, with Gotthold Lessing, about the historicity of Christian revelation.

The theological conservative positions exemplified by Goeze represented, however, a minority view in late eighteenth-century Europe. Most of the thinkers then who were concerned with religion held more progressive views. Cultural phenomena such as the deist controversy of the late seventeenth century, and the freethinking movement that had emerged in Britain and whose ideas subsequently became widespread throughout Europe, created a cultural climate that allowed for a critical approach to the biblical texts, and for a broadly rationalist view about religious beliefs.

In this cultural context, the main novelty of Kant's *Religion*, as it appeared to Kant's contemporaries, did not consist in the claim that religious beliefs should be justifiable on purely rational grounds—a position already widespread at that time among philosophers and religious thinkers—but rather, as already outlined by Beiser, relied on Kant's surprising conception that religious beliefs be justified exclusively by *practical* reason.[1] This position put Kant in contrast with the theologians and thinkers of his time, who traditionally conceived of the relation with transcendence primarily on *cognitive* or *spiritualistic* grounds. In addition, Kant's endorsement of the Christian doctrine of original sin (through his conception of human radical evil) alienated the sympathies of the most "secularized" thinkers—one can recall here Goethe's harsh judgment, according to which "Kant required a long lifetime to purify his philosophical mantle of many impurities and prejudices. And now he has wantonly tainted it with the shameful stain of radical evil, in order that Christians might be attracted to kiss its hem."[2]

This combination of emphasis on the exclusively practical justification of religion, radical evil, and a theory of grace (the latter analyzed in the previous chapter) created a situation whereby Kant eventually antagonized even the supporters whom he had previously acquired in the theological field. An emblematic case—one that was destined to have important implications for the philosophical directions taken by the post-Kantians—is that of Gottlob Christian Storr.

Storr was Professor of Theology in Tübingen; he followed Semler in the use of a critical method of approach to the Scriptures and intended to employ it to defend, rather than attack, the doctrinal system. We have a duty, Storr argued, to believe in the authority of revelation, but the content of revelation cannot be at odds with the demands of reason; hence, the recourse to textual criticism, which is meant to provide a confirmation of the authority of Christian doctrine. And, if one wanted additional confirmation, one could appeal to the miracles performed by Jesus as part of his revelation.

Storr was quite positively disposed toward critical philosophy—at least until Kant wrote the *Religion*. Storr's sympathy for Kant's thought was most likely originally determined by the work of one of his students, Johann Friedrich Flatt. Flatt welcomed the *Critique of Pure Reason* as the long-awaited and definitive confirmation that human reason could not solve fundamental metaphysical questions; and the fact that Kant had not, so far, made any attempt to philosophically address the content of religion seemed to him additional evidence of what he took to be the meaning of Kant's philosophy vis-à-vis religion. In order to provide content to religion, Flatt claimed, one should rather turn to a doctrine of revelation of the kind provided by his mentor, Storr. In various writings in the years 1792 and 1793, Storr endorsed the basic tenet advanced by Flatt, thus showing sympathy toward Kant's philosophy and outlining what appeared to him to be the compatibility of critical philosophy with his own doctrine of revelation. Now, if we agree with Kant that we can have no knowledge of the ultimate features or structures of reality (i.e., of things-in-themselves), then the alleged application of reason to criticize dogmatic religious truth, so common among Enlightenment thinkers, was totally misplaced.[3] The postulates of practical reason could not, Storr argued, provide us with a reasonable expectation of the forgiveness of sins, and therefore only Christian revelation could preserve us from moral despair.[4] In other words, Kant's critical philosophy could be endorsed, but it needed to be complemented with (Storr's own) proper theory of revelation, which Storr referred to as "pure supernaturalism."

When the first edition of Kant's *Religion* appeared in 1793, Storr was gutted with disappointment, as one of his favorite philosophers seemed to show that he was not as much of a "supernaturalist" as Storr had hoped he might be. He therefore decided to write a response to Kant, not only to raise his objections but to outline the direction that a philosophical inquiry in religion *should have taken* based on Kant's previous work. Such a response, also published in 1793,[5] was read by Kant, who effectively mentions it in the preface to the second edition of the *Religion*, published in 1794, but without explicitly engaging with Storr's critique, neither in the *Religion* nor elsewhere.[6]

The thesis that Storr advanced in his 1793 work was quite a simple one and basically an extension of his previous arguments. First, he objected to Kant's conception of a natural or rational religion being the core of revealed religion (a conception exemplified by the image of the concentric circles in the preface to the second edition of the *Religion*): it is evident that the distinction between those elements of revealed religion that are consistent with reason and deserve to be included in natural religion, and those that are not, can be made only by someone well educated, and that therefore the majority of people will have to rely on the authority of the few well-educated thinkers—but in that case, Storr rhetorically wondered, is it not much better to rely directly on the authority of Christian doctrine?[7] Second: with the introduction of the moral postulates about the existence of God and the immortality of the soul in the *Critique of Practical Reason*, Kant had implicitly admitted that the moral law, once deprived of fundamental religious beliefs (such as in God and immortality), had no sufficient motives.[8] If this is true, then we should do everything we can to reinforce such beliefs through a constant appeal to the Bible, whose reliability is demonstrated through the historical critical method, and through the supernatural acts performed by Jesus.

Storr's doctrine was clearly an *inversion*—or even a *perversion*—of Kant's original conception of the relation between morality and religion, and it surely appeared as such to most of Storr's students at the *Tübinger Stift*, which included a group of three friends who happened to share a room there in those years: Schelling, Hölderlin, and Hegel. They all disliked Storr's interpretation of critical philosophy, and they rather showed sympathy toward the position of Immanuel Carl Diez (an older student at the *Stift* who argued that a strict application of the limits of knowledge, as analyzed in the *Critique of Pure Reason*, had made the very possibility of a supernatural revelation unacceptable)[9] and toward the position of Fichte, who in 1792 had published his *Attempt at a Critique of All Revelation*, arguing that any revelation in relation to God must be consistent with morality. Both Diez and Fichte represented a radicalization of Kant's conceptions on religion in the direction of *naturalism*, and their positions were definitely very popular among the students of the *Stift*. Schelling, who among the group of friends was the most active as a scholar at the time, addressed the issue in one of his early works, *Of the I as the Principle of Philosophy*, arguing that Storr's position could not be considered a legitimate interpretation of Kant's philosophy, because it contradicted the true nature of freedom in the context of critical philosophy.[10]

Hegel kept a low profile in the context of such debate. He certainly had no sympathy for the "old guard" of theologians who did not want to give in to the new movement that Kant's philosophy represented, and the few sarcastic comments he makes in his mature writings on figures such as Goeze leave no doubt about the contempt he felt for the position

Goeze represented.[11] But at that stage he did not share the same level of enthusiasm that his friends Schelling and Hölderlin were showing for Kant either.[12] This does not mean, of course, that he liked what Storr and his disciples were doing to critical philosophy—that is, as Hegel later put it, "procur[ing] Critical building material to fortify their Gothic temple" (B I:16/31).[13] Rather than defending the "true" nature of critical philosophy, he opposed Storr by identifying a flaw in Storr's line of interpretation of Kant's moral theology: Storr connected the ethical freedom implied in one's commitment to the moral law (and also expressed by the postulates of practical reason) with the hope of personal happiness and salvation in the afterlife (which, in Storr's view, required a commitment to dogmatic religious truths); this connection had, however, no foundation.[14] Hegel's reluctance to directly defend Kant against Storr might also be determined by the consideration that Storr was not entirely wrong in pointing out that the distinction, advocated by Kant, between those elements of revealed religion that were rational and those that were not, even assuming that it was legitimate in itself, was abstract and required absolute trust in the "Critical philosopher" and therefore still relied on, rather than avoided, the appeal to authority.[15] Additionally, although there is no evidence to substantiate this claim, one might speculate that the young Hegel was starting to consider the possibility of restoring content to religion (a tenet that was proposed by Flatt and endorsed by Storr) while avoiding both Storr's "pure supernaturalism" and Fichte's "naturalism."

In the years between 1793 and 1796 (the so-called Berne period), the presence of both Storr and Kant is recognizable in Hegel's writings, as exemplifying respectively "the old" and "the new" in philosophical theology. In *The Positivity of Christian Religion*, Hegel defends the (Kantian) tenet that religion be proved through practical reason rather than through reasoned arguments—most likely an attack on Storr (FS, 1:108–9), and in *The Life of Jesus*, Hegel went so far as writing his own version of the Gospels, a version devoid of any supernatural act and in which Jesus appears as the Kantian prototype of pure moral perfection. It is, however, in the years between 1797 and 1801–1802 that Hegel developed his own view on religion and entered into what was destined to become his lifelong engagement with the subject, which eventually culminated in his four series of *Lectures on the Philosophy of Religion* in 1821, 1824, 1827, and 1831.

In the remaining part of this section, I can offer only the briefest survey of the development of Hegel's conception between 1801 and 1821, one that is exclusively concerned with a few topics that are relevant in the context of this book, and without the pretense of addressing even the major themes in each work. My analysis in the remaining part of this chapter, as well as in the next chapters, will be mainly focused on the *Lectures on the Philosophy of Religion*, although references to Hegel's other works will be made when relevant; therefore, it is appropriate to briefly mention the material in Hegel's earlier works that informs the reading of Hegel's discussion of God.

Following the publication, in 1801, of his first (short) book, the *Difference between Fichte's and Schelling's Systems of Philosophy*, in which Hegel introduced for the first time one of his everlasting concerns, namely, the dichotomy between God and the world, he took up another fundamental opposition in a long essay published in 1802 in the *Critical Journal of Philosophy*, entitled "Faith and Knowledge or the *Reflective Philosophy of Subjectivity* in the Complete Range of Its Forms as Kantian, Jacobian, and Fichtean Philosophy." Despite being a very "Kantian" work in the employment of some key arguments, this essay also marks Hegel's departure from a Kantian picture of religion. In the modern world, faith and knowledge, Hegel argues, seem to be opposed. But this apparent opposition is due to a shortsightedness in the faculty of the understanding. On one hand, the understanding considers reason to be concerned with a reality made of finite particulars and with a classification of such particulars according to abstract (universal) categories. On the other hand, the understanding considers any possible conception of finite particulars as internally related, and as a part of a larger "whole," as belonging to faith. If, however, we adopt a higher, dialectical conception of reason, which recognizes the particulars as internally related, then we see that there is actually no contradiction, and that the larger "whole" is nothing but God.

In 1805 Hegel, now *außerordentliche Professor* (without remuneration) at the University of Jena, began work on a manuscript (known as the "Third Jena System Draft") that he meant to use for his lectures on the philosophy of nature and the philosophy of spirit. This work is particularly interesting because it shows that Hegel's preoccupations about religion and the conception of God, which represented a significant, if not the main, aspect of *Faith and Knowledge*, were still very much on his mind in a time when he was also surely already thinking of his next work to be published, namely, the *Phenomenology of Spirit*; even more interestingly, in the Third Jena System Draft he introduces a few elements of the conception of God that will resurface almost twenty years later in the *Lectures on the Philosophy of Religion*. In the second part of the Third Jena

System Draft, Hegel addresses religion as the way of life in which spirit is directly concerned with the spirit itself. God is conceived here as spirit but also—and this is important for our purposes—as a *person*. Because we share personhood with God, our first approach to God is through representations (*Vorstellungen*); but in approaching God exclusively through representations, we create a distance between God and us (and the world in general). In fact, God is represented as spirit reconciled with itself; thus, the reconciliation is represented as happening in "another world"—not in *our* world. Therefore, in such a work we can see for the first time how Hegel thematizes the need for a *reconceptualization* of God, so that God can be presented as a self who is not, however, separate from the world and from us. And a central aspect in this reconceptualization is affirmed to be the sacrifice (*Aufopferung*) of God in the incarnation ("the sacrifice of divinity, i.e., of the abstract Being [*Wesen*] from 'beyond'" as occurring "in his becoming actual" [JS-III, 283/178]). The task of philosophy, Hegel suggests, is to complement and accomplish this process of reconceptualization of God that (Christian) religion had started in a representative way. Philosophy has the same content as religion, but it expresses such content in conceptual form.

This insight is consistent with the way in which religion is presented in the *Phenomenology of Spirit*, which appeared in 1807. The relevance of this work for Hegel's philosophy in general, and for his conception of religion in particular, is beyond doubt, and I will often refer to it in the following chapters. Here it is sufficient to emphasize that Hegel's account of religion does not depart from the strategy centered on the reconceptualization of God previously outlined. One of the most significant instances of a (phenomenological) display of such a dynamic can be identified in the section on the "Unhappy consciousness." Here the consciousness is longing for recognition by a transcendent God and tries to unite itself with the divine by disavowing its own activity. The unhappy consciousness turns out to be a thorough failure, as in the very act of thanking God for God's gifts, the unhappy consciousness is nonetheless active. And yet, the unhappy consciousness is the spirit's early attempt to think itself united with God through a recognitive dynamic. Such recognition will then be accomplished, at a representational level, in Christianity thanks first to the incarnation and then by speculative philosophy.

Hegel's project of a reconceptualization of God is not even absent from his later, more "systematic" works. In the *Science of Logic*, Hegel famously defined the content of logic as "the exposition of God as he is in his eternal essence before the creation of nature and of a finite spirit" (L I, 5:44/29)—a claim that puzzled many interpreters and that even today is still mentioned in debates about the status of God in the context of Hegel's philosophy of religion. George di Giovanni explains Hegel's claim as follows: "by 'world' we must now understand nothing physical but a universe of meaning instead, and by 'creation' the constitution of the conceptual medium that will make any reality, such as already exists or might exist, re-exist as intelligible. But of this universe it can also be said that it is a 'realm of shadows,' for it is made up of reflective abstractions only."[16] Surely the *Science of Logic* presents many challenges to an interpreter interested in Hegel's conception of God, because (as di Giovanni puts it) it "raises the broader issue of hermeneutic strategy—whether one should take the Logic as the norm for interpreting other parts of Hegel's system or, on the contrary, read some of the religious imagery that Hegel uses elsewhere back into the Logic."[17] In my view, these alternatives are not mutually exclusive. As I pointed out in the introduction, several of the analyses Hegel pursues in the *Science of Logic* are also expressed through representations; the point is rather whether such representations count as metaphysical content or whether the realm of metaphysics should be limited to what is strictly conceptual. That is, the point is what Hegel means exactly by "metaphysics" (something that I will address in more detail in the following chapters).

In the first volume of the *Encyclopedia*, effectively another version of his Logic, Hegel more strictly connects the reconceptualization of God with the argument that subjectivity itself is at the basis of the object-world, a position introduced with Kant's "Copernican" turn. And in the third volume of the *Encyclopedia*, this connection becomes even more explicit. Both Christianity and philosophy are concerned with subjectivity as such. Christianity tells a story about the intrinsic relationality of subjectivity through the conception of the Trinity and through the self-divestment of God in the incarnation: this is a groundbreaking moment in the history of spirit. Philosophy is called to accomplish this process by reconceptualizing the relation between God and human subjectivity, but this becomes possible only when human reason comes to grasp the interdependence between human subjectivity and God. Such interdependence does not imply, however, that God is a "fictional" character, or a mere human creation: it rather means that we would not be properly "human" if we lacked such a mutual recognitive relationship with God. I will come back to this important issue in chapter 4, in the context of my discussion of Hegel's defense of the ontological argument for the existence of God. Here it is interesting to note that Hegel refers precisely to the same dynamic in the *Elements of the Philosophy of Right*. In the context of his discussion of the legitimacy of monarchy, in fact, Hegel draws a parallel with the ontological argument for the existence of God, as he contends that what is at stake in both cases is a *translation of content from subjectivity*. In the ontological proof, in fact, we deal with the "transformation of the absolute concept into being"; this, however, has "recently been declared incomprehensible, which amounts to renouncing all cognition of the truth, for truth is simply the unity of the concept and existence" (R, 7:450/322). The reference to Kant is clear here, and it is evident that the danger of subjectivism that Hegel saw embedded in Kant's form of idealism was a lifelong concern for him, one that began with *Faith and Knowledge* (and perhaps even earlier) and never abandoned him. Therefore, in order to contextualize Hegel's project of the reconceptualization of God, it is now appropriate to address the question of Hegel's critique of Kant's subjectivism.

## The Problem of Kant's Subjectivism

The Kantian idea of moral perfection is to be applied to the world through transitional forms and symbolized in an archetype. Only God should properly be considered the archetype of the good; and Christ, being divine and human at the same time, is the prototype and the symbol of pure moral perfection. Therefore, it can be said that Kant's peculiar Christology is the condition of the applicability of the moral law.[18]

There are, however, at least two problems with the Kantian conception of God and Christ—problems that, as I will explain, shape the Hegelian response to Kant. The first problem is the abstract, theoretical status to which the idea of God is reduced by the "reflective philosophy of subjectivity" (as Hegel refers to the philosophy of Kant, Jacobi, and Fichte in the subtitle of *Faith and Knowledge*): theoretically, God is nothing but a "regulative idea" and thus cannot be known. But if God cannot be known, God might not exist at all and might be regarded as nothing more than a convenient epistemological metaphor.

The second problem is the role that Kant attributes to God in the realm of practical philosophy. As presented in *Religion within the Bounds of Bare Reason*, Kant's God is the "supreme legislator": a judge who commands "not mercifully" and "not forbearingly (indulgently) toward the weakness of human beings."[19] This "monarchical metaphor,"[20] which confers on God a "juridical and moral character," is heavily criticized by Hegel,[21] especially for the implications it has concerning the divine–human relationship, which, as is evident from the passages in the *Religion* where Kant addresses the issue of grace, is essentially a relationship between a creditor and a debtor.[22] After Kant, the space for faith seems to be reduced: either one agrees to keep religion "within the bounds of bare reason," or one comes to identify faith with feeling. In both cases, the outcome is a form of *subjectivism*. On one hand, to keep religion "within the bounds of bare reason" means to consider it from a moral perspective: as we have seen, Kant claims that we can recognize Christ as the symbol of moral perfection because the archetype is already in us. As Hegel argues, "It *ought* to be something unposited, an absolutely independent power; but in its not-being-posited, I do not forget myself, so that even this not-being-posited is itself a being-posited by me—I, my subjectivity, not absolutely self-united as absolute form but [obliged] to remain in this subjective antithetical relationship" (Rel III, 92/156).[23] Here Hegel shows how much subjectivism is still embedded in Kant's position, precisely when Kant, with the introduction of the archetype, seems to get closer to restoring content to religion. In recommending the moral agent follow the internal archetype, in fact, Kant inadvertently but inevitably generates an antithetical relationship between the moral agent and the archetype—a relationship that is still conceived *a parte subjecti*, from the point of view of the moral agent: a substantially subjective relationship.

On the other hand, if faith is identified with feeling, the surrender to subjectivism is even more evident,[24] and it certainly was very evident in Hegel's era, when several thinkers and theologians were advancing a direct and unconceptualized approach to God by grounding the divine–human relation in *feeling*. This attitude can be considered the theological translation of philosophical subjectivism, broadly defined as the tenet that the possibility of knowing God, or at least of establishing a relationship with God, depends on human feeling rather than rational thought—here one can think of Schleiermacher's notion of *Glaubenslehre*, that is, faith as the expression of the feeling of utter dependence, which for Hegel represented the paradigm for all conceptions that assert the superiority of feeling over thought: "We cannot know God as an object, we cannot cognize him, and it is the subjective attitude that is important" (Rel III, 101/166). Hegel wanted to react against this theological subjectivism by restoring *content* to religion.

Hegel's diagnosis of the problem of theological subjectivism cannot be disconnected from his diagnosis of the more general problem of philosophical subjectivism, conceived—to put it in very broad terms—as the philosophical tenet that the nature of reality as related to a given consciousness is dependent on that consciousness. As such, the notion has deep roots in the history of Western philosophy. The idea of a self-sufficient underlying subject was already central in Aristotelian philosophy, but it was Descartes who developed that conception into the idea of the "I" as the *thinking* subject—an idea that gave modern philosophy its peculiar *subjectivistic* twist. With its philosophical basis in Descartes's philosophy, this subjective account of the "I" dominated Western philosophy through the seventeenth and eighteenth centuries.

Even Kant was not immune from this subjective account. Kant's transcendental approach relied on a conception of experience as the succession of various contents—an idea that Kant borrowed from Hume. Kant argued that to be experiences, experiences must be combined or held together in a unity of consciousness—the unity of self, or "transcendental unity of apperception," that is, the "I think." In the "Transcendental Deduction," Kant argues that all objects, to be known, must refer to a unique and unifying mental center (the "I think") and that consequently (given that the "I think" unifies the representations using categories), objects cannot be perceived spatiotemporally without being categorized. In the "Transcendental Dialectic," then, Kant argues that the "transcendental ideas" of the soul, the world, and God are representations of an absolute unity and an unconditioned totality and hence can be *thought*, though not properly "*known*."[25] Transcendental ideas are not objects of knowledge, but regulative ideas that encourage us to organize our knowledge more systematically.

According to Hegel, Kant's philosophy is still affected by subjectivism. From the publication of *The Difference between Fichte's and Schelling's System of Philosophy*, Hegel criticized the Kantian "I think" as subjective, because the unity of experiences is realized in the subject.[26] Hegel was well aware that Kant was not an extreme subjectivist, and yet he saw a real danger in this conception, because if taken to its extreme, it could lead to the tenet that "the whole of experience is a construct from each individual subject and can reach no further than that subject's consciousness."[27]

Ironically, German idealism from Kant to Hegel (and, to some extent, even twentieth-century movements of European philosophy) has often been considered guilty of this very tenet. In his influential *German Idealism: The Struggle against Subjectivism, 1781–1801*, Beiser has shown that this interpretation is actually misleading and that from its very (Kantian) inception, German idealism was a reaction *against* subjectivism, "an attempt to prove the reality of the external world and to break out of the egocentric predicament."[28] Kant's critical philosophy was the attempt to react against Hume's skepticism and Berkeley's idealism (or, better, immaterialism) to safeguard the objectivity of human knowledge. Relying on the transcendental structure of the categories (a priori forms of the understanding), Kant managed to secure an objectivity that is, after all, only "universal subjectivity." Subjectivism had not been completely overcome; as Ameriks has appropriately pointed out, the German idealists, far from welcoming or, worse, radicalizing subjectivism "in the sense of any reduction of ontology to a set of mental states,"[29] tried different philosophical solutions to overcome the subjectivist load still present in Kant's idealism.

Let us go back to Hegel's critique of Kant, so that we can expand on Beiser's and Ameriks' assessments of subjectivism mentioned previously. The "Copernican revolution" in philosophy was groundbreaking because it demolished the traditional metaphysical view that the subject's cognition must conform to the object;[30] in other words, Kant put at the center of the philosophical scene the problem of the subject-object relation. However, Kant's suggested solution—namely, the conformity of the object to the subject's cognition—requires the unification of subject and object *in the subject alone*. Hence, the danger, already mentioned, that we can "reach no further than that subject's consciousness." It is this opposition that generates the well-known dualism between phenomena (appearances, things as they appear to us) and noumena (things in themselves).[31] As long as the opposition between subject and object is kept in place, the risk of a subjectivistic drift is unavoidable: this is, *in nuce*, Hegel's diagnosis of the question. A whole set of interconnected problems springs from here: maintaining this opposition leads Kant to see in experience the only real source of knowledge;[32] in turn, this generates the belief that "thoughts are only thoughts, meaning that it is sense perception which first gives them filling and reality and that reason left to its own resources engenders only figments of the brain" (L I, 5:38/45–46).[33] This is what Hegel calls "reflective understanding," a subjective way of thinking that falsely separates subject and object, whereas reason is, according to Hegel, characterized by the identity between concept and reality.[34]

Hegel, therefore, strongly opposes the subjectivism of modern philosophy and believes that it should be overcome, not—and this is the point—in the direction of a naïve pre-Kantian or (worse, in Hegel's eyes) pre-Cartesian realism but rather through an improved unification of subject and object, one that does not take place in the subject alone.

Beneath this seemingly vague strategy lies a complex mechanism of philosophical argument that I cannot anticipate here, for at least two reasons. First, as often happens in Hegel's philosophy, the response to a complex philosophical problem is not simply its "solution," because along the path that one follows while looking for a solution, one finds that the terms of the initial question were badly put or need reconsideration in light of a deeper analysis. Second, this book primarily deals with the *consequences* that Hegel's idea of God has *for* his understanding of an idealistically conceived metaphysics, and it therefore inevitably addresses the overcoming of subjectivism from one particular angle, that of Hegel's philosophy of religion. Admittedly, the choice of analyzing the consequences of Hegel's idea of God for his idealist metaphysics *prior* to the framing of the account of God in relation to his metaphysics can be questioned—the objection being whether it is possible to get an account of Hegel's view of God without situating it first in relation to his larger philosophical project. This is effectively the strategy followed in other recent critical works (most notably Redding's), which have clarified the consequences that an account of Hegel's metaphysics has for the interpretation of Hegel's philosophy of religion. Here, however, we move in a reverse but complementary direction, to examine the consequences that Hegel's idea of God, as elaborated in his philosophy of religion, has for his understanding of an idealistically conceived metaphysics. The main point here is that it is indeed possible to address Hegel's idea of God per se and then to analyze its consistency and relevance for the construction of his broader metaphysics.

It is clear therefore that one cannot address any important notion in Hegel's philosophy without considering the implications for other aspects of the system, and this is even truer when the notion in question is that of God. Thus, some considerations about Hegel's idealism, and the extent to which Hegel thinks it is possible to maintain and indeed extend the Kantian Copernican revolution, while at the same time realizing a unification of subject and object that restores nonsubjective content to philosophy, shall find a place in the next chapter. For now, we need to go back to pre-Kantian and (to some extent) Kantian conceptions of God, which can be seen as implications of the broader problem of a subjectivist understanding of the relation between subject and object.

Consider the relation between God and the human agent. This relation is usually subject to a polarized conception. In fact, *either* the *subjective* pole of the God–human relationship is emphasized, as in theological subjectivism and, more radically, in left Hegelianism (i.e., the human being exists, whereas God is a human projection), thus conceptualizing the existence of God as merely a human need; *or* the *objective* pole is emphasized, as in traditional theology and, to some extent, in pre-Kantian metaphysical realism (i.e., God exists as a kind of supernatural object), but any speech on God might be subject to the objections Kant advanced in the "Transcendental Dialectic."

Hegel does not accept this either/or conception. The only way to avoid the risks involved in the subjectivist (as well as in the objectivist) approach to religion is to *reconceptualize* God. The traditional (abstract and metaphysical) conception of God was still indebted to the Aristotelian idea of the immutable and fully actualized "unmoved mover" ("thought thinking itself"). Kant already challenged that idea with his emphasis on the practical (regulative) use of the idea of God and his Christocentric philosophy of religion; but, as already mentioned, his philosophy still required reference to a God's-eye view, on which both the possibility of the noumenal world (knowable by God only) and the ideal of pure moral perfection (and hence the possibility of conversion) are grounded.[35] Hegel wants to maintain Kant's achievement in getting away from that idea of God, while at the same time removing any subjectivistic residue. It is the conception of God as a supernatural transcendent object that generates both the ideal of the God's-eye view and, by contrast, the subjectivist drift that claims that such a view is impossible for human consciousness. What is required, therefore, is a reconceptualization of God (which is not, according to Hegel, a mere philosophical move, but the result of the historical development of collective consciousness—that is, "spirit") that can reduce the distance between God and the human subject by making the human subject more "divine" and God more "human."[36]

It is evident that a reconceptualization of the idea of God is a huge task, but it becomes even more challenging if one wants to pursue such reconceptualization while at the same time maintaining Kant's critical approach—in fact, for the reconceptualization of God to happen, it is necessary to restore *content* to that idea, a possibility that Kant's critical approach seems to *deny*.[37] How can Hegel restore content to the idea of God while maintaining Kant's critical attitude?

## Forgiveness, Kenosis, Perspectivism

Hegel's philosophy of religion can be read as an attempt to reconceptualize God—or, more specifically, to reconceive the relation between God and the human subject—by emphasizing the divine in the human and the human in the divine. It is in the unfolding of this process that the possibility of restoring content to religion will emerge, and this move will have significant consequences for Hegel's conception of metaphysics.

The process of the humanization of God was already started by Kant. Kant realized that God, as an ideal of pure moral perfection, was too abstract to effectively represent a symbol that could be used practically to apply the moral law to experience; hence, he introduced Christ as the prototype. This can be considered a move in the right direction; in fact, the former self / new self dynamic can be regarded as a first attempt to overcome subjectivism, at least insofar as it represents an attempt to provide a quasi-objective "theory of conversion" (it is, in other words, one of the moments where Kant comes closer to restoring *content* to religion).

However, and as already noted, Kant's theory still needs a God's-eye view, namely, an external standpoint from which the subject can be *judged* and, at best, justified, but not *forgiven*. It is Hegel who, carrying this issue further, suggested a way to solve this predicament. Consider the section of the *Phenomenology of Spirit* on forgiveness and reconciliation (PG, 3:665–71/403–9). Here the acting consciousness, the "beautiful soul," is imagined as confessing its being contingent on another shape of consciousness, a "hard-hearted judge," who initially "rejects any continuity with the other," that is, refuses to consider itself equally contingent, but eventually comes to forgive the beautiful soul. Pinkard nicely captures the deep meaning of the episode as follows:

> [E]ach is led to avow that, in Kant's terms, each is radically evil. That is, each comes to understand that he cannot easily pry apart the contingency of his own situated perspective (and thus his own individuality, or "self-love") and his own acquiescence to the demand for an unconditional justification of his actions. The mutual acknowledgment of radical evil is the prelude to forgiveness and reconciliation with the knowledge that what seemed like an insurmountable moral and metaphysical division can in fact achieve a practical resolution.[38]

One can compare this episode with the Kantian account of the story of Job that we considered in the previous chapter. Here, too, we have an initial opposition between truthfulness and truth: like Job's "friends," the hard-hearted judge initially refuses to forgive the counterpart because he claims to have a right to truth rather than simply truthfulness; in other words, he insists on speaking from a God's-eye point of view. As we have seen, Kant needs God to enter the scene and to condemn Job's friends for having (improperly) assumed the point of view of God, while, at the same time, he absolves Job because of his "truthfulness." It is God's act of speaking that makes Job's justification possible. In the Hegelian episode, the situation is similar, but unlike the Kantian episode, the "speaking" is via an *actual* speaking of another finite subject. This *Phenomenology* episode points toward a move that *could* follow from Kant's emphasis on truthfulness, but it is a move that Kant himself did *not* make: once the judgmental agent renounces any claim to judge from a position purporting to *represent* the law, real forgiveness becomes possible. The hard-hearted judge needs to renounce his own absoluteness and acknowledge his being equally contingent: this is the *sacrifice* that is required of him. However, there is no punitive aspect in this sacrifice. Rather than justification through the absolution imparted by an external omniscient God, here we have redemption through forgiveness granted by another finite subject. Hegel writes: "The reconciling *Yea*, in which the two I's let go [*ablassen*] their antithetical *existence*, is the *existence* of the 'I' which has expanded into a duality, and therein remains identical with itself, and, in its complete externalisation and opposite, possesses the certainty of itself: it is God manifested in the midst of those who know themselves in the form of pure knowledge" (PG, 3:671/409). Here "absolute spirit" is identified with reciprocal recognition of mutual forgiveness.[39] In other words, the act of forgiveness does not, for Hegel, merely express the agency of that concrete speaker: it is an act in which the voice of God is to be recognized—or, even better, it is God *Godself* appearing.

It is important to highlight the difference between this claim and Kant's claim that one has to listen to moral commands as if they had been spoken by the voice of God. The difference does not reside simply in the fact that here the voice of God does not command but *forgives*; the most important point is that here the voice of God needs to be conveyed *through another moral subject*. The forgiving agent is not simply a device that compensates for the lack of God's direct voice:[40] what is suggested here is a much deeper unity and interdependence between God and the human subject. I will come back to this point in the next chapter. For now, it is sufficient to remark that the Hegelian solution can be regarded as the development and radicalization of the Kantian idea of the internal archetype and its "activation" through the encounter with the symbol of Christ. This move is, however, only alluded to by Kant: Kant might have "foreseen the necessity of forgiveness,"[41] but he has proved unable to carry it further. Similarly, Kant has indeed introduced the kenotic idea that what is required to activate the internal archetype is "to make room for it," but this idea has remained somehow undeveloped.[42] Hegel radicalizes this idea; for Kant, grace was still a gift from a distant, transcendent, and "not-being posited" God, but this idea cannot escape subjectivism, because—as Hegel remarks—"even this not-being-posited is itself a being-posited by me";[43] in Hegel, conversely, legal justification becomes forgiveness exercised by God through the mediation of another moral agent who renounces any absolute judgmental standpoint by acknowledging her contingent status.

It might be objected that the transfer of the power to justification from a "posited-by-me" transcendent God to another moral subject amounts to dubious progress in the overcoming of subjectivism, and an even more dubious progression in the task of restoring content to religion. However, it has to be remarked, with Harris, that "the process of what Hegel calls *Verzeihung* is not that of ordinary 'forgiveness' at all. In essence, we are dealing with a logical forgiveness, exchanged between the agent and the observer, for the inevitable one-sidedness of being agent and observer."[44] "Logical forgiveness" is, in other words, not the *letter* but the *spirit* of Kant's Copernican revolution, that is, the idea that my view on the world is inevitably perspectival and one-sided. This is what I take to be the transcendental dimension that is maintained in Hegel's philosophy—that, after Kant, we can no longer aspire to a *directly objective* view on the world (and on God) is something that Hegel takes for granted. The point is to not stop at this reflective standpoint, and to not conclude (with Kant) that, given our view of the world is inevitably perspectival, then there cannot be (objective) knowledge that is not derived from (empirical) experience, and that, by resigning ourselves to a world of appearances, we can "reach no further than that subject's consciousness." Traditional metaphysics grounded objectivity on the subject's conforming to the object; Kant jeopardized this account and advanced an idea of universal subjectivity that required the unification of subject and object *in the subject*—but in so doing, he still maintained the traditional (Cartesian) conception of subject and object as originally distinct and in mutual opposition. But what if subject and object were *not* in original opposition, and the task of reason was to retrieve and consciously realize the unification of subject and object? If so, we could aspire not to a directly objective view but to a *mediately* objective view.

A comprehensive treatment of this issue will be essayed in the next chapter. For now, let us just consider this our working hypothesis. Assuming this mediated objectivity is indeed Hegel's goal, its achievement would first need the destruction of all the residues of traditional metaphysics still present in Kant's philosophy (being more "critical" than Kant himself, as it were) to enhance an authentically perspectival worldview. Only once this authentically perspectival standpoint has been affirmed would it then be possible to restore content to religion—a content that is (mediately) objective. It is to *this* dynamic of enhancement of perspectivism that we should therefore turn to contextualize the process of the reconceptualization of God.

Hegel concludes the "forgiveness and reconciliation" episode of the *Phenomenology* by claiming that both consciousnesses "display (*darstellt*) the power of the Spirit"[45] and that "the forgiveness which it extends to the other is the renunciation of itself [*Verzichtleistung auf sich*]" (PG, 3:669/407). This "renunciation of itself" signals not only the "recognition of our crucial mutual dependencies on each other"[46] but also—and even more importantly, for our purposes—the presence of a *kenotic* dynamic throughout the *Phenomenology of Spirit* and, in general, in Hegel's philosophy.

As I have argued elsewhere,[47] in the *Phenomenology* sacrifice can be considered a specific form of determinate negation phenomenologically conceived, in which recognition plays a central role. Besides *Verzichtleistung*, Hegel uses other terms to refer to this kind of kenotic sacrifice: *Aufopferung* (self-sacrifice in the sense of *giving something up*), *Verlassen* (which, interestingly, is often used in kenotic literature to describe Christ's act of relinquishing his own divinity in the incarnation), and *Freilassen* (literally, "to release" or "to set free," which Hegel uses in the *Encyclopedia of the Philosophical Sciences* to describe the final stage of the process of recognition: liberation from one's own self and, at the same time, a "leaving space" to the other).[48] In the *Phenomenology*, sacrifice appears to be the *Darstellung* of reciprocal recognition (of which forgiveness is the most developed form), in the sense that—in Hegel's own words—"This sacrifice [*Aufopferung*] is the externalization in which Spirit displays [*darstellt*] the process of its becoming Spirit in the form of free contingent happening" (PG, 3:807/492); in other words, sacrifice is an account of the distinctive movement of recognition.

In the *Phenomenology*, this kind of sacrifice is always associated with the endorsement of a perspectival view. One example is the phenomenological stage of the "unhappy consciousness," which represents the renunciation or surrender (*Aufgeben*) "first of its right to decide for itself, then of its property and enjoyment" (PG, 3:229/137); the intended aim of the consciousness is to reach "the certainty of having truly divested [*entäußert*] itself of its 'I,'" of its self-sufficiency. The unhappy consciousness, however, in the very act of showing itself to be the passive recipient of the gifts represented by its abilities and skills, proves itself to be active. As Pinkard nicely puts it, this episode is meant to show that the pursuit of independence does not consist in "completely disavowing one's own subjective point of view in favor of a forever distant, 'God's-eye' objective point of view," but in "fusing" multiple points of view into a unity.[49]

The section of the *Phenomenology* where Hegel's account of sacrifice appears more clearly is the one devoted to *cult*. Cult is the self-consciousness of the practical life;[50] those who perform sacrifice necessarily agree on that for which they are going to give up something without receiving anything in return. They agree on their recognition of something higher than mere contingent aspects of individual life—*idealities* such as values and beliefs. In the *Lectures on the Philosophy of Religion*, Hegel comes back to cult and distinguishes its three forms: devotion (*Andacht*), external sacrifice (*Opfer*), and its "highest" form," that is, interiorized sacrifice, according to which one "lays aside one's own subjectivity [*seiner Subjektivität abtut*]" (Rel I, 334/446).[51]

On the grounds of these and other passages addressing sacrifice in Hegel's works, it is possible to identify three fundamental features of sacrifice. First, sacrifice is a conscious negation—it has to be performed consciously. Second, it needs to be considered as a selfless act that does not expect anything in return. The sacrifice performed in cult presents both these features; however, it is only *close* to being a real and genuine sacrifice, as it lacks the third feature. In cult, the agent deprives itself of something, but the object of sacrifice is external; conversely, a genuine sacrifice implies the giving up of something *essential* to the subject, that is, something that *constitutes* the subject. Hegel is quite explicit in identifying the exemplar of genuine sacrifice in Christ's incarnation and death (PG, 3:724/438 and 3:749/753). Christ represents the overcoming of the abstract opposition between the divine and the human. This overcoming can be realized only through a sacrifice that consists in a *withdrawal*. Effectively, in becoming human, God sacrifices his own divine absoluteness in an act of self-divestment or relinquishment (*Entäußerung*) and accepts most human limitations.

I will not enter into the labyrinthine issue of the influence exerted on Hegel by the thought of the seventeenth-century German mystic Jacob Böhme;[52] here it would suffice to say that, as I have argued elsewhere, it is a Böhmian conception of kenosis that is at work in interiorized sacrifice.[53] One of the most original features of Böhme's account is that God's incarnation and self-sacrifice is a gratuitous act of love. Hegel endorses this Böhmian idea: Robert Williams even defines self-sacrificing divine love as "the fundamental speculative intuition of Hegel's thought."[54] Williams has emphasized the relevance of this issue in Hegel's reconceptualization of God more than any other contemporary interpreter. The conception of God that Hegel advances is not that of an immutable being, a "monopolar absolute,"[55] "lifeless and solitary [*leblose Einsame*]"; Hegel's God is a God who gratuitously decides to sacrifice Godself, who can suffer, and who is "reciprocally related to and can be influenced by the world."[56] According to Williams, it is this conception of God that allows Hegel to overcome the abstract opposition between the divine and the human: "Both God and the human are united in a community of forgiveness."[57] Thus, Williams brings us back to the notion of forgiveness. As we have seen in the "forgiveness and reconciliation" episode of the *Phenomenology*, the renunciation of one's absoluteness (kenotic sacrifice, in theological language) is an unavoidable presupposition for the act of forgiveness. Both are gratuitous,[58] and it is in this gratuitousness that recognition has its epistemological and existential grounds. The process of recognition *requires* a willingness to renounce one's own absoluteness. It might seem puzzling that a *required* sacrifice is also *gratuitous*. However, such puzzlement is only illusory: it is precisely the *gratuitousness* of sacrifice that is *necessary* for recognition. Recognition is intrinsically a *free* act—it might also not happen; but in order for it to happen, a gratuitous act of self-giving is required. This renunciation can indeed be named "sacrifice" in the kenotic sense, of which Christ is considered by Hegel as the prototypical expression. The centrality of the incarnation of Christ in Hegel's philosophy can be fully grasped only if its function as model of kenotic sacrifice is taken into consideration.

## A New God, a New Metaphysics

The reconceptualization of God—in Hegel's words, "The sacrifice of divinity, i.e., of the abstract, transcendent Being [*des abstrakten jenseitigen Wesens*]," which "has already occurred in his becoming actual [*Wirklichwerden*]" (JS-III, 258/178)[59]—has several implications. First, it has *ethico-political* implications. This has already been noted by Pippin, who refers to the "insufficiency of a God merely contained with himself" and to God's "need to 'empty' [*entäußern*] himself in creating the world"[60] and reads this in light of Hegel's claim (in the 1827–1828 *Lectures on the Philosophy of Spirit*) that "precisely [in] this condition of self-externality [*Äußerlichkeit*], of being beyond the limits of one's individuality, one gains one's substantial self-consciousness. This is the condition of being recognized" (VPG, 174/194). Human subjects are required to imitate Christ in his kenosis, which, being the condition for recognition, has a distinctive *normative* value, insofar as it represents a normative idea in ethics and politics. Pippin therefore argues that "the deeper point here" is "ultimately politico-ethical."[61] While I agree with Pippin that this dimension is undoubtedly there, it would be a mistake to read this claim as meaning that the role of the idea of God in Hegel's philosophy is *merely* that of an ethical metaphor. The "deeper point" is not only "politico-ethical," but it is also *epistemologico-metaphysical*.

In Western thought, the idea of God has always been indicative of the knowledge aspired to in philosophy. The Aristotelian God, the immutable and fully actualized unmoved mover, was indicative of the goal of philosophy as a metaphysical knowledge of an "ultimate" reality. In the domain of epistemology, this image is connected with a conception of metaphysics as expressed by the phrase "God's-eye view."[62] Hegel's emphasis on the figure of Christ, that is, on God's emptying Godself of divinity[63] to become human, suggests a conception of metaphysical knowledge different from traditional pre-Kantian metaphysics. Hegel's kenotic Christian God (who renounces the "God's-eye view") is consistent with an account of metaphysics as *perspectival* knowledge of *ideal* objects, thus representing the *idealistic* standpoint in the domain of epistemology and metaphysics.

The claim here is that a reconceptualized, kenotic conception of God has important implications for metaphysics insofar as it enhances a *perspectival* standpoint. Conceiving God as affected by the same partiality in perspective that we as humans suffer means to undermine the traditional idea of metaphysical knowledge as "the omnicomprehensive point of view" and to replace it with an idea of knowledge as an expression of all different (and even contradictory) points of view.

Other scholars endorsing the so-called "revisionist/post-Kantian" interpretation of Hegel have addressed Hegel's perspectivism. Commenting on the "forgiveness and reconciliation" episode of the *Phenomenology*, Pinkard had remarked that forgiveness only becomes possible when "those perspectives are seen for the partial, contingent perspectives they are";[64] and more recently, he came back to the same episode, stressing that "[e]ach acknowledges his own finitude and partiality, and in doing so, in the give-and-take of their encounter, each forgives the other for having claimed such an absolute status for himself."[65] As with Pippin, for Pinkard what is at stake here is predominantly the ethico-political dimension. Building on these readings, Redding has started to show the relevance of Hegel's perspectivism beyond the ethico-political dimension, pointing out that for Hegel "we cannot think of rational thought as working its way through changing perspectives onto a single, stable world."[66] Redding's recent work has been seminal in mapping the consequences that a perspectival account of Hegel's thought has for his conception of God and for his interpretation of religious practices and beliefs. The perspectival interpretation of Hegel advanced by Redding would not be complete, however, without a move in a *reverse* but *complementary* direction—to examine the consequences that Hegel's (kenotic) idea of God has for his understanding of an idealistic metaphysics. In other words, Hegel's perspectivism has both an ethico-political *and* an epistemologico-metaphysical dimension; they are both direct implications of the logic of kenosis. Thus, not a *regression* into pre-Kantian metaphysics but only a *progression* into a post-Kantian idealist metaphysics is able to restore content to philosophy and religion—and thus, to overcome subjectivism.

At this stage, a certain degree of skeptic puzzlement toward Hegel's strategy reconstructed earlier is understandable and even unavoidable. Assuming that our reconstruction is correct, how can a metaphysics grounded in perspectivism be capable of overcoming subjectivism? Does not perspectivism, rather than lowering the risk of subjectivism, make it worse, and even turn it into relativism? And more fundamentally, how can a metaphysical thought be perspectival—isn't it a contradiction in terms?

These (legitimate) questions are relevant not only in themselves but also for a correct understanding of Hegel's philosophy of religion. A response to these concerns, which we use here as our working hypothesis, has already been provided by Redding. Redding regards Hegel as conceiving of the content of metaphysics as entirely normative (rather than as a type of "scientific" or "naturalistic" knowledge about the way the world is "anyway"). But the norms are themselves fallible and subject to finitude (*hence*, for Redding, the necessity that God becomes a finite, suffering mortal); what "rescues" Hegel's "cognitive contextualism from any threat of relativism and connect[s] it back to the unifying conception of reason in

Kant" is, according to Redding, the rational "revisibility" of norms—that is, their self-correcting nature, which enables thought to "work its way through a logically governed, or at least logically reconstructable, order" in the world of ever-changing and even contradictory norms. If this interpretative model is correct, it should also work in the *reverse* direction—that is, the kenotic reconceptualization of God (God incarnate in a finite and suffering mortal being) should have consequences *for* an understanding of metaphysics (Hegel's philosophy of absolute spirit) conceived as the realm of self-realizing and self-correcting norms.

In the following chapters, we will therefore move in that (reverse) direction. This requires us to go through a number of steps: (1) if the reconceptualization of God is to have consequences for metaphysics, it is indispensable to understand the degree of objectivity of this concept (clearly, if the reconceptualization of God is merely the result of a subjective process, that is, nothing more than a change in *our* way of thinking of God, then the resulting metaphysics would be exposed to subjectivism, and the entire project would collapse)—in Kantian terms, an *analytic*; (2) the objectivity of this concept will need some justification, such as that provided by Hegel in his defense of the ontological argument; (3) a structure will be needed to make this reconceptualization applicable to the world: the trinitarian structure[67]—in Kantian terms, a *schematism*; (4) a critique of the traditional conception of God will also be needed, and Hegel provides such critique with his notion of the death of God—which thus plays the role of a Kantian *dialectic*; and finally (5) an explanation of the proper function of the concept of God for the "I" will be needed—something analogous to the Kantian *Doctrine of method*; such explanation will show how the reconceptualization of God has consequences for an understanding of idealist metaphysics in its overcoming of subjectivism.

This is precisely the path that we will follow in the ensuing chapters.

# 3

# The Reality of Religion in Hegel's Idealist Metaphysics

## Metaphysics and Picture-Thinking

What degree of objective reality does the concept of God have for Hegel? Is the reconceptualization of God attempted by Hegel the result of a subjective process—that is, is Hegel diagnosing a change in our way of thinking about God in modernity? Or is Hegel reestablishing the objective reality of God, thus reconnecting with the pre-Kantian theistic tradition that sought to prove the reality of God?

The question of God is clearly central to an analysis of Hegel's philosophy because it is bound to influence countless other notions that he uses. Moreover, in the context of his philosophy of religion, Hegel uses several terms and notions that derive from Christian theology (such as the incarnation, the Trinity, and the death of God); here, therefore, the question becomes whether Hegel is using them as images that inadequately anticipate a philosophical content, or as images that have an ontic status—that is, as having a factual existence.

On closer inspection, and as already noticed by some Hegel scholars,[1] the relevance of the question of the reality status of God (and, by extension, the reality status of other religious notions employed by Hegel) is not limited to an assessment of Hegel's philosophy *of religion* but has huge repercussions for the general interpretation of Hegel's metaphysics. In other words, what is at stake here is the understanding of Hegel's *idealism,* and the extent to which it maintains (and possibly extends) the

Kantian Copernican revolution, while restoring nonsubjective content to philosophy (and to religion).

The question is anything but new. As is known, the right Hegelians, representing the theist faction of Hegel's followers, considered Hegel a *realist*, and not an *idealist*, concerning God. On the other side of the interpretative spectrum, the left Hegelians (such as Strauss and Feuerbach) opposed the theistic reading of Hegel and turned Hegel's thought into a "humanist" critique of theism.

Today, we witness a similar debate in Hegel scholarship, which, while being more focused on the general interpretation of Hegel's idealism, has relevant implications for his conception of God. Recent approaches generally share the idea that Hegel's philosophy cannot be simply considered a *regression* to *pre-Kantian* metaphysics. After all, Hegel describes pre-Kantian metaphysics as a "naive way of proceeding" because it "regarded the thought-determinations" it uses "as the fundamental determination of things" ("Grundbestimmungen der Dinge," E I, 8:94/68). Hegel therefore considers Kant's conception of thought-determinations qua mind-dependent as an important turn in the approach to metaphysics. Recent approaches, however, often differ in their interpretation of Hegel's attitude toward the possibility of a *post-Kantian* metaphysics. In the context of this debate, interpretations range from views that the main purpose of Hegel's system is to articulate a metaphysical account of the world and of history (the "conceptual realist" interpretation) to "revisionist" (also referred to as "deflationary") readings, which largely question the metaphysical nature of Hegel's system.

The "conceptual realist" interpretation reads Hegel's idealism as an inquiry into the world's fundamental "features" or "structures," which include a conceptual dimension; thus, it rejects any transcendental interpretation of Hegel.[2] Thus, for example, Stern argues that "the characteristic feature of Hegel's absolute idealism is his freeing of the Idea from Mind and from the thinking subject"—a distinction (that between Idea and Mind) that, according to Stern, was "impossible for Kant's merely subjective idealism."[3] Similarly, Kreines sees Hegel as reestablishing metaphysics in a revised form by exploiting a sense of the "thing in itself" as knowable: such "features of the world" accessible to thought are seen as having an "in itself" status in the sense of being "mind-independent"[4]—but in a way that such knowledge would not be equated with the transcendent God's mind presupposed by Kant. Beiser holds similar views and maintains that Hegel's philosophy has an unavoidable metaphysical dimension.

Conversely, the "post-Kantian" or "revisionist" interpretation[5] considers Hegel's thought as an extension of Kant's transcendental philosophy, with the conditions of human rationality not limited to mental formal structures but including historically and socially determined conditions. For example, Pippin argues that Hegel followed Kant in "attempting to deduce the categories from the condition of self-consciousness" to "'ground' them in the 'I.'"[6] Also, employing Hegel's notion of recognition (*Anerkennung*),[7] the revisionist Hegelians conceive of the norms as holding between agents: "The rules exist there only to the extent that agents actually do hold themselves and others to them, and in this sense they are 'mind-dependent.'"[8] This interpretation is sometimes referred to as "non-metaphysical": the proponents of "conceptual realism" are, in fact, concerned that the "revisionist" reading might lead (or effectively leads) to the conclusion that Hegel's philosophical project is substantially anti-metaphysical. The word "deflationary" is also occasionally used to describe these readings, suggesting—as Hammer explains—that they "deliberately refrain" from taking Hegel's "claim to possess metaphysical knowledge of the essence of reality seriously. [. . .] In Pippin and Pinkard, for example, much of the gist of Hegel's project has to do with the attempt to provide a social epistemology that, while remaining committed to Kant's account of rational self-legislation, bases its normative orientation on criteria derived from concrete historical communities rather than individual minds."[9]

To complete this brief taxonomy of recent approaches to Hegel, one should add the "qualified revisionist" interpretation. The term was coined by Redding[10] to refer to Longuenesse's tenet that Hegel's philosophy is a *post-Kantian* metaphysics, insofar as "metaphysics after Kant is a science of being as being thought"; that is, it is "an investigation of the universal determinations of thought at work in any attempt to think what is."[11] The definition of "qualified revisionist" can be extended to Redding himself: in fact, by treating Hegel's recognition as primarily an epistemological notion,[12] Redding suggests that it is possible to regard Hegel's thought as being in continuation with the Kantian project and, at the same time, as maintaining a metaphysical dimension—or, better, as proposing a *different* kind of metaphysics: an *idealist* metaphysics. Redding sees Hegel as preserving the empirical realism of Kant's account and yet denying (contra Kreines) that thinking allows us to access a mind-independent reality—thus retaining something of Kant's transcendental idealism. In other words, and as already noted in the previous chapter, Hegel is regarded as conceiving of the content of metaphysics as entirely normative.

We know that Hegel is not short of claims asserting the need to take seriously the cognition of God (Rel I, 5–7/86–87). Thus, Hegel's philosophy of religion is, unsurprisingly, often appealed to in criticizing the post-Kantian interpretation, which can effectively be said to constitute the hardest test case for such a reading.[13] Williams offers a reading of the implications of the two interpretative streams mentioned earlier. There is an undeniable theological dimension, Williams claims, in Hegel's philosophy. Does the presence of a theological dimension imply a commitment to pre-critical metaphysics? If so, and if Hegel rejects pre-Kantian metaphysics (as Pippin and the post-Kantian interpreters contend), then he should also reject theology and embrace atheism—something Hegel never ventures. Both Pippin and Beiser, Williams states, agree that Hegel's philosophy, including his metaphysics, is *post*-critical.[14] However, Pippin, by offering a "Kantianized" version of Hegel, seems to Williams to be implying that a post-Kantian theological Hegel is an "impossibility." Beiser is critical of such a view; but, Williams continues, he "seems unsure what that might be or whether it includes theology."[15] Effectively, Beiser is explicit in claiming: "The incarnation and the trinity, Hegel believed, were simply metaphors, intuitions and feelings about this fundamental truth of reason."[16] Therefore, Williams concludes, "In this respect Beiser agrees with the non-metaphysical interpretations he criticizes."[17]

Both the conceptual realist and the revisionist/post-Kantian readings of Hegel seem to offer a detheologized version of Hegel. On the conceptual realist side, Kreines maintains that the metaphysical knowledge advanced by Hegel cannot be equated with that of a divine intuitive intellect: the theological elements seem not to be present at all. On the post-Kantian side, Pinkard regards Hegel as arguing that in Christianity "we acknowledge that we worship not ourselves, which would be absurd, but the 'divine principle' within ourselves [. . .]. The divine in Christianity is the rational structure of the whole in which we live and work, are born and die, not some transcendent entity beyond human life and concerns."[18] Thus, Hegel is seen as taking religion in general, and Christianity in particular, seriously—but such an account also seems, as Lewis suggests, to require viewing much of the doctrines such as creation and the fall "as metaphors for claims that philosophy expresses discursively."[19]

The "qualified revisionist" interpretation does not offer a unique response to the question of God and religion in Hegel—precisely because the "qualifications" vary for each of its proponents. On one hand, Longuenesse recognizes the presence of metaphysical-theological elements in Hegel's idealism but seems reluctant to embrace them. On the other hand, Redding, in virtual conversation with Kreines, suggests that if Hegel has no use of the transcendent God's mind presupposed by Kant, it is because he thinks he has a better concept of God available—that is, that God's mind is "distributed across the minds of finite human beings" and "reliant on the acts of those finite beings."[20] That God's mind is distributed across the minds of finite human beings does not, Redding argues, "disqualify it from being a mind in its own right, nor does this reduce it to the status of a mere fiction."[21] This argument requires some unpacking. In what sense can God be a mind "in its own right" while being distributed across the minds of finite human beings? Is that a form of concealed collective consciousness residing in everybody's mind? No—or, better, not exactly. This conception of God is rather based on Redding's distinctive "epistemology of recognition."

In the previous chapter, I mentioned that Redding regards Hegel's metaphysics as entirely normative. This means that Hegel might be regarded as transforming the Platonic world of ideas,[22] which are supposed to exist "anyway," into the "realm of reason," in which objects are "idealities" (which include, but are not limited to, values, norms, and beliefs); in the realm of reason, objects exist qua products of reason. Clearly, a problematic aspect of such an approach is specifying which criterion should be used to determine which objects belong or do not belong to that "realm of reason." In Redding's view, Hegel's answer to this question is forged out of an assimilation of the Kantian conception that ideas play a regulative and normative role in human cognition and morality, with the Fichtean concept of recognition (*Anerkennung*). The main idea emerging from Redding's work is that to be an idealist about metaphysical objects is to recognize that their reality (their existence as objects of reason) is *conditional* upon human recognition. This means that human beings *themselves* must be regarded as products of reason; as Redding puts it, "Without this system of recognition, there is no self, just a natural organism."[23] The first implication of such an approach is that if I, as a subject (or, to use Hegel's terminology, as a subjective spirit), do not recognize others as human beings (and, as such, as being equally capable of recognizing me as a human being), the very possibility of a realm of reason made up by values and norms (whose existence depends upon a joint act of recognition) disappears. In fact, if metaphysical objects exist only insofar as human subjects recognize them as existing, and if the existence of human beings (as distinct from mere natural organisms) is, in turn, dependent upon mutual recognition, it follows that recognition is the fundamental organizing principle of Hegel's metaphysics.

Redding's interpretation seems to have extensive and interesting consequences for the conception of God in the context of Hegel's philosophy of religion: "Read as an 'absolute' idealist in a post-Kantian sense, then," Redding argues, "Hegel might be seen as extending such a non-realist approach to both the individual soul and to God."[24] I will return to this issue of the non-realist approach to God in the final section of this chapter, where I will advance a distinction that falls outside Redding's interpretation but rather follows from a further qualification that I have already introduced in the previous chapter: an interpretation of the objective reality that Hegel wants for God as *mediated* objectivity. Before proceeding further, however, it is first appropriate to establish the terms of the question by briefly considering the nature of religion, the role of Christianity, and the kind of problem an interpretation of religious (Christian) representations posits in the context of Hegel's philosophy of religion. I will accomplish this by referring to definitions provided in the existing scholarship, which I take to be (relatively) undisputed, and building on them to pave the way for the application of the "mediated objectivity" to religious representations in the next section.

According to Magee,[25] religion for Hegel is "the truth grasped in picture-thinking" (*das vorstellende Denken*). Hegel's analysis of religion is indeed characterized by a frequent use of the term *Vorstellung*. This term comes from the German verb *vorstellen*—literally, "to represent" or "to put forward"; *Vorstellung* is the result of this activity. Before Hegel, the term "representation" was used in philosophy in a wide sense: Locke, for instance, used it as equivalent to "idea," and Kant often seems to have done the same with his use of *Vorstellung*. Hegel significantly transforms the use of this term by employing it in a much narrower sense, primarily insofar as it contrasts with "concept" (*Begriff*).

*Vorstellung*,[26] for Hegel, is, according to Williams's definition, "consciousness as a representational system" that "is based upon and constituted by the dichotomy between subject and object."[27] Hegel's use of *Vorstellungen* is not restricted to his writings on religion; the main reason why Hegel often uses this term in the context of his discussion on religious issues is because the content of religion, despite being the same as that of philosophy, is presented in a form that is not properly conceptual (JS-III, 260/181): *Vorstellungen* are representations of objects perceived to be *external* by the consciousness. In fact, in religion, God is often conceived as a *Gegenstand*, an object-that-stands-over-and-against human consciousness: that is, God is represented "without proper consideration of its relation"[28] to the human subject. Such opposition has to be overcome: God is to be thought of as being in an indissoluble relation with human consciousness. As an implication, the human subject cannot properly think of God outside of the set of historical and cultural categories that have determined God's representation. I take this to be the general strategy employed in Hegel's *Lectures on the Philosophy of Religion*, which effectively represent an analysis of the transformations of religious *Vorstellungen* through the various ages and cultures. The question of what God is for Hegel, therefore, inevitably implies wondering whether Hegel is suggesting that we should consider all of the representational accounts of God to be vestiges of the past, which are thus destined to be overcome by a pure conceptual understanding of God (similarly to what other philosophers had suggested before Hegel). As I am going to argue, Hegel's understanding of the relation between the representation(s) of God and the concept of God is actually much more sophisticated.

Historically, the traditional philosophical conception of God derived from the Aristotelian idea of the immutable and impassive "unmoved mover," which also represented the "view from nowhere" typical of traditional metaphysics. In modernity, the philosophical idea of God was made to coincide with the source of norms, that is, the source of a normativity that transcends the acts of individuals. Against this background, Christianity represents, in Hegel's view, a "complete revolution" (Rel III, 62–65/127–29): "substance becomes subject" (PG, 3:571/476). This claim appears after Hegel's account of the incarnation, which represents the death of the ancient (Aristotelian) God, that is, God as substance. There is no doubt that Hegel has Aristotle in mind here, and the Aristotelian definition of God as "thought thinking itself." The Aristotelian God, as well as Spinoza's God, which is also defined as substance, is not a person or a subject.[29] Christianity captures an aspect of God that is missing in both the Aristotelian and Spinozan accounts: God is a person, that is, a subject. Christianity represents this move through the emphasis on the self-divestment (*Entäußerung*) that occurs in the incarnation and death of Christ. That is, God is not immobile, static, and motionless but is rather active and self-transforming, *alive*.

The revolution of Christianity calls for a *reconceptualization* of God because it introduces, with the notion of incarnation, the conception of a God who assumes the finite viewpoint and renounces his absoluteness to the point of death. Hegel's great insight here is to understand that although God does play a fundamental philosophical role, God cannot be thought of in isolation from the historical and cultural transformations of the conception of the divine, because God needs to be thought of in conjunction with the movements of self-consciousness that is thinking God. Whether the Christian God that Hegel refers to is a more or less orthodox Lutheran God or, more likely, a heterodox God whose conception is influenced by the mystical tradition of Meister Eckhart and Jacob Böhme,[30] two considerations are relevant for our purposes. First, in the context of a philosophical analysis of religion, representations and concepts must be conceived in mutual relation; religious representations lead to philosophical concepts, and the corresponding concepts reconstruct "the genetic move that made it [the concept] possible"—a strategy that O'Regan calls, with an appropriate expression, "a special kind of dialectical shuttle."[31] Second, Hegel's endorsement of a kenotic conception of God (a God undergoing self-divestment) is, as remarked by Williams,[32] "unfoundational." Hegel's discourse on God, I argue, can be defined as "unfoundational" in a twofold sense: first, because there is no ontotheological necessity guiding this process; and second, because the process cannot occur outside of the relation between God and humanity. Williams particularly focuses on the theological justification for such nonfoundational discourse.[33] Here, I am interested in developing the *philosophical* justification of such a nonfoundational discourse. In fact, if the central question is, as previously stated, whether Hegel considers God and the objects of other religious notions as having an ontic status (and hence as being, at least potentially, the object of an objective knowledge), or as being unreal metaphoric images (and hence as having a mere subjective value), then we should wonder whether a rational philosophical thought can effectively support a conception of God that entails such an understanding of religious representations as ontic (that is, as being objectively real) without being foundationalist (in a pre-Kantian and traditionally theistic sense).

Prima facie, the question seems to be whether the religious representations and particularly the conception of the Christian incarnated God (which clearly plays a pivotal role in Hegel's conception of the "consummate" religion) merely belong to the history of thought and culture (that is, they are relevant insofar as they are meaningful to understand a change that has occurred in *our* way of thinking about God) or whether, having an ontic status, the incarnation, death, and resurrection are events that effectively occurred to a being distinct from us, which we refer to as "God." Put in these terms, the distinction is between an *anthropological* reading and a *realist* reading of Hegel's conception of God—in other words, it is a more sophisticated version of the old split between "left" and "right" Hegelians.

The qualified revisionist interpretation, broadly defined by Longuenesse's basic tenet that "metaphysics after Kant is a science of being as being thought," potentially provides, I suggest, an interpretation of Hegel's metaphysics within which the question of the objective reality of God for Hegel can be answered beyond the impasse represented by the opposition between the anthropological and the realist readings. For the qualified revisionist approach to provide a philosophical justification of Hegel's conception of God and religious representations as objectively ontic and yet not foundationalist (in the sense of pre-Kantian metaphysics), we need, I contend, to introduce a further qualification, which I have already referred to as the "mediated objectivity" of metaphysical knowledge. In the remaining part of this section, I will argue that the objective reality that Hegel attributes to God in particular and to religious representations in general, considered as metaphysical objects, is a *mediated* objectivity, that is, an objectivity that does not reflect the reality of an object-that-stands-over-and-against human consciousness but rather takes into account the contribution of our self-conscious mind for the establishment of the content of that metaphysical object and thus reflects the relational unity between subject and object.

Hegel clearly maintains (and this is indeed something that is hard to deny) that Western philosophy started from a *realist* metaphysical view (that is, the view that knowledge requires the subject's cognition to conform to the object). Kant's critical philosophy has jeopardized this view, which was destined to collapse, according to Hegel. However, the collapse of traditional metaphysical realism led to the rise of subjectivism. Traditional realism and subjectivism generate two conceptions of God (and of religion in general) that are mutually exclusive: either God exists as a mind-independent external object (realism) or God is a concept completely dependent on our subjective activity (subjectivism, which, pushed to its extreme consequences, can turn into fictionalism). What both traditional realism and subjectivism (including Kant's idealism, insofar as it is not immune to a type of subjectivism) fail to recognize is that, as remarked by Redding, human beings *themselves* must be regarded as products of reason. As Hegel puts it, self-consciousness itself—that is, the standpoint from which the world and God are approached—"exists in and for itself when, and by the fact that, it so exists for another; that is, it exists only in being acknowledged" (PG, 3:145/111). In other words, self-consciousness *emerges* from the process of recognition, and it is not even really *distinguishable* from it.

Hegel is definitely not committed to a peculiar "immaterialism" à la Berkeley; indeed, he is very far from it—as evidence of this, one might recall the master/slave episode in the *Phenomenology*, which features the slave as *physically* interacting with objects. In Hegel's view, conceptually mediated recognition between minds is predicated upon a practical involvement with a world of things in which objects are transformed by *labor*. In this context, recognition is the interaction with spatiomaterial objects; some objects that are recognized as having their existence not entirely exhausted by spatiotemporal properties (human beings) are posited as part of a framework that explains the very possibility of transforming spatiotemporal ones. In other words, a community of cognizers ("minds") is built on the presupposition of a community of beings physically interacting with each other and with objects. This narrative picture of the Hegelian system is based upon a primordial account of ourselves (human beings) as shapes of life that recognize each other and interact with the world and with each other in such a way that these intersubjective acts of mutual recognition make possible the genesis of concepts—for instance, when human beings agree on the recognition of "idealities," that is, something higher than mere contingent aspects of individual life.[34] In other words, as has been argued by Redding,[35] Hegel is an idealist about that which a metaphysical realist is a realist, namely, the capacity to know things in themselves, that is, through a "God's-eye view" of the world. Hegel maintains that concepts cannot be known *independently* of human recognitive activity.

One could charge Hegel with what we might call the "Munchausen fallacy," that is, to think of self-consciousness as emerging from a process, that of recognition, which seems to already imply the existence of self-consciousness might remind one of Baron Munchausen, who famously tied a rope around one of the horns of the moon and slid down to the end of the rope, but given that the earth was still a long way beneath him, he unhooked the rope from the moon, swung it beneath him, slid down the length of the rope again, and again threw the rope down—and by this process he reached the earth. In other words, someone might wonder how can there have been a "first" (self-conscious) human being, if no "human being" (properly speaking) exists without recognition from another human being. However, such an objection would entirely miss the point that it is *mutual* recognition we are talking about here. There is no such thing as a "first" human being, but human beings collectively come into existence, as it were, through the ongoing process of mutual recognition. That is, to claim that self-consciousness is dependent on recognition means that it depends on its own development.

The consideration of self-consciousness as dependent on recognition also sheds some light on the extent to which Hegel's idealism can be considered transcendental. In the previous chapter, I mentioned that Hegel scolds Kant for being resigned to a world of appearances (that we can "reach no further than that subject's consciousness"). However, Hegel's reproach can be considered to be consistent with (what Hegel takes to be) the spirit of Kant's transcendental philosophy, that is, the idea that our cognition is not passively modeled on the external world; our self-conscious mind contributes something to it. For Kant, the contribution was only formal: our mind contributes the form of knowledge, whereas the content comes exclusively from the empirical world. However, limiting the contribution of the mind to the form of knowledge still reproduces, to some degree, the traditional metaphysical distinction between subject and object, splitting the object into an accessible (*phenomenon*) and an inaccessible (*noumenon*) aspect and thus paving the way to subjectivism. Being radical in the conception that our cognition is not passively modeled on the external world means affirming, with Hegel, that our mind contributes not only the form of knowledge but also some of its content; for there is, properly speaking, no "metaphysical" world prior to self-consciousness and no self-consciousness prior to recognition (that is, the process that produces the metaphysical world). This is the reason why objectivity can only be *mediated* objectivity: self-consciousness does not passively receive the content of cognition (which constitutes its objectivity) from a preexisting mind-independent external reality. If consciousness "restricts itself to the scope of perception," no objectivity can be reached. It is rather in "the content of thought in and for itself" ("der Inhalt des Gedankens für sich," E I, 8:125/92)[36] that objectivity can be reached, that is, by embracing a conception of (metaphysical) reality as the result of an ongoing process of mediation between subject and object that is always already in place. Figuratively speaking (and, as I will show in the next section, this is not inappropriate in this context), we might say that our gaze is always already part of reality, and reality is such because it includes our gaze. Hegel's metaphysics does not look at the nature of reality "from a position of supreme insight" but "from the center of the action," that is, "in the middle of things."[37]

Kant's modesty is the path to Hegel's ambition. If, on one hand, by "transcendental" we mean that our cognition is always perspectival, then Hegel's idealism is still transcendental and is even more transcendental that Kant's idealism because, for Hegel, all our attempts to keep our consciousness distinct from the world (and the world distinct from our consciousness) in the process of cognition are destined to fail.[38] If, on the other hand, by "transcendental" we mean a philosophy concerned exclusively with the conditions and forms of our knowledge, then Hegel's idealism is not transcendental, because he wants to restore content to nonsensible (metaphysical) knowledge; that content, however, is not independent of human activity, because, being "content of thought," it inevitably includes (to the point of being indistinguishable from) "conceptual determinations as have been developed throughout the history of human thought."[39] Beyond any debate of the use of the term "transcendental," if the preceding reconstruction is valid, then Hegel is a post-Kantian philosopher with a *post*-critical metaphysics.

So far, I have sketched an account of Hegel's metaphysics as being concerned with a reality that, precisely because it is metaphysical, is the result of an ongoing process of mediation between subject and object that is always already in place and therefore aims at giving an account of metaphysical objects conceived as the products of this indissoluble relation between self-consciousness and the world. The view suggested here differs from its competitors in a twofold sense. This view does not read Hegel's idealism as an inquiry into fundamental "features" or "structures" of the world aiming at reaching a type of "scientific" or "naturalistic" knowledge of the way the world is "anyway."[40] At the same time, this view avoids any anthropological or subjectivist drift of the post-Kantian revisionist interpretation, which might lead to an account where the possibility of a post-critical metaphysics is drastically reduced (or even impossible) and where there is no other function for God beyond that of being a philosophical metaphor or, at best, a figural representation of the source of norms. Conversely, the view I am advocating safeguards the presence of an unavoidable metaphysical dimension of Hegel's thought, which is conceived as being an expression of Hegel's mediated objectivity, consistent with the principle of the indissolubility of the relation between self-consciousness and the world.

The mediated objectivity of metaphysical knowledge is to be considered an important (in my view) qualification of the post-Kantian interpretation. This qualification would, in fact, allow the post-Kantian interpreter to defend a post-critical metaphysics and, equally important for our purposes, it would provide a philosophical justification for Hegel's religious nonfoundational discourse: the conception of God entails a mediately objective (and not merely metaphorical) understanding of religious representations.

From this point of view, the question of the reality of God as presented before, which seems to push the interpreter of Hegel to choose between an anthropological and a realist (theological) reading of his thought, is misleading as it is presented in *pre-critical* (pre-Kantian) terms. Presenting the alternative between an anthropological and a realist reading would mean conceiving of God in a pre-critical way, that is, as an entity absolutely transcendent and separated from humans, whose properties could be discussed regardless of the way God is thought of. In Hegel's view, Kant was right in emphasizing the practical relevance of the idea of God for us but was wrong in maintaining that any (theoretical) knowledge of God was therefore inaccessible. Hegel regards Christianity as the "consummate religion" precisely because of the centrality of the incarnation, which is, conceptually, the unity between the finite and the infinite, a unity realized religiously in the incarnation, and that reason is called upon to realize at a conceptual level. On this ground, to wonder whether the events of the Christian narrative—the incarnation, the death of God, and the resurrection of Christ—occur only "for us" or in "external" reality is a pre-critical question because, in the spirit of Kant's critical revolution (or, better, in the spirit of what Hegel *considers* to be Kant's critical revolution), we cannot "step out" of our finite perspective on the world (and on God) to have a *directly objective* reading of the world.

Embracing a *mediately* objective reading of religious representations means that we should conceive of those *Vorstellungen* neither as *inadequately objective* representations of the structures of reality (later destined to be overcome by adequately objective philosophical conceptualizations of the same structures) nor as mere metaphors of the rational structures of the whole in which we live. Thus, the next question is how the conception of mediated objectivity can be applied to religious representations. If Christian doctrines are the result of historical elaboration and transformation (and Hegel is certainly aware of this fact), it should be explained how their historically determined nature can be reconciled with Hegel's ambition to rescue them from subjectivism and to restore content to religion.

## Figural Reading of Religious Representations

In the previous section, I sketched a qualified post-Kantian reading that, thanks to the introduction of the notion of mediated objectivity, is consistent with the possibility of a post-critical metaphysics while allowing for an account of Hegel's thought that is not detheologized. The conception of objectivity as *mediated* objectivity, I argued, philosophically justifies Hegel's nonfoundational religious discourse because it implies that the human subject cannot properly think of God outside of the set of historical and cultural categories that have determined God's representation. One of the benefits that flow from this reading is, I now contend, an approach to religious representations that avoids the (supposedly) mutually exclusive choice between their literal and their metaphorical meaning—that is, a choice between an account that straightforwardly attributes an ontic status to those representations and an account that does not attribute to them any factual reality beyond their status as metaphorical instruments.

Nowadays, when we are confronted with a text, we usually distinguish between a literal and an allegorical sense. In most of the texts we are exposed to, we are able to make that distinction fairly quickly. If I read about pigs' habits in a book on farm management, I assume that I have to take its recommendations quite literally; but if I read George Orwell's 1945 dystopian novel *Animal Farm*, I quickly realize that the events narrated should not be taken literally but as an allegory of the historical events leading up to the Russian Revolution of 1917 and then on into the Stalin era in the Soviet Union. The ease with which I make the distinction depends on the fact that both the author of the book on farm management and Orwell wrote their respective texts adopting that very same distinction between a literal and an allegorical sense. When we read Hegel's work, and especially the *Lectures on the Philosophy of Religion*, however, we cannot make the distinction with the same ease—hence, the interpretative debate about the status of religious representations in Hegel's philosophy. But are the literal and the allegorical the only two meanings that can be applied to a text? This distinction is quite common today, but this has not always been the case.

In the mid-twentieth century, some philologists and literary critics addressed this issue, especially (although not exclusively) in relation to the interpretation of medieval literary works, most prominently, Dante's *Commedia*. These scholars developed interpretive approaches that had, despite their own respective specificities, a few important elements in common:

they are Auerbach's figural hermeneutics,[41] Singleton's allegorical theory of interpretation,[42] and Charity's typological exegesis.[43] In slightly different ways, they have all contended that, besides literal and allegorical readings, there is at least a third kind of reading, which has been almost completely abandoned in modernity, but which was quite prominent in the Middle Ages. For the sake of simplicity, I will refer collectively to the ways in which this third kind of reading has been described as "figural reading."

Most of the medieval texts were concerned with or had important references to the Christian Bible. This obviously posed the problem for medieval authors of the extent to which some events narrated in the Bible had to be taken literally. Early Christian theologian Origen (as well as others of the so-called Alexandrian school) claimed that the Bible's true meaning could be found only by reading it *allegorically*.[44] In most cases, this reading was justified by the attempt to read stories in the Old Testament as anticipations of Christ's coming: thus, for example, the three days Jonah spent in the great fish symbolize the three days before Christ's resurrection (something already suggested in the Gospel according to Matthew 12:39–40).

However influential, Origen's allegorical interpretation, which is the most familiar to us, was not the most prominent in the Middle Ages. In fact, "the medieval exegetical tradition inherited primarily Tertullian's historical method which promoted figural interpretation."[45] By the term *figura*, Auerbach defined an account of reality whereby one historical figure or event signifies a second one. He argues that figural readers, unlike allegorical readers such as Origen, preserved the historicity of biblical figures. As Auerbach explains, "Since in figural interpretation one thing stands for another, since one thing represents and signifies the other, figural interpretation is 'allegorical' in the widest sense. But it differs from most of the allegorical forms known to us by the historicity both of the sign and what it signifies."[46] In other words, the two characters or events (the first one, and the second one that is signified by the first) remain distinct, and the meaning is to be identified in the figural *relation* between them. This "figural realism," as Auerbach calls it,[47] was dominant in the Middle Ages: it is "the idea that earthly life is thoroughly real, with the reality of the flesh into which the Logos entered, but that with all its reality it is only *umbra* and *figura* of the authentic, future, ultimate truth, the real reality that will unveil and preserve the *figura*."[48] In Auerbach's view, Dante's *Commedia* is the paradigmatic instance of figural realism. "For Dante," he explains, "the literal meaning or historical reality of a figure stands in no contradiction to its profounder meaning, but precisely 'figures' it; the historical reality is not annulled, but confirmed and fulfilled by the deeper meaning."[49] "Is the *terrena Jerusalem*," he concludes, "without historical reality because it is a *figura aeternae Jerusalem*?"[50]

Singleton's allegorical theory of interpretation makes a similar point. Singleton appeals to the distinction, quite widespread in the Middle Ages, between the "allegory of poets" and the "allegory of theologians." The former, substantially analogous to Auerbach's "allegory," is the allegory of "this *for* that"; the latter, which corresponds to Auerbach's *figura*, is the allegory of "this *and* that, of this sense plus that sense." Singleton explains: "Its first meaning is meaning *in verbis*; its other meaning is a meaning *in facto*, in the event itself. Words have a real meaning in pointing to a real event; the event in its turn, has meaning because events wrought by God are themselves as words yielding a meaning, a higher and spiritual sense."[51]

As Auerbach remarks, "The strangeness of the medieval view of reality has prevented modern scholars from distinguishing between figuration and allegory and led them for the most part to perceive only the latter."[52] To Auerbach's conclusion, another more strictly philosophical point can be added. The figural reading appears "strange" to modern scholars mainly because they are unfamiliar with it; and this unfamiliarity is determined, in turn, by the affirmation of a philosophical conception that arose precisely in the (late) Middle Ages—that is, nominalism. Nominalism was one of the two main philosophical tenets in the so-called "dispute of the universals." Against the realism of Thomas Aquinas and Duns Scotus, who argued that universals (what is predicated of multiple entities, according to a definition inherited from Aristotle) are real, that is, they exist and are distinct from the particulars that instantiate them, nominalists generally asserted that only individuals or particulars exist and deny that universals are real. William of Ockham, probably the most influential nominalist, distinguished himself from the other thinkers of the same stream because he argued that there is something in common among similar particulars; however, he argued that universals are not real and do not exist independently of the mind, but only as mental contents: universals are only mental ways of referring to sets of particulars. A universal, Ockham states, "is nothing other than a content of the mind";[53] and a real science "is not about things, but about mental contents standing for things."[54] The distinction between "things" and "mental contents" was destined to be one of the milestones of modern philosophy; one can think here of Descartes's theory of ideas and its reception and transformation in the tradition of British empiricism.

This distinction, substantially alien to medieval realism (which was the dominant view until the late Middle Ages), fits better with the allegorical reading ("this *for* that") than with the figural reading ("this *and* that").

Interestingly, Auerbach claims that the figural realism he theorizes in his masterwork *Mimesis* "arose from the themes and methods of German intellectual history and philology; it would be conceivable in no other tradition than in that of German romanticism and Hegel,"[55] and elsewhere he explicitly says that his figural conception "is already to be found in Hegel."[56] Here we are not interested in scrutinizing Hegel's influence on Auerbach; it is much more interesting, for our purposes, to explore whether it is a conception similar to Auerbach's figural realism that is at work in Hegel's treatment of religion. Should we find enough evidence to support this reading, we will find ourselves equipped with a conceptual tool that would allow us to avoid both the realist and the fictionalist interpretations of religious representations in Hegel's philosophy and to clarify Hegel's application of mediated objectivity to them.

Hegel addresses the issue of the status of religious representations in the *Lectures on the Philosophy of Religion*. The content of the certainty of God (the objectivity of religion), Hegel claims, is first given to us in the form of representation ("a consciousness of something that one has before oneself as something objective," Rel I, 292/396). However, Hegel argues, representation (*Vorstellung*) has two forms. The *first* form of representation occurs by way of the image (*Bild*). Images have a double meaning: the immediate meaning primitively expressed by the image and then "what is meant by it, its inner meaning" (Rel I, 293/397). Thus, Hegel's account of the first form of religious mode of representation does not particularly differ from Kant's: religious doctrines, notions, and stories appear to be metaphorical, allegorical, or symbolic expressions of an "inner meaning" that is attributed to them.[57] Hegel does not draw strict distinctions between metaphor, allegory, and symbol;[58] rather he is interested, as Redding remarks, in stressing that "the distinction between the literal and the figurative is one made within the mode of representation"[59] (rather than between representation and thought). The account provided by Hegel so far therefore seems to support a metaphorical, or even fictional, reading of religious propositions. In an oft-quoted passage of the section of the *Lectures on the Philosophy of Religion* that we are analyzing, Hegel proclaims, "For example, if we say that God has begotten a son, we know quite well that this is only an image; representation [*Vorstellung*] provides us with 'son' and 'begetter' from a familiar relationship, which, as we well know, is not meant in its immediacy, but is supposed to signify a different relationship, which is something like this one" (Rel I, 293/398). He also mentions other examples, such as "God's wrath" and the "tree of knowledge" of Genesis; a religious representation of the kind that these phrases exemplify "is not to be taken in the literal sense" and "is merely an analogy, a simile, an image [*Bild*]" (Rel I, 293/398). However, taking these claims as evidence of a fictional approach to religion would be a gross error. The church fathers would not say anything different. Origen, the champion of the allegorical reading, offers plenty of examples along the same lines, and even Tertullian, who pioneered the figural reading, does not apply it indiscriminately: some biblical phrases, such as the tree of knowledge, are just allegorical, whereas others are *figural*. Hegel seems to make a similar distinction when he introduces the *second* form of representation by saying: "However, it is not merely things that are manifestly metaphorical (*bildlich*)[60] that belong to the mode of representation in its sensible aspect, but also things that are to be taken as historical [*Geschichtliches*]" (Rel I, 294/399). Hegel refers here to the story of Jesus, a story that "does not merely count as a myth, in the mode of images [*Bilder*]," but as "something completely historical." Its historical dimension is twofold: it is an "outward history"—the "ordinary story of a human being"—and, at the same time, an "inward history," which is the genuine, substantial dimension of this history, "a divine happening, a divine deed, an absolutely divine action"; Hegel concludes that "this is just what is the object of reason [*Gegenstand der Vernunft*]" (Rel I, 294/399). This is a very clarifying claim in the context of our investigation. The story of Jesus is depicted as not simply an allegory but as having a twofold value: first, it has value as a historical event (the life of Jesus, a specific human being living in a specific place in a specific time); and second, it has value for what it figures, that is, "divine history."[61] The first form of representation is the allegory of "this for that"; the second is the allegory of "this and that"—or *figura*.

If one considers the passage that we have just examined, it is puzzling how someone might have considered Hegelian religion as "disfiguring" the truth or, at best, as giving a very inadequate (because representational) account of truth.[62] Conversely, as Houlgate argues, religious representations "are appropriate—and, indeed, necessary—ways of picturing the truth."[63] However, truth here, I suggest, is not the truth of the old metaphysics of the "God's-eye view" but rather the "mediated objectivity" that results from the ongoing process of mediation between subject and object, which is always already in place. Thus, the meaning of a religious representation is to be identified neither merely in the historical nature of that represented character or event nor merely in the spiritual meaning that that character or event is meant to signify but in the *figural relation* between this historical nature and spiritual meaning. In other words, a figural relation is meant to capture the organic unity of outward (objective) history and inward (subjective) history.[64]

Picture-thinking (*das vorstellende Denken*) as an activity is not distinctive to religion: at a certain cognitive level (say, the level of our everyday experience), everything is, to some extent, experienced as a mere representation *first*. *Vorstellungen* can encompass both the metaphorical uses of a predicate and the "literal" uses on which the metaphorical extension depends. Concepts are the hinges on which inferences are made, not elements of linguistic representations, which can be literal or metaphorical. In the context of religion, however, some representations are not merely images but expressions of what Hegel calls "divine history": these representations deserve a *figural* reading. My argument here is that Hegel appropriates this type of reading because he sees it as the most appropriate way to reach what I have called "mediated objectivity," that is, an objectivity that reflects the relational unity between subject and object.

A closer inspection of the language used can be of some help here. As Nuzzo reminds us, Tertullian's Latin term *figura* was rendered in German by Luther with *Gestalt* in the context of his critique of Zwingli's allegoric interpretation of Holy Communion to restate the real presence of Christ's body in the bread. Nuzzo maintains that the reality of *Gestalt* (as the German rendering of *figura*) "is not lost in the abstraction of allegory or symbolism."[65] This is an important observation. The notion of *Gestalt* has, for Hegel, a very specific meaning. Objects that have a *Gestalt* "are thought of as organic unities, appreciable only as a whole, not by the piecemeal consideration of their parts."[66] A rose, Mozart's *Requiem*, or ancient Greek culture are all examples of objects that have a *Gestalt*. Some religious representations are simply metaphorical images (*Bilder*), but others have a *Gestalt*, because in them, to quote Nuzzo again, history is not "eliminated" but rather "repeated."[67] These are the religious representations that properly constitute a *religion*. In the *Phenomenology*, Hegel uses the term *Gestalt* for the shapes of consciousness in general, but religion is that particular *Gestalt* in which Spirit is fully self-conscious (PG, 3:499/414). What Hegel is saying here is that the human spirit cannot become fully conscious of itself without knowing the divine spirit;[68] but the divine spirit cannot be properly known by abstracting the conceptual from the sensible because it is given to us in religious representations that are *figurae* or *Gestalten*, that is, organic unities of the sensible and the conceptual, the historical and the eternal, the finite and the infinite—the subject and the object. In fact, the overcoming of the distinction between things and mental contents that emerges from a figural reading of Hegel's philosophy of religion is not a regression to a pre-Kantian, "anti-nominalist," or even realist position, but quite the opposite. A religious *Gestalt* is the evidence that metaphysical reality is the result of an ongoing process of mediation between subject and object: to some extent a religious *Gestalt* is the result of our *geistlich* activity, but, at the same time, our identity is also constituted by the religious *Gestalten* that populate our cultural world.

Therefore, when Hegel talks about those religious representations that are not merely images, but are *Gestalten*, we should interpret them neither literally nor metaphorically but rather *figuratively*. To treat a religious representation as *figura* means, to paraphrase Auerbach,[69] that the individual earthly event is not regarded as a definitive self-sufficient reality but rather in immediate connection with a divine order; however, for Hegel the divine order needs individual earthly events to fully realize itself. Thus Hegel, in the 1824 introduction to the *Lectures on the Philosophy of Religion*, claims that "[God] has no other figure or shape [*Gestalt*] than that of the sensible mode of the spirit that is spirit in itself—the shape of the *singular human being*. This is the one and only sensible shape of spirit—it is *the appearance of God in the flesh*. This is the monstrous reality [*das Ungeheure*] whose necessity we have seen. What it posits is that divine and human nature are not intrinsically different—God [is] in human shape" (Rel III, 146/214). Indeed, Christ is for Hegel the religious *Gestalt* par excellence. In the previous chapter, we saw that Hegel's Christocentric philosophy of religion can be viewed as the development and radicalization of Kant's idea of the internal archetype. A figural interpretation of Christ confirms that: for Hegel, spirituality (conceived as the expression of *Geist*) is "ultimately a matter of the impact of the historical Jesus on historical human beings."[70]

We find an extensive clarification of this dynamic in the introduction to the *Lectures on the History of Philosophy*, a consideration of which allows us to appreciate how, in Hegel's view, religious *Gestalten* should be interpreted neither literally nor metaphorically but rather, to use the term that we have introduced to capture this interpretative relation, *figuratively*. There is a "see-saw," Hegel writes, in our relationship to Christ: on the one hand we have an "imaginative consciousness" of Christ, conceived as an object outside us and separated from us, that is, a historical personage who lived in Palestine two millennia ago; on the other hand, worship and the cult express, and indeed provide, a "sense of unity with this object" (GP, 18:95 / ILHP, 134).

The vital role of *cultus* merits some attention here. Cult is the self-consciousness of the practical life, and it aims at recomposing the unity of nature and spirit. The central aspect of *cultus* is a "sacrificial dedication [*Hingabe*] of a possession which the owner, apparently without any profit whatever to himself, pours away or lets rise up in smoke" (PG, 3:718/434). In pre-Christian forms of *cultus*, however, "Spirit has not yet sacrificed itself as self-conscious Spirit to self-consciousness, and the mystery of bread and wine is not yet the mystery of flesh and blood' (PG, 3:724/438). In *cultus*, the subject is self-conscious, but the object (of sacrifice) is not. In Christian *cultus*, however, self-consciousness "surrenders itself consciously" (PG, 3:749/453).

Understanding the vital role of *cultus* helps us understand why Hegel claims that we should not focus exclusively on the imaginative consciousness of Christ, an attitude that, Hegel adds, equals "lying against the spirit," that is, "saying that the spirit is not universal, not holy, i.e. that Christ is only something apart, separated from us, only one person differing from another, only someone who once existed in Judaea, or who yet exists still but beyond, in Heaven, God knows where, not actually present in his community" (GP, 18:94 / ILHP, 135). A few pages later, Hegel draws the consequences of this line of reasoning: "Man and God, the subjective Idea and the objective Idea are one here": it is the principle of the unification of subject and object (GP, 18:128 / ILHP, 179). Then Hegel concludes that "the unity of knowing and truth, is not an immediate unity but a process; it is the process of the spirit" (GP, 18:128 / ILHP, 179).[71] For once, Hegel could not be clearer than this. It is through the "process of the spirit" that the mediated unity that constitutes objectivity can be achieved and content can be restored to both philosophy and religion.

Further evidence to support this reading can be found in the third part of the *Encyclopedia*, where Hegel remarks that in order to elucidate the "unity of form and content present in mind, the unity of revelation and what is revealed, we can refer to the teaching of the Christian religion" (E III, 10:28/18). Here, Hegel mentions once again the Christian doctrine according to which God "has begotten a son." Taken in isolation this is only an image (*Bild*) that allegorically signifies that Christ is the organ of God's revelation; however, if we consider Christ as a *Gestalt*, that is, in its organic unity with the concept of God *and* with the sensible world (we might also say, using the terminology that we have adopted so far, if we interpret Christ not simply allegorically but *figuratively*), then we realize that "the Son is not the mere organ of the revelation but is himself the content of the revelation": and the content is that God "in differentiating himself" made Godself "finite" (E III, 10:29/18). In other words, the content of revelation consists in that *kenotic* conception of God that we saw at work in the previous chapter, which, we can now argue, fits well with a qualified revisionist reading of Hegel (especially one that employs the recognition-theoretic approach and interprets Hegel's metaphysics as *mediately* objective), as well as with a figural reading of religious representations. In particular, a figural reading of Christ as *Gestalt* can be taken as expressing a conceptual content (while fully preserving the historical Jesus and his religious value), namely, that "objectivity" and "subjectivity" should not be conceived as mutually exclusive but, on the contrary, that "objectivity's 'self-emptying' is a condition of its appearing for subjectivity; and subjectivity's 'self-emptying' is a condition for it genuinely attending to the objectivity of objects."[72]

As Hegel claims, "what is speculative is not separate from religious ideas" (GP, 18:95 / ILHP, 134). The unity of divine and human—"reconciliation" (*Versöhnung*) in the language of religious representations—that Kant only postulated, becomes objective for Hegel; but its objectivity is mediated, that is, achieved through a learning process (the process of spirit): unity, already figuratively realized by Christ, must be "appropriated" (*zu eigen gemacht*) by us (Rel I, 65/154).[73] How?

*First*, we should not forget that Christ is one person in a Trinity of *Gestalten*.[74] The notion of reconciliation plays, in Hegel's view, an important role in fulfilling the trinitarian dialectic: the Father represents abstract universality, but "[t]he abstractness of the Father is given up in the Son" (Rel III, 286/370), who represents the moment of individuality. The third person of the Trinity, God as Spirit, finally expresses the reconciliation between God and the finite world, and therefore represents the moment of concrete universality: the divine Spirit is, from this angle, the community of mutually recognizing "selves." As such, the third hypostasis of the Trinity is the concrete fulfillment of the process of grounding human norms of thought and action, and therefore also the appropriation of the unity between the divine and the human in the sensible (social) world. I will explore Hegel's conception of the Trinity in more detail in chapter 5.

## The Reality of Religion in Hegel's Idealist Metaphysics 77

*Second*, to restore content to philosophy and religion for Hegel means that the unity between the human and the divine needs to be realized in *thought*. I previously argued that recognition is the organizing principle of that "realm of reason" in which the human cultural *and normative* world consists. By "normative" here I mean that the generation of norms that make up and guide the realm of reason is dependent on recognition and that without recognition there is no cultural world. Because the incarnation of Christ is the representation of the kenotic conception of God (God self-emptying and embracing the finite perspective), the affirmation of this conception *in that same realm of reason* really is a turning point in the history of spirit, a turning point that hence sheds light on how metaphysics (conceived as that discipline concerned with the realm of reason) is to be interpreted.

The fact that a figural reading is possible clarifies the idealistic overcoming of the opposition between subject and object. Subject and object should be thought of not in isolation but as both contributing to (metaphysical) reality: thus, the truth of a religious representation is to be found neither in its literal (historical) meaning nor in a mere metaphorical meaning but rather in the relation between them.

The figural hermeneutics developed by Auerbach might in itself be simply considered to be an isomorphic model of Hegel's dialectical self-negation: for any spiritual content to be real, it has to become manifest, be expressed, and ultimately be articulated at the level of finitude or otherness. What I am suggesting here is that the general interpretative approach to religious representations that Auerbach and others had the merit of formalizing—that is, an approach that focuses on the relation between the subject and the object of interpretation rather than exclusively on the objective (literal reading) or subjective (metaphorical reading) pole of the relation—is more than an isomorphic model. It is, I contend, the expression of an idealist metaphysics that conceives the entirety of nonempirical reality (the cultural world, we might say) as being the result of an ongoing relation between subject and object. In other words, we cannot escape that figural system because we, as human agents, are inevitably part of it.

This is the reason why a figural interpretation is so central to Hegel, that is, because an interpretation that focuses on the relation between subject and object (that is, one that aims at a mediated objectivity) is the only proper way to "read" metaphysical reality while avoiding both a precritical objectivism (which is constantly exposed to the Kantian critique) and a subjectivism that waives the content of religion (as happens with romanticism). In Hegel's view, in fact, (post-critical) metaphysics needs to be dialectical, that is, it must take into account the historical development of self-consciousness (in Hegel's jargon, the life of the spirit). Insofar as Christian doctrines (such as the incarnation, death, and resurrection of Christ) are part of such development, a figural interpretation of them enables the establishment of a post-critical metaphysics.

For Hegel, God becomes actual only in the thought of human agents (subjective spirits) as a result of human *interaction*, especially in the recognitive practice of reconciliation that characterizes the religious community.[75] God's self-actualization is not independent of that which determines our *relation* to God, such as historical, social, and cultural dimensions, but these dimensions actually shape God's self-actualization. There is, therefore, a sense in which Hegel's God differs from the merely philosophical God of the (pre-Kantian) metaphysical tradition, insofar as, for Hegel, God cannot be completely abstracted from those religious *Vorstellungen* that represent God's relationship with human subjects. Any attempt to think of God independently of those historical, social, and cultural dimensions, as in the traditional (pre-Kantian) metaphysics, would constitute a regression to the abstract conception of God as substance and is ultimately destined to fail.

The figural reading has proved to be a better alternative to both the realist and fictionalist interpretations of religious representations in Hegel's philosophy of religion and has allowed for a clarification of Hegel's application of mediated objectivity to them. But can the figural reading also be applied to the concept of God *itself*? Is God a representation (in the sense of *Gestalt*, or *figura*, as we can now concede) among others? Or is there a sense in which God is more than a representation?

## God: Concept and Idea

As Hegel explains in the *Encyclopedia*, to have a representation (*Vorstellung*) of an object does not necessarily mean to be "familiar with the meaning" that this representation has "for thinking"—that is, with its concept (*Begriff*) (E I, 8:44/30–31). We can, therefore, have a *representation* of God without being familiar with the *concept* of God. In this sense, the concept of God is "the result of the other branches [of philosophy]"; but in the philosophy of religion, "this end is made the beginning." Hegel explains:

"*That* God (as result) *appears* is what we make into our particular object—God as the *utterly concrete idea* [*Idee*] together with its infinite appearance, which is identical with the substance, with the essence of reality; this is the content, the specification of the content" (Rel I, 37/120). The *Idea* of God[76] is the full actualization of the *concept* of God realized through a dynamic overcoming of the opposition between subject and object.[77] Philosophy "does not thereby place itself above religion but only above the form of faith as representation" (Rel III, 289/374): "It still relies on religion for content."[78] In summary, God might well be regarded merely as a representation in our everyday use of the term, but this does not prevent God from being considered as a concept. Moreover, the fact that this concept is the *result* of philosophy does not mean that now philosophy can do without religion: it is religion, in fact, that provides the concept of God with the content that is required for its full actualization in the Idea (*Idee*). Let us now consider the reality of the concept (*Begriff*) of God; this shall lead first to a further distinction, and then to a proper consideration of what the actualization of the *concept* into the *Idea* entails.

As already mentioned, read as an idealist in the context of the "qualified revisionist interpretation," Hegel may be seen as conceiving of metaphysics as the discipline in which reason is concerned with its own products. Hence, the *concept* of God should be regarded as having an *ideal* rather than a "naturalistic" or—to quote Redding—a "there anyway" existence.[79] This interpretation seems, prima facie, to conflict with some of the claims Hegel makes about God—for instance, that God is "absolutely self-sufficient, unconditioned, independent, free, as well as being the supreme end unto itself" (Rel I, 4/84). This conflict, however, is only apparent, because even this claim should be taken *idealistically*—that is, Hegel's claim should be applied to God as *a product of reason*; and, because of the peculiarities of *this* product of reason, it might well be defined as self-sufficient, unconditioned, and so forth. The main argument here is that, from a Hegelian perspective, everything that is not a natural object is a product of reason—including human beings. As we have seen, human beings *themselves*, qua knowing subjects, must be regarded as products of reason, and exist as such only in as much as they mutually recognize themselves as existing.[80] Considered in this way, the concept of God can be said to be a human "creation"—but only in the same way in which it is possible to say that human rights, or human beings (considered as free and rational beings), or even reason itself, are human "creations."

At this point, one might object that, if we take Hegel as regarding God as a human "creation" (even with the preceding qualifications), then the left Hegelians, who considered Hegel's thought a "humanist" critique of theism, were correct. Consider the case of Feuerbach, with his anthropological reading of God as a human "creation," that is, as a *mere projection* of human desires. If Hegel does not attribute to God any existence external to reason, he can, after all, be considered an atheist. In this reading, the concept of God might be regarded as *merely* a representation, or at best a translation, in nonfigurative and conceptual terms, of a content that is better and more clearly presented within philosophy. However, this account represents a serious misunderstanding of Hegel's approach to God. Hegel is explicit in calling God "an idealization [*das Ideelle*]," but he also remarks that to call God "*only* an idealization, presupposes the standpoint according to which finite existence counts as the real, and idealization or the being-for-one has only a one-sided meaning" (L I, 5:177/129; my emphasis). In other words, any crude anthropological reading of God, such as that of Feuerbach, is a regression into pre-Kantian metaphysical realism insofar as, although it identifies God as a "mere" projection, it regards the "human being" as a metaphysical entity that is there "anyway," independent of any act of human recognition. However, from an idealist standpoint, this distinction simply does not make sense because nothing, in the realm of reason, can be regarded as totally independent of human recognitive activity.

How can we go beyond the "one-sided meaning" of the concept of God? In which sense is God "more" than an idealization? So far we have distinguished between the image (*Bild*) of God, the concept (*Begriff*) of God, and the Idea (*Idee*) of God; now, as anticipated, another distinction is to be posited, to distinguish "God" from the image, concept, and Idea of God. That "God" is distinct from God's image is something that has emerged quite clearly from our previous analysis. The distinction between "God" and "the Idea of God" is more complex, and we will deal with it later. Now, consider the distinction between "God" and "the concept of God." Why should there be a need for such a distinction?

Hegel considers God as the object of the *philosophy* of religion. The object of this *philosophical* analysis is not *God* and God's existence *external* to reason; Hegel is neither committed to affirming its independent existence as a natural object (right Hegelians) nor its nonexistence (left Hegelians) simply because *it would not make any sense* to claim anything about the *independent existence* of an *object of reason* (the *concept* of God), which by its very nature is dependent on human reason.

Prima facie, this distinction might appear puzzling. One might object that either (1) absolute idealism literally means that God, *tout court*, is a construct of human reason, and so there is no need for the distinction between "God" and "the concept of God"; or (2) that the latter distinction is important—but then we have a less than absolute idealism, and God's existence beyond human reason remains a metaphysical possibility. However, such an objection would overlook the fact that the very notion of metaphysics has been radically transformed since Kant. Hegel's idealism is *absolute* because everything that is not a natural object cannot be thought of *independently* of human recognitive activity that makes it possible for the object to be *thought*. In other words, while a natural object (say, a stone) depends on human activity only in terms of its conceptual determination (the Kantian cognitive synthesis between the intuition and the concepts of the understanding), but not in ontic terms (the stone is there "anyway," even if it is not "thought"), the existence of an ideal object—an "object or reason" or, to use the Hegelian term, a "concept" (*Begriff*)—is not independent of human recognitive activity (the existence of "marriage," for instance, is not independent of the ways marriage is practiced and thought of). At the same time, Hegel's absolute *idealism* implies that metaphysical objects cannot be thought of independently of the human reason that is thinking them. If human reason is called to say something about God, its object is inevitably the *concept* of God qua product of human reason. An ultra-metaphysical existence of God (considered, as it were, as a "[super-]natural" object) is something that simply falls outside the domain of reason; but this makes Hegel's idealism *more* (and not *less*) "absolute." Considering the *concept* of God as having no existence external to reason makes Hegel neither a *theist* nor an *atheist* concerning *God* (at least not in the traditional sense). Regarding the *concept* of God as indissolubly interconnected with human recognitive activity does not make God a merely *fictional* character; it rather binds its *metaphysical reality* (its existence as an object of reason) to the way that the concept has been (historically and culturally) thought of. Consider, for example, the notion of the resurrection of Christ: Hegel is equally resistant to those critical approaches that regarded it as a cultural-fictional product, and to those interpretative standpoints that considered it as it were a natural fact. In Hegel's view, the resurrection needs to be thought of as bonded to the development of (cultural) history, of which it is an integral part. Consistently, conceiving God's existence from within human reason does not necessarily imply a purely *immanent* conception of the divine; rather, it implies that the transcendent features of God cannot be thought of independently of the (human) mind thinking them.

The distinction between "the concept of God" and "God" does not in any way reproduce Kantian dualism at a metaphysical level, with an allegedly phenomenal "concept of God" (God as being known by us), and a "noumenal" unreachable God (which remains beyond our rational abilities). Hegel consistently opposes any dualism of this type—in the *Lectures on the Philosophy of Religion*, which constitute our main focus in this chapter, as well as in any other work. The concept of God, as "object of reason," is the outcome of the "other branches of philosophy," as Hegel reminds us; however, we need the philosophy of *religion* to turn that end into the beginning of the dynamic that overcomes the opposition between subject and object, which can eventually restore full content to that concept, namely, the process that will lead to the *Idea* of God. The process of full actualization of the concept of God requires the resources of both religion and philosophy.

Now, consider what religion and philosophy contribute to the actualization of the concept of God as Idea. These remarks are meant to clarify the extent to which "the Idea of God" is *God*.

The *Religion* is always driven, for Hegel, by a tension toward the full actualization of the concept of God, which implies and indeed coincides with the unity between the human and the divine. If Christianity is regarded as the "consummate religion," this is because, in Hegel's view, Christianity realizes that the concept of God needs a concrete (historical and bodily) actualization. The various versions of the *Lectures on the Philosophy of Religion* can be read as presenting an increasing emphasis on the arguments for the necessity of the incarnation. In the last series of *Lectures*, delivered in 1831, Hegel maintains that individual human subjectivity is the only proper *Gestalt* in which God can appear (Rel III, 146/214).[81] This explains the figural necessity of the incarnation of Christ; moreover, the religious (representational) reality of the incarnation of Christ is confirmed and fulfilled by a deeper meaning, that is, "the true idea of God," which "entails that God is not a beyond, over and against which stands consciousness" (VPW, 87/188). When I think of *God*, I think of this conceptual object (God) figuratively: I might well refer to the Christian God but, Hegel maintains, the incarnated Christian God is a *Gestalt*, that is, it is to be thought of in its organic unity with the *concept* of God.

This is where religion is to be complemented by *philosophy*. As object of reason, the conception of God is the result of the other branches of philosophy; as such, it might be considered to be a figurative representation of a philosophical content (the source of norms). Kant had conceived of God as an idea of reason, that is, a nonempirical concept that has the regulative function of unifying the various claims of the understanding into a systematic whole (which we can subsequently identify as "knowledge"). Hegel's concept of God can be considered the successor of this conception, thus turning the formal regulativity of Kant's God as an "idea of reason" into a more concrete regulativity. In other words, Hegel's concept of God unifies the realm of reason as a whole, and in this way it regulates what is entailed for recognition to be the ground of the human and cultural world: it is, in other words, the source of norms. However, this is only half of the story, because when *I* think of God, even the subject of this action (the "I") is to be considered figuratively: in the everyday use, when I say "I," I usually refer to a *representation* of my thoughts, perceptions, desires, and body as an individualized unity, but, Hegel argues, the *true objective self* is this representation made consistent with its content—that is, self-consciousness. Self-consciousness does not exist in isolation:[82] being a product of reason, it requires others to recognize it to exist *as self-consciousness*, and to collectively make identity-conferring commitments to idealities such as norms. No identity can be formed without participation in that realm of reason that is unified by the idea of God.

Therefore, the process of actualization of the concept into the Idea of God is both religious and philosophical. On one hand, (Christian) religion, with its representations, *Gestalten*, and cult, makes the incarnated God "actually present" in the community (GP, 18:95 / ILHP, 135): it is the identity-conferring commitment of the community that makes God actually "present" (the Hegelian version of the Gospel's claim, "where two or three are gathered in my name, there am I among them," Matthew 18:20); thus, it can be said that God is not fully actual outside of the human community and its recognitive activity. On the other hand, it would be a mistake to deduce from the previous point that the concept of God plays a mere social function in Hegel's account, because the actualization of the concept into the Idea is also philosophical: if the concept of God, as the source of norms, unifies the realm of reason as a whole, and if the self is an object of reason, it follows that the development of self-consciousness implies consciousness of the interdependence between the self and God. It is in this process that the *concept* of God is fully actualized in the *idea* of God. The concept of God, in fact, is not merely a product of reason among many others: the *content* of that particular concept requires that it be understood to exist in a way that goes beyond the true point that the concept of God, like any concept, exists only insofar as it belongs to the realm of reason: for God to be seriously considered as the source of norms, we have to think of God as necessarily existing. As I will show in the next chapter, Hegel's "infamous" defense of the ontological argument can be considered as providing an argument for the necessary existence of God.

In light of these considerations, to what extent it is possible to distinguish "God" from "the Idea of God"? Such a question cannot be fully answered until we progress in our inquiry and consider other important aspects of Hegel's conception of God, such as his version of the ontological argument, his account of the Trinity, and his use of the expression "death of God"—I will, therefore, come back to this issue at the end of chapter 6. For now, it is sufficient to say that the distinction between "God" and "the Idea of God" can *and* cannot be made, depending on the angle from which we consider the question. If, on one hand, we take "God" to mean a (super-)natural entity that can be known and/or with which it is possible to establish a connection bypassing our rational faculties—the conception of God grounded in feeling rather than rational thought advanced by thinkers such as Jacobi, Fries, and Schleiermacher—then the distinction between "God" and the "Idea of God" is evident. For Hegel, conceiving God in a direct and unconceptualized way is simply impossible, and pursuing that path inevitably leads to subjectivism, which is precisely that which Hegel is trying to avoid. If, on the other hand, we follow Hegel in his conception of God as "not a beyond" but as necessarily intertwined with the human self through the recognitive activity of the community and as a commitment that one necessarily undertakes when thinking of norms, then "the Idea of God" *is* God in its full (idealistic and mediated) objectivity, and we no longer need such distinction.

To conclude: a proper, figural approach to Christian religion is consistent with the idealistic, mediated objectivity of the concept of God, that is, to its understanding as Idea, but it is philosophy that can, and should, provide a *justification* for this objectivity and show that the Idea of God necessarily involves its existence. Indeed, this is what Hegel appears to be offering us with his defense of the ontological argument for the existence of God. As I will show in the next chapter, Hegel regards the ontological argument as playing an important function in the context of such a justification, which represents an important strategic move against the danger of subjectivism.

# 4

# Hegel's Version of the Ontological Argument for the Existence of God

## From Anselm to Kant

In the tenth century, Anselm of Canterbury proposed an argument for the existence of God in his *Proslogion*. Since then, the so-called "ontological proof" has been one of the most famous philosophical arguments, often revived and often criticized. Even in contemporary philosophy, the ontological argument (OA) is a very lively subject that keeps attracting attention in philosophical debate.[1]

Hegel is usually counted among the supporters of the OA. There is no doubt that a reading of Hegel's work shows a favorable attitude toward it. And yet his position, even when superficially considered, seems different from other modern "revivals" of the OA—like, for example, those of Descartes and Leibniz. Strictly speaking, Hegel does not seem to provide an "argument," at least not in the classical sense. This has led several scholars to be skeptical about the real presence of a proper OA in Hegel's work.[2] This skepticism is somewhat understandable: if one expects to find in Hegel's works a traditional "argumentative support" (at least by contemporary ordinary standards of arguing) for the OA, one would be disappointed. There is a simple reason for that: Hegel does not want to defend the *traditional* OA, neither in Anselm's formulation, nor in one of its modern revised versions. In fact, he thinks that the traditional OA does *not* work. So in what sense does Hegel maintain that the OA is successful?

To answer this question, we need to go back to Anselm's formulation of the OA, to its reception in modern philosophy, and—importantly—to Kant's refutation of the OA in the *Critique of Pure Reason*, because only against the background of the history of the OA in the modern era is it possible to truly appreciate in what sense Hegel maintains that the line of thought implied in the OA is important.

The first historical version of the OA appears in Anselm's *Proslogion*. It has to be recalled that the *Proslogion* was meant to be a work of meditation, and the idea of a rational demonstration (in the modern sense of the word) of the existence of God fell outside Anselm's original intention.[3] Nevertheless, it is possible to identify Anselm's argument on the basis of the two definitions of God he provides. The first one is *id quo maius cogitari nequit*, "that than which nothing greater can be thought" (IQM). Later on, in chapter 15, Anselm gives another definition of God: *quiddam maius quam cogitari posit*, "something greater than whatever can be thought" (QM). The second is implicit in the first: God must be QM; otherwise he would not be IQM.

Anselm's argument for God's existence is based on the definition of God as IQM. The demonstration proceeds as follows:

The one who denies the existence of God refers to God as IQM.

Therefore, the denier has the idea of God in mind (that is, God exists as an idea in the mind).

But the IQM cannot exist only in the mind, because an IQM that exists would be greater than a being that exists only in the mind, and this is a contradiction.

Therefore, God exists.[4]

In modern philosophy, the OA was first revived by Descartes. He provides a set of interconnected arguments rather than a single proof. For our purposes, it is sufficient to consider his main three points.

First, Descartes starts from the assumption that we all have the idea of God, and from the definition of the idea of God as the idea of an infinite substance (eternal, omniscient, omnipotent, etc.). As I do not possess any of the perfections that are represented in this idea, it is difficult to suppose that I created it. In fact, the cause of an idea must have at least the same amount of perfection as the idea represented. Therefore, the cause of an idea of an infinite substance can only be an infinite substance. It follows that the simple presence in myself of the idea of God demonstrates the existence of God.

Second, the existence of God can also be demonstrated, according to Descartes, by a consideration of my finitude. That I am finite is demonstrated by the fact that I doubt. That I am not the cause of myself is further demonstrated by a simple reasoning: if I were the cause of myself, I would give myself all the perfections I can think of (and that are included in the idea of God). Since this is not the case, it is evident that I have not created myself, and therefore my creator must be a Being who has all the perfections I can think of. In other words, human constitutive finitude implies a causal relation between human being and God—and the idea of God is the expression and immediate revelation of this relation.[5]

Third, Descartes maintains that the existence of God has the same kind of necessity as a geometrical demonstration has. If I have a genuine concept of a triangle, Descartes argues, I can infer that a triangle's internal angles add up to 180 degrees. Such an inference holds whether or not any triangle exists in the actual world; denying such an inference would imply a contradiction. Similarly, I can clearly and distinctly conceive God as a supremely perfect being—that is, a being that has every perfection. From this idea I can infer various facts about God, just as I can about triangles—facts that hold whether or not God actually exists. I can infer, for example, that God is omniscient and omnipotent, for I would contradict myself if I thought that a being with every perfection lacked a perfection. But existence is a perfection, and I can therefore infer that God exists.

Leibniz's argument is a variation (but a significant one, for our purposes) of the third version of Descartes's proof. Leibniz identifies a flaw in Descartes's reasoning. Before following Descartes in his demonstration, in fact, it is first necessary—Leibniz argues—that a supremely perfect being indeed be possible. In other words, the idea of a perfect being needs to be shown to be coherent. This is possible, because perfection cannot be analyzed; therefore, it cannot be demonstrated that perfections are contradictory or incompatible. It follows that there can be an entity that possesses all the perfections. Once this move has been made, then Descartes's argument is, according to Leibniz, valid.[6]

Subsequently Kant, in the *Critique of Pure Reason* (in the "Transcendental Dialectic"), offered a refutation of the OA that was destined to have an everlasting impact on further philosophical discussions. Kant's confutation is well known; however, it is useful to briefly go through Kant's reasoning, as Hegel's position cannot be really appreciated without taking Kant's refutation into account.

Kant's argument is twofold. First, Kant objects that if we include existence in the definition of something, then asserting that it exists is a tautology. If we say that existence is part of the definition of God (an *analytic* judgment), then we are simply repeating ourselves in asserting that God exists. We are not making a *synthetic* judgment that would add new information about the real existence of God to the purely conceptual definition of God.

Second, Kant objects that existence is not a predicate. The claim that an object *exists* does not mean that it has an additional property that is part of its concept; rather, it means that the object is to be found *outside* of thought and that therefore we can have an *empirical* perception of it *in space and time*. In other words, we can ascertain existence only *empirically*, not deduce it *intellectually*. Kant provides the example of horses and unicorns: there is no difference between the concept of a horse and the concept of a unicorn. What is more, there is no difference between the concept of a horse and the concept of a *really existing* horse: the concepts are identical. The reason we claim that horses exist (and unicorns do not) is simply that we have spatiotemporal experience of them: concepts have corresponding objects. The famous example of the hundred thalers serves the same purpose: "A hundred real thalers," Kant writes, "do not contain the least bit more than a hundred possible ones. [. . .] But in my financial condition there is more with a hundred actual thalers than with the mere concept of them (i.e., their possibility)."[7]

In Kant's view, it follows that any demonstration of the existence of anything that relies on predicating a property (in this case, existence) of that thing is fallacious; and this includes God. In fact, Kant claims, we cannot even determine the possibility of any existence beyond that known in and through experience; Kant clarifies his position by claiming that "for objects of pure thinking there is no means whatever for cognizing their existence, because it would have to be cognized entirely a priori."[8]

Now, consider Hegel's position in relation to the history of the OA. Hegel's attraction to the Anselmian formulation of the OA can be explained by the presence of something characteristically ancient and, at the same time, of something peculiarly modern in Anselm's argument.[9] The OA wants to capture the unity of thought and being (the IQM cannot exist only in the mind, so it must exist in reality): this aspect of the proof harks back to that which can be considered as the default position in ancient thought. For example, Aristotle's idea of how the mind comes to have thoughts of things effectively *presupposes* the reality of the things about which the thoughts *are* thoughts. This feature is found throughout Aristotle's logical and epistemological works, but it is also a common assumption throughout ancient philosophy as a whole.[10]

The unity of being and thought represents the outcome of the argument; but its starting point is a purportedly determinate concept of God understood as a *possible* existent, and only then is the actuality of God argued for on the basis of what can be derived from features of that initial concept. Hegel points out that such a type of argument that starts with a concept and tries to infer to being was unknown to classical thought, and that it implies an advanced stage of thought in which spirit "has arrived at its highest form of freedom, namely subjectivity" (Rel I, 324/434), a stage that starts off from a *separation* of thought and being, which was destined to become most obvious later in the early modern period.[11] That is, the OA considers the concept "God" and attempts to find in that concept some subconcepts, such as that of perfection, from which the actual existence of God can be deduced (because an existing God is considered as better exemplifying perfection than a nonexisting one).

The reason why the argument, in its Anselmian form, does *not* work—Hegel states that clearly (E I, 8:349/268)[12]—is that it *implicitly assumes* a distinction between the conceptual realm (the allegedly subjective set of our ideas, or mental representations) and the realm of being (the allegedly objective set of objects that populate the world independently of the knower), and it subsequently attempts to bridge that distinction by *presupposing* that (for the idea of God) being was always already there *in* the thought of God (because of his perfection). The "deficiency in Anselm's argument" is that the unity (of thought and being) is simply presupposed, that is, assumed only "in itself," as potential: it is an abstract unity. To this abstract unity, it is then easy to oppose the (likewise abstract) distinction (which was already assumed in the consideration of the idea of God in the mind, as disconnected from being) to argue that the argument is faulty.[13]

The "deficiency in Anselm's argument" is also "chargeable" against Descartes and other modern philosophers who employ the OA. Descartes needs to be praised for his "sublimest thought, that God is that whose concept [*Begriff*] includes his being within itself" (L II, 6:402/625), but the thought was "degraded into the faulty form." Two interconnected issues need to be stressed here. First, Descartes's version of the OA features a conception of subjectivity (typical of modernity) according to which representational states can be considered in abstraction from the existence of that which is purportedly represented in them, but something like an embryonic conception of subjectivity was already presupposed in Anselm's version of the OA. Second, and as a consequence of this subjectivistic approach, the idea of thought as the "realm of possibilities" becomes more explicit in Descartes's account. It has been recalled that the core of Descartes's "geometrical" version of the OA is that it is possible to infer various proprieties of God (just as it is possible about triangles), *whether or not* God actually exists. Again, this idea was already implicit in the Anselmian version of the argument, which starts from the *thought* of God conceived as *possibly* existing, and then argues for the *actual* existence of God on the basis of what is derived from features of that initial thought. In such accounts the mind is conceived of as knowing itself—that is, its own states or processes conceived of as "ideas" or "thoughts"—*first*, generating the familiar skeptical questions about the reality of the apparent world "external" to the mind. As I pointed out in the previous two chapters, Hegel strongly opposes any conception that considers self-knowledge or self-consciousness as independent of interactions with the external world and other self-consciousnesses.

The conception of thought as the realm of possibilities becomes even more radical with Leibniz. For Leibniz, possibility is simply the absence of contradiction—an idea that was destined to become standard in modern and contemporary philosophy.[14] Thus the existence of God becomes, in Hegel's words, "only an inference from eternal truths," and thus we can again have the "wearisome" (*langweilige*) proof of God's existence, consisting in the inference that "He has the prerogative of existing immediately in His potentiality" (GP, 20:247 / LHP, 3:339–40). Once again, the unity of thought and being is presupposed (this time as possible) but not yet demonstrated.

Against this background, it is possible to understand why Hegel's position in relation to Kant's refutation of the OA is ambivalent. One of Kant's points is that the conceptual content of an object that is only thought and the conceptual content of the same object as it is experienced are the same; thus, Kant argues, the existence of the corresponding object can only be experienced in external reality, and all those arguments that try to demonstrate the existence of the object by simply treating existence as an additional property that is supposed to be added to the object a priori inevitably fail. Kant is *right* according to Hegel, because his refutation finally makes explicit the assumption that was implicit in the traditional versions of the OA, namely, the (distinctively modern) separation between thought and being. The conception according to which we have "thinkables" that are independent of whether they exist or not is certainly an important achievement with respect to the ancient Aristotelian "realist" approach that *immediately presupposes* the reality of the things about which the thoughts are thoughts. Kant's refutation is effectively a radicalization of the modern viewpoint, namely, that of the separation between thought and being: as such, Kant's refutation is, to some extent, legitimate, because once a sharp distinction between thought and being has been drawn *for all the objects of thought* (as it happened in modern philosophy), the gap seems to be filled only by ascertaining the *empirical* existence of the object. And yet, it is *incorrect*, in Hegel's view, to stop at this distinction and conclude that "being" can only be ascertained empirically *for all the objects of thought*.

In Hegel's view, Kant's fundamental error here resides in his misunderstanding of "being," when it is taken—Hegel claims—as something occurring "in the form of sensuous perception," like the hundred thalers, and thus often confused with "existence." Conversely, the expression "being" (*Sein*) as the copula of the judgment and the expression "to exist actually" (*existieren*) are not interchangeable (L II, 6:407/629).[15] In other words, Kant's refutation still assumes the separation between thought and being, and it explicitly applies it indifferently to sensible, empirical objects, *and* conceptual objects (that is, objects of reason). The major flaw that Hegel identifies in Kant's view is precisely this *gegenständlich* view of reality[16]—that is, a view that considers reality as a set of objects opposed to a subject: a view still marked with subjectivism.[17] It should not come as a surprise, then, that this view legitimizes the use of "being" and "existence" indifferently for sensible, empirical objects *and* conceptual objects (that is, objects of reason). "Calling something like a hundred thalers a concept [*Begriff*]," Hegel says, is "barbaric" (E I, 8:136/100). And in the *Lectures on the Philosophy of Religion* he explains: "In ordinary life we do indeed call a representation [*Vorstellung*] of a hundred dollars a concept [*Begriff*]. It is no concept, however, but only a content-determination of my consciousness; an abstract simple representation [*Vorstellung*] [. . .], or a determinacy of the understanding that is within my head, can of course lack being" (Rel I, 325/436). A hundred thalers is a representation, and as such can obviously exist only in my mind; but a *concept* is, for Hegel—as we know from our analysis in the previous chapter—something entirely different. In other words, Hegel has developed a "conception of concept" different from that of Kant.[18]

Hegel's alternative conception of concept, which will be the subject of the next section, preeminently applies to the concept of God and clearly has repercussions on the OA. In the *Encyclopedia Logic*, Hegel remarks that the elevating of God "*from* and *out* of the empirical view of the world" is not possible on the basis of the "merely sensory or animalistic observation [*Betrachtung*] of the world," but only on the basis of the "thoughtful [*denkende*]" study of the world (E I, 8:131/97). This means to remember, Hegel explains a few pages later, that when we speak of God, we are dealing with an object "of a different kind from a hundred dollars and from any sort of particular concept [*Begriff*], representation [*Vorstellung*], or whatever one wants to call it" (E I, 8:136/100). Then Hegel concludes: "God, on the other hand, is explicitly supposed to be what can only be '*thought as existing*,' where the concept includes being" (E I, 8:136/100).

At this point, one might wonder: is Hegel's line of reasoning plausible? Was not the unity of thought and being a naïve assumption of ancient thought, finally overcome with the modern separation of the two realms? Does not Hegel's argument, not differently from the more traditional proofs, take us any further than the concept of God?

The objection is legitimate and, in fact, is acknowledged by Hegel himself. The outcome of the proof is the unity of thought and being, but the *implicit* starting point is a conception of God understood as a *possible* existent. As such, the OA does not take us further than the *representation* of God,[19] as 'to presuppose means to accept something immediately as primary and unproved' (Rel I, 328/440). Therefore, Kant is incorrect, in Hegel's view, in claiming that the OA fails *because* of the unity of being and thought; it fails only because the unity of being and thought is *presupposed* rather than *demonstrated*. "The defective feature," Hegel explains, "is the fact that this is a presupposition and therefore something immediate, and so one does not recognize the necessity of this unity" (Rel I, 328–29/440). In other words, the argument *could* work, according to Hegel—provided that we are able to demonstrate the unity of being and thought—namely, the *transition from the absolute concept to existence*. Is that transition possible?

## The Concept as Unity of Subject and Object

In the previous chapter, we familiarized ourselves with the concept (*Begriff*) of God, as distinct from the representation (*Vorstellung*) and the Idea (*Idee*) of God. We also contextualized Hegel's approach to the concept of God in what we have called his mediately objective view—that is, his ideal of an objectivity that takes into account the contribution of our self-conscious mind for the establishment of the content of a metaphysical object, or *concept*. Now, on the grounds of the preliminary considerations of Kant's refutation of the OA that have been the subject of the previous section, and with the aim of showing why the OA represents, for Hegel, a central move in the translation of the absolute concept of God into existence, it is appropriate to introduce some further clarifications about Hegel's conception of concept.

The first consideration that is suggested by Hegel's critique of Kant's refutation of the OA is that it is a mistake to think of "concepts" like words or any other kind of pictorial representations. Hegel has told us that we cannot call something like a hundred thalers a concept. This is because concepts are, for Hegel, the objects of metaphysics: and we have already stressed, in the previous two chapters, that Hegel's metaphysics is *normative*. Traditionally, the normative status of a concept represents (as it happens in Plato's philosophy) its *telos*, goal, or purpose:[20] hence, an object might or might not fully fit its concept. Objects such as a hundred thalers, or, say, a chair, however, do not have an *intrinsic* purpose; *we* attribute to a chair the purpose of being something on which we can sit, but—and this is the point—we do not assume that the chair has the intrinsic purpose of *being* a chair. "Where there is the perception of a purposiveness," Hegel writes in the *Science of Logic*, "an intelligence is assumed as its author; required for purpose is thus the concept's own free concrete existence" (L II, 6:436/651). This is the reason why, according to Hegel, it is not proper to use the term "concept" to refer to a hundred thalers, or to a chair. Conversely, we should properly call "concepts" those entities that have the capacity to fulfill their goal or normative status, according to a scale of gradations. We can legitimately refer, for instance, to the concept of a flower—which is not our mental representation of a flower but its normative ideal—but the concept of a flower will never achieve self-consciousness. Human beings, conversely, are capable of self-consciousness and can therefore consciously fulfill their concept. However, as I argued in the previous chapter, Hegel has connected the conception of normativity with that of recognition, in the sense that the generation of norms is dependent on recognition. This is because concepts are not sharply distinct from the "I" and from objects: therefore, we should call "concepts" not only the human mind but also those organic systems that are capable of developing self-consciousness through recognition—such as a community, a society, or (even more pointedly) the state, which Hegel compares to the solar system (E I, 8:356/273).[21]

The objectivity of content is the coincidence, for concepts, of existence with the normative status they are meant to express.[22] All of this is very relevant for a correct understanding of the OA. In fact, when we talk about the "concept of God" and we wonder how that concept can translate into existence, we should not refer to the conception of concept as (mental) representation but to the (distinctively Hegelian) conception of concept explained previously.

At this point, it might be argued that a preliminary, more direct discussion of Hegel's account of God would be helpful to better understand what Hegel is up to here and to follow more closely his philosophical moves with respect to the OA. However, I argue that it is precisely through his discussion of the OA that Hegel sheds some light on his conception of God, and we can adequately answer the question of why God deserves to be called a "concept" according to the preceding definition.

In the previous chapters, I have already mentioned that historically the idea of God has always been indicative of the knowledge aspired to in philosophy. And once again it was Kant who made that implicit idea explicit. As early as in *Faith and Knowledge*, Hegel criticizes Kant for his consideration of the OA as "nothing but an unnatural scholastic trick," but then he reminds us that Kant also established the idea of God as a necessary *postulate*. Kant famously defined the postulate as "a theoretical proposition, though one not provable as such, insofar as it attaches inseparably to a practical law that holds a priori [and] unconditionally."[23] Therefore, the idea of God already had for Kant an explicitly normative status. The problem, in Hegel's view, is that Kant's postulate "is supposed to have necessary subjectivity [*Subjektivität*]" but not "absolute objectivity [*absolute Objektivität*]" (GW, 2:302/67). But what is the "absolute objectivity" of a concept, and why is it philosophically justified to claim that objectivity for the concept of God?

The answers to these questions can be found in a passage of the *Lectures on the Philosophy of Religion* (Rel I, 323–29/433–40), where the argument from *Faith and Knowledge* mentioned earlier is proposed again and explained more fully—and it is therefore appropriate to analyze that passage closely.

The implicit distinction between thought and being inevitably qualifies our relation to God as subjective: we do not treat God as a *subject* but merely as a *subjective* content.[24] This content is "afflicted with one-sidedness," because it is merely a *representation*. To deal with God as a representation is not incorrect in itself: in everyday life, everything is dealt with as a representation *first*. God, however, is not only a representation: God is a concept, and a self-conscious being—a subject. The relation I can have with a representation can only be a passive one, whereas with a subject there is the potential to establish a mutually active relationship.

We need to keep this reflection in the background while we consider the OA as trying to bridge the distinction and unite (the thought of) God with being. Anselm's move is to appeal to the perfection of that representation; and because "that which is perfect is something that is not merely represented but also is, actually is," the traditional OA concludes that "God is not only a representation" (Rel I, 324/434–35). To this argument, it is easy to object that adding the quality of perfection to a representation does not effectively bridge the distinction (between thought and being), as representation and being remain distinct from one another. Thus Kant is, to this extent, right—but he is right because the OA was originally flawed by its consideration of God as a representation rather than as a concept (in the Hegelian sense). Conversely, if we consider the concept as "what is alive," we can then claim that "one of its determinations is also being" (Rel I, 325/436). According to Hegel, this can be shown in two ways. *First*, "As spirit or as love, God is this self-particularizing." Here we notice that Hegel is not referring to an abstract, philosophical God but to the *Christian* God. This is consistent with Hegel's own conception of concept, which is not simply a mental content but something "alive" that cannot be disconnected from culture and history. Thus, Hegel refers explicitly to the incarnation, defined as the process according to which God "produces his Son, posits an other to himself" (and we will see in the next chapter that this self-differentiation plays a central role in Hegel's trinitarian conception). *Second*, we can prove that the concept of God involves being as follows. Of course, Hegel maintains, "the concept is different from being," because the concept is precisely what "sublates" the difference: the concept is "the movement or process of self-objectifying." The concept, Hegel reminds us, is "the purpose of an object": as I outlined earlier, a flower (here Hegel uses the sun and an animal as examples) *is* the concept but does not *have* the concept: it is not self-aware, it is not an "I." Human beings, conversely, *have* an "I" that is active: and "this activity is a self-objectifying" ("what we call a drive"). In other words, the "I" does not exist without the act of self-objectifying, or self-positing, precisely because it is that very act that establishes the "I." As Hegel explains elsewhere (Rel III, 274/355), when "human beings realize their purposes [. . .] what was at first only ideal is stripped of its one-sidedness and thereby made into a subsisting being": the ideal becomes real.[25] In the realm of metaphysics, the "I" and the world cannot be thought of in opposition: the concept, then, is the overcoming of the false opposition between the subjective and the objective: "To posit itself not only subjectively but also objectively, or even neither subjectively nor objectively—that is what the concept is" (Rel I, 328/439).

Why is Hegel addressing the "I" and its process of self-objectifying in this context? Because only in the light of the self-objectifying activity of the "I" can we correct the flaw in the OA. We can now better appreciate that the deficiency of the Anselmian proof consists in starting from a representation of God, and then "binding up with it" the being of God (Rel I, 328/439): but as long as we deal with a representation of God, the argument cannot work, because "[i]n the case of the concept, being is not supposed to be a mere *esse in idea* [being in thought] but also an *esse in re* [being in fact]" (Rel I, 328/440). The representation of God cannot be "immediately conjoined with the being"; otherwise, we would go no further than Anselm's argument, and no further than subjectivistic faith.

We are now in a position to answer the question about the absolute objectivity of the concept, and the legitimacy of claiming that objectivity for the concept of God. The objectivity of the concept is not an *immediate* objectivity—the objectivity that we presuppose when we "bind up" the representation of God to being—but that "mediated objectivity" (to use the explanatory term that I introduced in the previous chapters) that is "the unity of subject and object" (Rel III, 275/356).

I concluded the previous chapter by stressing that the process of the actualization of the concept into the idea of God (or absolute concept) is both religious and philosophical. We have now seen that Hegel is referring to both those dimensions in his "proof" that the concept of God involves being. *First*, the proof works at the religious level because Hegel is referring to the *Christian* God; the concept of God is self-objectifying *in* the *religious* relationship between the human being and the divine subject—a relationship that takes place in *cultus*, to which significantly Hegel turns in the following section of the *Lectures* (Rel I, 330/441). *Cultus*, properly conceived, is not a set of external actions of devotion but presupposes the "reconciliation of God with humanity" (Rel I, 332/443). The reconciliation that happens in *cultus* is the accomplishment, in religious terms, of the overcoming of the abstract opposition between the human and the divine; in normative terms, it means that human subjects collectively agree on norms higher than human norms (such as love and kenotic withdrawal), and yet informing them (the Eucharist is thus conceived as this assimilation of the divine). *Second*, the proof works at the philosophical level because, once we rightly understand the concept of God and the concept of the "I" beyond the subject/object opposition, we also understand that there is a necessary relation between the two concepts. In fact, once the subject/object opposition has been overcome, we come to see that concepts form a "system,"[26] within which the relative relevance of each specific concept is determined by their degree of self-consciousness (the capacity not only to be a concept but to have a concept, to use Hegel's terminology) and, as an implication, by their normative capacity. That the concept of God and the concept of the "I" are the key players in this system should not come as a surprise then. God and the "I" are intertwined: and the development of self-consciousness implies the consciousness of the interdependence between the self and God.

The interdependence between God and the self serves the purpose of making "the movement of the concept as activity" *palpable* (Rel I, 327/438); however, as Hegel specifically indicates, to "grasp" it "is a task that clearly belongs to logic." We now know that the demonstration of a concept means to grasp the unity of being and thought—that is, to follow the movement of transition from the absolute concept to existence. It is in logic, therefore, that we should look to find an argument that shows the philosophical necessity of the self-actualization of the concept in order to complement the religious necessity previously outlined.

## The Transition from Concept to Existence

In the *Encyclopedia Logic*, Hegel argues that "there are *two* possible paths or forms" to the unification of thought and being in the concept of God: "one can begin from *being* and from there make the transition to the *abstractum of thinking* or, conversely, the transition can be effected from the *abstractum to being*" (E I, 8:130/96). While the latter approach is the one adopted in the OA, the former represents the direction taken in the a posteriori proofs for the existence of God, such as the cosmological and teleological proofs.

The a posteriori proofs start from some conception of determinate being ("an infinite variety of determinations, a world completely full") that is regarded as unproblematic, and then "ascend" via a type of stepladder of concepts in an attempt to reach the *thought* of some highest being—by asking, for example, after the cause of those determinate beings. Thus, in fact, these proofs end where the OA starts—the highest *concept*, "God." The OA "starts from the *abstractum of thought* and proceeds to the determination for which only *being* remains" (E I, 8:135/100). However, we have seen that the concept of God to which the OA in Hegel's account arrives is not an abstract, merely philosophical God; rather, it is the God of the Christian tradition, the creator of the world. Therefore, the OA does not simply end with the being of God but also with the being of the finite world as God's creation—which is the position from which the cosmological and teleological proofs start. But the classical OA also starts with the assumption of a finite subject capable of having and reasoning about concepts, such as the concept of God. Taken together, then, the proofs seem to exhibit a *circular structure*.

One might object that if Hegel's arguments for the existence of God have a circular structure, then they are as disastrous as the traditional ones; in any case, they do not have the form of *linear* proofs. Also, one might wonder why Hegel's strategy, which we have seen so far as concerned exclusively with the OA, now also includes the a posteriori proofs. Isn't that a sign of desperate argumentation?

Not necessarily—let us give Hegel some credit; let us follow him through his thinking of logical structures and how they can show the transition from concept to existence. In the section on "syllogism" in the *Encyclopedia Logic*, Hegel distinguishes three kinds of syllogism: the qualitative syllogism, the syllogism of reflection, and the syllogism of necessity. Hegel's analysis of the first two forms of syllogism also shows the inadequacy of traditional proofs for the existence of God by looking at the two types of inference structure that one has in judgments of existence (the Aristotelian *qualitative syllogism*) and of reflection (the Leibnizian *reflective syllogism*). As I argued in the first section of this chapter, Leibniz makes explicit a logical assumption that was already implicit in Anselm and then Descartes, namely, the assumption that it is possible to distinguish the abstract form (the concept of God) from the consideration of content (the existence of God). Out of these two forms of syllogism then comes the syllogism of necessity, which is the appropriate logical form for Hegel's own version of the OA. In fact, the syllogism of necessity is meant to indicate the transition to the thinking of logical structures as already "embodied" in metaphysical objects (as objects of thought). The logical movement here is from the concept to being, which is the movement of the OA. A convincing way to grasp the legitimacy of this movement is that suggested by Redding. He argues that Hegel essentially "repeats at the level of logic his diagnosis and resolution" of the problem of circularity: the syllogism of necessity, conceived in this way, represents "the concrete and pragmatic recognitively circular context within which finite thinking subjects necessarily exist": a circle "in which both the thinking subject and the thought object are included such that there can be no idea of some absolute place *outside* the circle."[27]

Let us expand on Redding's interpretation. There is no doubt that Hegel's argument here needs to be contextualized within his conception of knowledge, because it applies to the concept in general. Hegel is critical of *certainty* (*Gewissheit*), which he opposes to *truth*. Linear forms of proofs require a starting point that is regarded as "unproblematic" in the way the primitive *certainty* (with which, one can remember, the *Phenomenology* begins) sees claims as unproblematic. Starting points are considered immediate rather than derived, or *mediated*. Likewise, religious faith, in its primitive or naïve dimension, flows from the standpoint of certainty. For the OA, the implicit assumption is the distinction between thought and being; but this assumption is, in Hegel's view, problematic. Such a conception cannot just be "assumed" but needs to be conceived as being *posited* (*gesetzt*). In Hegel's view, there are no unpresuppositional starting points, and certainty does not guarantee truth. Descartes's assumption represents the standpoint of subjective certainty, that is, a standpoint that is typical of modernity and that represents a huge step forward from the primitive, Aristotelian, and unmediated assumption of the unity between thought and being (a unity that was just assumed but not yet *posited*). However, the standpoint of subjective certainty is equally unmediated and therefore needs to be overcome, not in the direction of (Kantian) skepticism but in the development of a self-correcting way of thinking of that starting point as deduced *within* the circle of knowledge. Conceived as a moment of this "cognitive circle," the unity of being and thought is neither the same assumption that we find in the Aristotelian standpoint, nor a faith-belief that needs to be accepted as such, but a coherent reconceptualized version of that unity between thought and being.

Once again, one might object that, if this is the case, one could never get out of that circle and get a type of "view from the outside." If the interpretation outlined earlier is correct, then Hegel would probably reply to this objection by simply agreeing to it. The Hegelian OA is valid precisely *because* it expresses the circular structure that is the structure of knowledge itself. Both the unity *and* the separation of being and thought need to be thought of as posited, that is, *mediated*: if we now consider the OA and the a posteriori arguments together in this light, we can see that they effectively represent this kind of circularity. The a posteriori arguments implicitly assume an unmediated, nonposited unity between thought and being (qualitative syllogism); the traditional OA implicitly assumes an equally unmediated, nonposited separation between thought and being (syllogism of reflection); finally, the Hegelian version of the OA (syllogism of necessity) recognizes the unity neither as immediately assumed, nor as subjectively posited by the thinking subject, but as a moment in the circle of knowledge.

The syllogism of necessity, with its move from "inference" to "objectivity," is essentially a redetermination of *perspective*: by overcoming the distinction "between mediator and mediated, and between subject and object,"[28] it removes both the old metaphysical illusion of an immediate unity *and* the modern subjective illusion of an immediate separation, to reach an idealist, *mediated* standpoint that acknowledges the intrinsic and unavoidable circularity of knowledge and finally allows us to grasp the coincidence, for concepts, of their existence with the normative status they are meant to express. It is this redetermination of perspective that allows the thought's normative capacities to confer existence on the concept.

The concept of God, therefore, exists *in* the recognitively circular context (to use Redding's expression), because that is the only context in which finite thinking subjects exist; nevertheless, far from proving that, as a consequence of such position, God is only a fictional character, this is rather evidence that God and finite human subjects are in a relation of *interdependence*—which is not, however, a relation of mutual full dependence.

*First*, therefore, divine self-consciousness can realize itself only through the mediation of the knowledge of the recognizing community. The existence of God (as concept and Idea) is bound up with the existence of human beings. God is necessarily self-conscious, but this self-consciousness is not achievable in a direct way: God's thinking of Godself is dependent on the way God's creatures think of God, and when God's creatures think of God, they are properly thinking thoughts that are God's. Something like this is what we have seen, in chapter 2, in the conception of God as manifesting Godself in certain speech acts of subjects as when, for example, they forgive each other—acts that do not merely express the agency of that concrete speaker but in which the voice of God is to be recognized. Clearly, Hegel cannot be identified as a theist in the (traditional metaphysical) sense, by which God's existence can be grasped as entirely independent of human beings. The God of the pre-Christian cosmological and teleological proofs might be conceived as independent of the existence of "objective spirits," but the conception of God at work in those proofs is not the same as that of the Christian God. The Christian God, as interpreted (in a quite heterodox way, one must admit) by Hegel, requires the thought processes and communicative actions of humans within which God can manifest Godself so as to become self-conscious, to become a *subject*—an attribute that is essential to God.

*Second, we* are not independent of God. As I argued in the previous chapter, if the concept of God unifies the realm of reason as a whole, and if the self is an object of reason, it follows that the development of self-consciousness implies consciousness of the interdependence between the self and God. We are now better positioned to appreciate this claim. Because of the circularity of knowledge, we need, in Hegel's view, to commit to the existence of God. Pinkard has stressed this aspect by remarking that Hegel's concept of God "could in fact be shown to be a commitment that one implicitly undertakes when thinking about 'being' in general."[29] There is also *another* aspect of our dependence on God. As I argued in the previous two chapters, Hegel considers Christianity as being crucial for having made explicit a conception of God as the model of both epistemological and practical openness—leading to perspectivism and recognition, respectively. This openness is what makes us humans. Humans cannot be extricated from their relation to God on this model and properly *be* humans. This is also the reason why the Christian God cannot be reduced to being a mere projection of "proper" human existence—and Hegel is adamant that God cannot be reduced to a state of dependence on human beings (VBD, 382/66): because the conditions of that existence require the use of the concept of God. This might be taken to be the ultimate meaning of Hegel's OA.

In Hegel's own revised version of the OA, therefore, the logical aspect and the religious (Christian) aspect cannot be disjoined. Hegel thinks that an argument for the existence of God should provide satisfaction not only for the speculative consciousness but also for the religious consciousness. In other words, faith and thought cannot be assumed to be antithetical, as they have come to be regarded in modern times. Rather, it is more a matter of faith requiring a proper understanding of God in order to be properly "satisfied": to use a formula of which Hegel was fond, in the raising of one's mind to God from the level of feeling to that of thought, something that had hitherto been simply *presupposed* must come to be "posited." Hegel's revaluation of the OA can be considered, from this point of view, as a strategic move in his ongoing polemic against the danger of subjectivism in theology, which—as already mentioned in chapter 2—he saw expressed in the thought of those among his contemporaries (such as Jacobi, Fries, and Schleiermacher) who grounded the relationship to God in *feeling*. Hegel, conversely, insists that *thought* is the proper medium for God. In other words, the stance of mere faith must be raised to the level of thought, in as much as the proper human stance is one mediated by thought. The same can be said, I argued, against the default assumption of the unity of thought and being in classical thought, which has to be mediated by thought in order to gain the objectivity of content of the Christian religion.

Therefore, Hegel's OA (which is a revaluation, not devoid of criticisms, of the traditional OA) is a crucial step in his strategy to restore *content* to religion. With the transition from concept to existence, Hegel can now dismiss Kant's objections against the knowledge of God, as much as he dismissed the traditional versions of the OA: in fact, Hegel's objections equally apply to those traditional versions *and* to the Kantian reply they lead to—they all treat God as a *Gegenstand*, an object-that-stands-over-and-against human consciousness. Only once God is reconceptualized in the circular context of interdependence with the human subject—once, in other words, the subject/object opposition has been overcome—the knowledge of God becomes possible.[30] Actually, the OA has not only shown the *possibility* of the knowledge of God but has also told us something about the *content* of that knowledge. The concept of God that has turned into existence in the OA—God as the "absolute Idea," to use Hegel's jargon—has been shown to be in an intrinsic relation with human subjects. Also, the interdependence of God and human subjects resulting from the OA confirms, in a circular fashion, the normative features of this conception of God, both epistemologically (perspectivism) and practically (recognition). Both these features are grounded in *relationality*. The Kantian monarchical metaphor is thus completely replaced with another model, that of the divestment (*Entäußerung*) of God in the world. As remarked by Hodgson, "The abiding unity that forms God's infinite subjectivity does not dissolve differentia into sameness but holds them in a play of productive relationships, as symbolized by the play of the trinitarian persons."[31] The relationality of God, in fact, is not only its *outward* relationality, which is expressed in God's relationship with human subjects, but is also an *inward* relationality: the play of the trinitarian persons is, therefore, the relational content of the knowledge of God. As I will show in the next chapter, the trinitarian structure, far from being merely a set of religious representations (*Vorstellungen*), if properly reconstructed, is to be regarded as another step in Hegel's enterprise of restoring content to religion—and specifically, of making the reconceptualization of God applicable to the world.

5

# The Trinity and the "I"

Walter Kaufmann wrote that when one examines the tables of contents of Hegel's works, one necessarily notices a "very decided preference for triadic arrangements."[1] Given this preference, Hegel's interest in the Christian notion of the Trinity (*die Dreieinigkeit*) may seem obvious. Thus, Hegel has sometimes been regarded as seeing, in Christianity generally and in the Trinity specifically, "a kind of allegory depicting the central truths of his own philosophy."[2] However, defining Hegel's interest in Christianity and the Trinity exclusively in terms of an allegory is reductive. To grasp the importance of the Trinity for Hegel, the definitions he provides must be examined: the doctrine of the Trinity is not only "the fundamental characteristic of the Christian religion" (Rel I, 68/157), but it is also the "axis on which the History of the World turns" and "the goal and the starting point of history" (VPW Lasson, 3:722/331).[3] In this respect, the correspondence of the three parts of the *Encyclopedia* (Logic, Philosophy of Nature, and Philosophy of Spirit) to the structure of the Trinity suggests that the relevance of this notion in the context of Hegel's system extends beyond its role as an allegory.[4]

The Hegelian account of the Trinity has attracted increasing scholarly attention over the last few decades. Some interpreters, such as Jaeschke[5] and Hodgson,[6] have stressed the *rationalist* dimension of Hegel's view on religion, whereas others, such as O'Regan,[7] have stressed the *mystical* features of Hegel's thought. However, until recently, most studies on this topic tended to consider the Trinity strictly in the context of Hegel's philosophy of *religion*, without considering the implications of this emphasis on Hegel's idealism (or by considering them to a limited extent).

Since 2000, some important books on Hegel's philosophy of religion have been published that have also devoted some attention to the notion of the Trinity. Calton seemingly considers Hegel's thought to be committed to pre-Kantian metaphysics and yet presents notable insights, particularly regarding the role, in Hegel's account, of human consciousness in complementing the Trinity (through the reasoning that takes place in the ontological proof).[8] Desmond argues for the importance of the question of God and the Trinity within Hegel's thought;[9] however, his work adheres to the old-fashioned account of Hegel's absolute spirit as a totalizing substance (as noted by Hodgson[10]), and although Desmond seems to argue that Hegelian thought cannot do justice to the religious conception of God, he does not identify a specific fallacy in Hegel's strategy, apart from an alleged "reduction" of God to the "immanent self-transcendence" of the dialectic. Hodgson offers a valuable analysis of Hegel's speculative reconstruction of various Christian themes and considers the Hegelian notion of absolute spirit as representing a radical departure from the traditional metaphysical concept of God and the Trinity as the highest substance, but nevertheless he seems to argue for the importance of Hegel's philosophy of religion to *theological* rather than to *philosophical* discourse.[11] Wallace offers a highly detailed account of Hegel's logic as providing the fundamental structures that constitute Hegel's account of God as irreducible to either traditional theism or to Enlightenment naturalism and atheism, but he does not consider the trinitarian account of God (most likely because he openly disregards Hegel's *Lectures on the Philosophy of Religion*).[12] The connection between Hegel's *Science of Logic* and his *Lectures on the Philosophy of Religion* is instead central in Wendte's work.[13] Wendte makes the Chalcedonian formula (the twofold, human and divine, nature of Christ) central to his account of the relation between logical and theological investigations. In the context of this account, the doctrine of the Trinity is conceived as the fundamental framework of a relational ontology that is dynamic and dialectic. Finally, Lewis has recently reinterpreted Hegel's philosophy of religion in light of the post-Kantian/revisionist reading of Hegel. Lewis regards Hegel as advancing a distinctively modern, nontheistic account of Christianity that is integral to fostering social and political cohesion; in this account, however, the notion of Trinity is considered a representation of philosophical content and therefore remains in the background.[14]

These books, together with several other papers and book chapters published in recent years, have significantly advanced our understanding of

Hegel's conception of the Trinity. Nevertheless, the net of complex relations linking the Trinity to other aspects of Hegel's thought, particularly the implications of the relevance of this notion on Hegel's metaphysics, remains underdeveloped.

It is impossible to provide, in the space of a chapter, a novel or a revised interpretation of the Trinity in Hegel's philosophy. More modestly, and consistent with our general purposes, this chapter aims to show the relevance of Hegel's notion of the Trinity with respect to two specific aspects of Hegel's idealism. The first is—and this is hardly a surprise, at this point in our journey—the overcoming of subjectivism. The second, perhaps more surprisingly, is Hegel's conception of the "I." I argue that these two issues are interconnected and that the notion of the Trinity is important to Hegel's philosophical strategy in addressing these aspects.

I will first focus on the problem of subjectivism by considering Hegel's philosophy against the background of modern philosophy from Descartes to Kant and I will do so with an emphasis on the conception of God. I will argue that the recognitive structure of Hegel's idealism effectively led him to consider the Christian Trinity as having a decisive role in his philosophical account. Then I will briefly analyze the three divine persons of the Trinity. Using this analysis, in the conclusive section of this chapter, I will argue that the Trinity represents a model for rethinking the "I" in a way that overcomes a "naïve realist" and a "subjective" account of the "I." Hegel's absolute idealism, I will suggest, can be conceived as an approach to the "I" that considers the role of intersubjective acts of mutual recognition for the genesis of self-conscious thought and the Trinity as the *exposition* or *presentation* (*Darstellung*) of the relational and recognitive structure of the "I."

## Subjectivism and God

Since its inception, German idealism was a reaction—or a "struggle," as defined by Beiser[15]—against subjectivism, conceived as the philosophical tenet that claims that the nature of reality as related to a given consciousness is dependent on that consciousness. As we have seen (in chapter 2), Hegel considers the Kantian approach to experience as leading to a conception of the "I" marked with subjectivism, and he advances a different understanding of the mind/world relation. We also know that Hegel's account of the mind/world relation is one of the deciding factors (or even *the* deciding factor) differentiating various interpretations of Hegel's philosophy (chapter 3). Some scholars see Hegel as approaching the mind/world relation in terms of a kind of *conceptual realism*, that is, as suggesting that Hegelian metaphysics is an inquiry into fundamental "features" or "structures" of the world itself, independently of the "I."[16] Hegel explicitly maintains that "thoughts are not merely our thoughts but at the same time the in itself [*das Ansich*] of things and of the object-world [*des Gegenständlichen*] in general" (E I, 8:116/85).[17] The question is: can thoughts constitute the essences of things *prior to being thought*—that is, independently of the mind? In the context of an idealist metaphysics, can "an object" really be distinguished from what that object is "for us"—that is, from the object *as it is thought* by us? According to the post-Kantian/revisionist interpretation, concepts are not regarded by Hegel as completely independent of the mind, and it is necessary to consider the role of intersubjective acts of mutual *recognition* for the genesis of self-conscious thoughts. As remarked in the previous chapters, a way to describe the role of recognition in the establishment of a concept is to think of it as *contributing* to its *positing*: a concept is neither something merely given nor exclusively posited by an absolute "I" (as in Fichte); the intersubjective acts of mutual recognition contribute to its positing by making a representation (*Vorstellung*) consistent with its content—thus generating a concept (*Begriff*). Considered in such a way, the Hegelian move can be regarded as bypassing the approach iconically exemplified by the Cartesian doubt, which considers *first* the "I" as a reality independent of the world, and *then* the problem of the "I's" cognitive activity.

After the mind/world relation has been reconsidered from an idealist standpoint—that is, after the ideal aspired to has become that of a system of absolute knowledge, or absolute idealism (i.e., a system that overcomes the subject/object distinction)—then the knowledge (not merely the moral postulate, as Kant suggested) of God becomes not only possible but also internally required. In fact, God represented, for Kant, the idea of the absolute totality of internal and external phenomena and therefore the necessary ideal of an architectonic unity of knowledge as an entirety; this ideal, however, was only *formal*, because of the subjectivist component of Kant's transcendental idealism. After the mind/world relation has been reconsidered from the standpoint of absolute idealism, then the unity of knowledge expressed by the idea of God is to be conceived not only as a formal regulative ideal but also as achievable (at least to some extent). Hegel, in fact, approaches God not as a natural object but as a *concept*:

if the "world" philosophy is concerned with is primarily the world of "objects of reasons," then God is not to be considered as severed from the world. If we can know the world, then we can know God.

This approach raises the question of *how* we can know God. I have already mentioned, in the previous chapters, that Hegel is critical of a conception that grounds the relationship to God in *feeling*. The 1824 *Lectures on the Philosophy of Religion* are usually regarded as advancing a polemic against the danger of subjectivism in theology, particularly as expressed by the thought of Jacobi, Fries, and Schleiermacher. Against all of them, Hegel objects that we do not simply *believe* in God; we also *think* God, God *is* thought. Hegel also blames theological subjectivism for its implications, among which he identifies *both* a turn to a historical attitude (Rel I, 76/166), unconcerned with the question of whether a religious claim or doctrine "is true in and for itself" (Rel I, 68/157n17), *and*—importantly, for the purposes of this chapter—a dismissal of the doctrine of the Trinity. The target here is again Schleiermacher, who, in the conclusion of the *Glaubenslehre*, described the Trinity as an "appended proposition" to Christianity.[18]

Theological subjectivism is dangerous, in Hegel's view, because its implications, such as an overemphasis on history and a dismissal of central doctrines, such as the doctrine of the Trinity, enable the reduction of the conception of the divine to a reflection of the finite mind (Rel III, 168/238). This conception is defined by Hegel as the "reflective philosophy of subjectivity"; its historical incarnation first arose in the Enlightenment, though it is not limited to it, as it extends to incorporate the thought of idealist philosophers, such as Fichte. Hegel is concerned that a reflective critique of religion that questions central doctrines and tends to consider God a mere product of the human mind may lead to an empty deism or even to atheism.[19] Hegel's concern indicates a predicament constitutive of Hegel's philosophy that was destined to have consequences for the further development of post-Hegelian philosophy and for the split among Hegel's followers, that is, between "right" and "left" Hegelians. On one hand, Hegel reacts against theological subjectivism and its idea of an immediate relationship with God by stressing the mediated nature of the knowledge of God that must be accessed rationally. Hegel's reason is not, however, Kant's *individual* reason, but it is a *socialized* form of reason that relies on recognition. Considered thus, our knowledge of God cannot be said to be completely independent of the rational and social practices involving the recognition of God's existence. On the other hand, Hegel seeks to safeguard God's independence against the reduction of God to the status of a fictional character or a human production—a tendency common among the subset of his followers subsequently identified as "left Hegelians," such as Strauss and Feuerbach.[20] Hegel's final unfinished work, written in his own hand in 1831 (*Lectures on the Proofs of the Existence of God*), shows an increasingly strong concern in this respect. "If in fact," Hegel writes, "we are to understand by religion nothing more than a relationship on our part to God, then God is left without any independent existence. God *would exist only in religion* as something *posited* by us, produced by us" (VBD, 382/66).[21] Such statements most likely prompted right Hegelians (and a few later interpreters) to conclude that Hegel was regressing to the idea of a pre-Kantian, metaphysical God. However, as explained, this possibility is eliminated by Hegel's insistence on mediation in his polemic against theological subjectivism. "Mediation," in fact, does not only signify "conceptual" mediation (according to the common definition of concepts as "mental contents") but also, more broadly, cultural and historical mediation: the concept of God is not, and cannot be, independent of the historical development of that idea in Western culture.

If this analysis is correct, Hegel is then regarded as simultaneously maintaining three claims: God exists independently of our positing God, God becomes self-conscious, and God's self-consciousness is mediated through the knowledge of the socially recognizing community. Prima facie, it might look like there is a problem here: how can the existence of God be separate from the knowledge of individuals, if God knows Godself only in the knowledge of the socially recognizing community? Nevertheless, this contradiction is only apparent in Hegel's view, as it relies on a notion of God operating like a *name* rather than as a *concept*. As we know from the analysis carried on in chapter 3, at a certain cognitive level (the level of, say, our everyday experience), everything is, to some extent, experienced as a mere name, that is, as a representation (*Vorstellung*)—and God is no exception. However, as soon as one starts to consider God as a concept rather than as a name, and starts to rationally analyze it in its connections, one recognizes that the concept is mediated—that is, that it cannot be thought without thinking of it in relation to the world and to human beings. Unlike Kant, Hegel does not believe that there is another world beyond that of representations, but he maintains that conceptual thinking allows continual undermining of the *independence* that names illusorily suggest for what they refer to, and it shows their *dependency* on each other. In other words, the concept of God needs to be such to allow this type of differentiation: God exists independently of our positing God, but, if one properly considers God as a concept, one realizes that the divine self-consciousness can realize itself only through the mediation of the knowledge of the socially recognizing community.

This was effectively one of the outcomes of our analysis in the previous chapter, where, going through the implications of the ontological argument, we started to identify a strict connection between God and the "I." God represents the unity of knowledge, but real knowledge, for Hegel, is the spirit's self-consciousness, that is, the rational human "mindedness" considered not only in its "Kantian" individual and formal aspects but also in those historical and social aspects of concrete human existence that depend on mutual recognition.[22] Hence, God exemplifies the spirit's structure.[23] Hegel's strategy in addressing the mind/world opposition is a refusal to consider the two "poles" of the relation in isolation and as opposed. Similarly, the traditional account of the human being (subject) as knowing God (object) is regarded as inappropriate: in Hegelian terms, the relationship would be more properly described by claiming that God knows Godself through humanity's self-consciousness.[24]

The three series of *Lectures on the Philosophy of Religion* are usually regarded as characterized by different concerns or preoccupations: specifically, the 1824 lectures by the polemic against subjectivism, and the 1831 lectures by a major focus on the trinitarian structure of God. For instance, Hodgson, commenting on the 1831 lectures, writes: "The polemic against the subjectivism of present-day theology is past, and Hegel now faces a different challenge."[25] But despite the indubitable change in focus, the polemic against subjectivism is not simply "past" in the 1831 lectures.[26] The emphasis on the trinitarian structure of God that characterizes that series of lectures is rather a further step within Hegel's strategy in addressing the same challenge. The suggested way to avoid the risk of subjectivism and to overcome the subject/object opposition in the human–divine relationship is to show that God exemplifies the structure of the spirit, because the medium through which self-consciousness is realized is recognition—and this claim remains valid for both the development of *divine* self-consciousness *and* for the development of *human* self-consciousness. In other words, the nature of God and the nature of the human "I" mirror each other. Williams has shown that the spirit's fundamental structure is "self-recognition in other"; if God is intended to exemplify this structure, then God is necessarily "social and personal," and "since God requires an other," Williams continues, "but no other can be given to God, God is his own other."²⁷ Hence, Hegel's interest in the trinitarian structure of God can be explained. Furthermore, because the trinitarian God is the prototype of a personal, intersubjective relationship, knowledge of the Trinity will also represent knowledge of the recognitive "I" and its relation to the world. The internally recognitive structure of God leads to the Trinity, and the Trinity in turn represents a model for the self-development of the "I." Therefore, the next two sections will be devoted, respectively, to a brief account of Hegel's conception of the Trinity in light of his ongoing opposition against subjectivism, and to some conclusive remarks about the recognitive structure of the "I" and the Trinity as mirroring each other.

## Hegel's Trinity

Hegel is adamant regarding his view of the centrality of the trinitarian doctrine within Christianity. In this context, the target of his polemical attacks was not only Schleiermacher, who had described the Trinity as an "appended proposition" to Christianity, but also those "pious theologians" (Rel I, 68/157n17) who regarded the Trinity as a mere historical product and traced its origins back to late Greek philosophy and Neoplatonism and, on this ground, dismissed it as a "decorative timbering."²⁸ Hegel is willing to concede that, as a human-developed historical product, the notion of the Trinity entered Christianity through external cultural influences, and especially through the Neoplatonic tradition. However, stopping at this claim would, in Hegel's view, miss the point. Hegel thinks that religious representations can find their *sublation* (*Aufhebung*) in the conceptual language of philosophy. But, insofar as they are *representations*, they are inseparable from the cultural history that has produced them. Therefore, it is "immaterial where that doctrine came from," Hegel claims, and he continues: "The question is solely whether it is true [*wahr*] in and for itself" (Rel I, 68/157n17). In this regard, one must remember that Hegel thinks that the traditional (Aristotelian) correspondence theory does not exhaust a comprehensive theory of truth; for Hegel, truth (*Wahrheit*) is, first and foremost, "the agreement of a content with itself [*Übereinstimmung eines Inhalts mit sich selbst*]" (E I, 8:86/62).²⁹ Therefore, the question is whether the religious representation of the Trinity is consistent with the concept of God. To answer this question, Hegel's dialectical method requires an "unpacking" of the notion. The dialectical method, rather than being simply "applied" to an inquiry, gives "form" to the subject matter; in other words, that "unpacking," which clarifies the internal and external connections of a notion or representation, permits the "truth" of the Trinity to be discovered.

The standard Christian doctrine of the Trinity defines God as three divine persons, distinct but coexisting in unity: God the Father, the Son, and the Holy Spirit. Hegel clarifies that, taken literally, this description of the Trinity is a "childlike" (*kindlich*; Rel I, 43/126 and Rel III, 127/194) and imaginative (*bildlich*; Rel III, 209/284) expression. Here, Hegel distances himself from the traditional doctrine of the Trinity and expresses a dislike for the emphasis on the representation of three "persons." For Hegel, "we must be aware that all three are spirit" (Rel III, 128/195), an awareness that should help us to develop a more appropriate understanding of the Trinity as represented by a unity, that is, a unique "personhood,"[30] which expresses itself in a range of relationships—those relationships traditionally expressed by the inadequate images of Father, Son, and Spirit.

To explore this range of relationships, it is useful to employ a distinction that is traditional in trinitarian theology but that is not explicitly mentioned by Hegel, yet it seems to be implied in his analysis: that between *immanent* and *economic* Trinity.[31] The immanent Trinity is the pre-worldly Trinity, that is, the idea of God prior to the creation of the world—"the show of finitude," Hegel remarks, "has not yet taken place" (Rel III, 16/77–78). It is an "abiding unity" (Rel I, 272/374),[32] but this unity is pre-characterized by a set of internal relationships: identity (represented by the Father), difference (represented by the Son), and mediation (represented by the Spirit).[33] The economic account, by contrast, expresses the Trinity in its outward relationships: respectively, the creation of the finite world, the incarnation of Christ, and the consummation of everything in God; it is the *diremption* (*Entzweiung*) of the immanent Trinity. To consider the two "trinities" in such a way that the economic Trinity temporarily or logically follows the immanent Trinity would be inaccurate. There is only *one* Trinity, and the distinction depends on our finite nature, which is forced to distinguish between inward and outward relationships to grasp their complexity. However, after this distinction is clarified, it is appropriate to claim, albeit inadequately, that the immanent differentiation enables the economic differentiation. In other words, precisely because God is, *ab aeternum*, self-identity, self-differentiation, and self-return, divine history features the creation of the world, the incarnation of Christ, and the consummation of all finite things in the Spirit. The Trinity is "true" because it is a representation of God's essence, which can also be logically expressed as unity, differentiation, and return.³⁴ However, these logical "structures" of God would remain abstract without their outward "translation." Therefore, the *drive* of the outward relationships of the economic Trinity is *self-revelation*—which is represented more accurately by the *second* hypostasis but is not limited to it, as all three forms represent the movement from the *inner* to the *outer*—from logical categories to their applications in the spatiotemporal world. In the context of the economic Trinity, Hegel regards the *first* hypostasis, God the Father, as subsuming in itself the logical stance of the *immanent* Trinity as an entirety.³⁵ The Son represents, simultaneously, the "eternal Son," that is, self-differentiation, and God becoming human in the person of Christ, whereas the *third* hypostasis, the Spirit, represents the reconciliation between God and the finite world. Therefore, God's self-revelation is required for God's *self-realization*. *Logically*, God is complete as immanent Trinity, but it is through those internal relationships that it is externalized and concretized in the spatiotemporal domain.³⁶ As previously stressed, Hegel opposes a clear separation between God and the world. Thus, it would not be completely correct to claim that, for Hegel, God "needs" the external world to realize Godself; rather, the relationships expressed by the economic Trinity are part of a process that God undergoes to properly *be* God. This "absolute unity," Hegel states, which is "self-identical in its differentiation, [is] *eternal love*" (Rel III, 16–17/78). Love is "already implicit"³⁷ and indeed constitutes the relational structure of the immanent Trinity in which—to quote Williams again—"God is his own other" (because no other can be given to God); however, love becomes explicit and "concrete" only in the moment of differentiation, or diremption.

Consider the three hypostases of the Trinity in their respective specificity as they emerge from Hegel's treatment. As previously stated, the Father represents the immanent Trinity as an entirety, that is, an all-encompassing universality or ideality. Hegel defines the Father as "*actus purus*," "the activity of pure knowing" and significantly refers to the Scholastic age (Rel III, 209/284n93), in which the idea of God was modeled on the Aristotelian "unmoved mover." Given that God is also conceptualized as the unity of knowledge, the Father represents, within the Trinity, the moment of an a-perspectival ideal of knowledge—a proper "God's-eye view."³⁸

The second person of the Trinity, the Son, represents the moment of self-differentiation, diremption, "infinite particularity" (Rel III, 128/195). The idea of a "descent" of God into the world is not in itself a novelty of Christianity, as in Hegel's view, the idea can be traced back to the Neoplatonic "nous"; however, the nous as spiritual force is not "individualized" yet.[39] According to Hegel, the real novelty of Christianity is God self-differentiating Godself and becoming human in the incarnation. Redding has noted that the movement from the "Aristotelian" god represented by the Father to the Son of the Christian tradition is the movement from "the perspective of a transcendent god to one 'fallen' into the realm of objectified living existence on earth."[40] When Hegel maintains that Christ is not "the mere instrument of the revelation but is himself the content of the revelation" (E III, 10:29/18), he is emphasizing the relevance of the incarnation over the preaching of Jesus. For Hegel, Christ's incarnation is important because it prevents the reduction of the conception of the divine mind in one subject to the merely human point of view. God *is* the unity of knowledge, a unity that Hegel seeks to preserve; but the Hegelian strategy for preserving a conception of the divine mind (including its role of model for human knowledge) is to relinquish the idea of the "God's-eye view" not only for humans but *also for God Godself*.[41]

To further understand the centrality of God's incarnation to Hegel's account of the Trinity, it is useful to mention the attention he reserves for the theological view of the German mystic Jacob Böhme in the *Lectures on the History of Philosophy*.

Commenting on Böhme's theology, Hegel first stresses that God's self-revelation happens through the *differentiation* of God within Godself.[42] Without this differentiation, God (the Father) is, in its abstract self-identity, pure undifferentiated nothing (*Nichts*).[43] By contrast, the Son is the source of all differences, as he is "the Separator": being an *individual*, he is the negation of that undifferentiated unity that is God the Father. As "selfhood," he is an "I," and simultaneously he is "nothing" with respect to the divine unity—an idea that Böhme tries to convey through the wordplay *Icht* by fusing the German words "I" (*Ich*) and nothingness (*Nichts*).[44] Finally, the Separator must yield to fulfill his destiny of "negation of negation" to allow the separation within God to be annulled and to allow God to live as Spirit (VGP, 86/3:129).

This brief description indicates that Hegel emphasizes various aspects in Böhme's theological account. The first aspect is, as previously stressed, the centrality of the incarnation, conceived as the process of God's relinquishing God's absoluteness to become human. The second aspect is the "analogy" between the Son and the "I." The third aspect is the Son's death to fulfill the process of God's self-realization.

This idea of Spirit as resulting from a "negation of negation" is a conception endorsed by Hegel and is expressed in a passage of the 1831

*Lectures*: "The abstractness of the Father is given up in the Son—this then is death. But the negation of this negation is the unity of Father and Son—love, or the Spirit" (Rel III, 286/370). In other words, the love implicit in the immanent Trinity—or, which is the same, in the Father—has now become concrete; the Father has been somehow "opposed" by the Son's self-differentiation, and the Son has died, together with his individuality. However, as is usual within the Hegelian system, the previous "moments" are not merely "left behind" because they effectively constitute the final "form" of God–Spirit.[45]

Therefore, Christ's death is the "negation of the negation," and this double negation is love, or Spirit. When Hegel mentions love, he usually refers to a highly specific conception grounded in recognition: "When we say, 'God is love,' love signifies a distinguishing of two, who nevertheless are absolutely not distinguished for each other" (Rel III, 201/276). As Hegel clarifies in the *Philosophy of Right*, the first "moment" of love consists in the acceptance that complete independence cannot be achieved and that we therefore should be willing to be "open" to others.[46] The second "moment" of love consists in a renewed self-discovery *in* the other.[47] The Trinity represents a model for both these "moments" of love: first, the Father recognizes the need for an "other," represented by the Son (from the point of view of the immanent Trinity) and the world (from the point of view of the economic Trinity); then, through the incarnation, God achieves in the Spirit reconciliation on the part of human beings and God's own self-realization, thus constituting "the realized identity of objective world and eternal thought."[48]

Hegel's emphasis on the Trinity's third hypostasis is therefore strictly connected with the mutual recognition between the individuals who form a community. In this context, the novelty of the Christian church, considered as a prototypical community, is its willingness to perform a twofold withdrawal that mirrors the trinitarian dynamic: first, each individual surrenders her subjectivity to establish the community's intersubjectivity, and second, the community gives up its spirituality (the religious community's traditional spiritual component) to engage with the world.

Before proceeding further, we should briefly pause and wonder what role Hegel's account of the distinction between representation (*Vorstellung*) and thought (*Denken*) plays in how we interpret Hegel's use of Böhme's language, and how transformed this language is by Hegel's conception of such a distinction. Here we should recall what we anticipated in chapter 3: representations and concepts have to be conceived in mutual relation.

We inevitably start from representations (in everyday life, and in dealing with religion). Some representations are, however, more adequate than others for capturing reality—and here Hegel does not significantly distance himself from Kant (for Kant, Christ, for example, is to be considered the prototype of pure moral disposition because it is the most adequate representation of that idea). Thought then "purifies" and "frees" the content "from the contingencies of representation."[49] However, Hegel's dialectic would not be complete if it stopped at this point. There is, in fact, a further movement of thought, by which concepts reconstruct the genetic movement that made the concept possible—what O'Regan calls "a dialectical shuttle": "The philosophical concept is arrived at through religious representation, yet the concept that presupposes representation, reconstructs, even redescribes, the genetic moment that made it possible."[50] It is this additional movement that marks the novelty of Hegel's approach in dealing with religious representation (differentiating him from Kant, for example, as for the latter this additional movement is completely absent); and this is precisely, I contend, what is happening here in relation to Böhme's language. Böhme's mystical language has the merit of capturing some philosophical content prior to philosophy itself and presents it in a representative form of language; thought then "purifies" these representations and extracts their conceptual content; but thought then goes *back* on the religious representations to grasp the "genetic moment"—which consists in the *relationality* of God.

Therefore, Hegel's account of the Trinity leads to the conclusion that God's essence, as long as it is trinitarian, is intrinsically *relational*. Of course, one might object that the validity of this claim is culturally limited, that this claim is true only if we refer to the idea of the *Christian* God as it has been culturally developed during history and that this claim has no conclusive value. However, this objection is unacceptable from a Hegelian point of view because the history of the cultural development of ideas *is* the history of the development of self-consciousness itself—that is, it has a value for "reality" itself. The value of the trinitarian representation of God is its capacity to capture the intrinsic relationality *of the world*—that is, to provide a picture of the world that overcomes the subject/object distinction. Hegel believes that God is the unity of knowledge; hence, God is not severed from the world. If we can know the world, then we can know God, but also the converse is true: if we can know God, then we can know the world. Given this relation, one can better understand Hegel's interest in Böhme's thought (one that "permeates all his works," in Hegel's words) that the Trinity can be perceived "in everything" and that everything can be recognized "as its revelation and manifestation" (GP, 20:98–99 / LHP, 3:196). Thus, the relationality of the Trinity can be perceived in the world, and the world is *relational*. The world is relational because *we* "create" the world as relational, in the sense not that the world is a human fictional projection (a view that sometimes has been wrongly attributed to Hegel's idealism), but that there cannot be a sharp distinction between subject and object, between our mind and the metaphysical world (that is, the culturally and historically determined world of concepts and "idealities," contrary to the natural world), the main point being that the "I" and the world cannot be thought of independently of each other.

Although the Trinity can, in its traditional understanding, be considered a "childlike" expression, Hegel can be considered as suggesting that, once it is properly "unpacked," the Trinity indeed provides a *figural* account of the "I" and of its relation to the world. In other words, the meaning of the Trinity is to be identified neither in its literal religious reading nor merely in a supposedly abstract content that that *vorstellung*-ish account is meant to signify, but in the figural relation between the religious account (the three persons of the Trinity) and the *geistlich* structure of the "I."

Therefore, in the final section of this chapter, I will briefly analyze Hegel's conception of the "I" for which, I suggest, the Trinity can be considered a figural model—one that emphasizes Hegel's ongoing attempt to overcome subjectivism.

## The Trinity as the Model for the "I"

I previously suggested that Hegel's idealism can be regarded as an ongoing fight against subjectivism, conceived as the philosophical tenet that holds that the nature of reality as related to a given consciousness is dependent on *that* consciousness. However, Hegel's idealism must not be perceived as a regression to pre-Kantian realism, but as an overcoming of subjectivism whose central moment is the rejection of the polarizing mind/world distinction. In this way, Hegel does not refuse Kant's transcendental idealism but surpasses it, specifically by requiring the "I" to be approached through a consideration of the role of mutual recognition for the genesis of self-conscious thought.

Hegel's conception of the "I" aims to circumvent the subjective account of the self that is typical of modern philosophy. His strategy to pursue this goal consists in his theory of recognition: rather than relying on the "I-versus-world" distinction typical of pre-Kantian philosophy, Hegel advocates an understanding of the world in which values, norms, and other "idealities" (in the Hegelian language, "concepts") do not exist without the recognition of individuals—that is, without a community of mutually recognizing "selves." However, with respect to understanding the notion of the self (the "I"), the idealist philosopher is presented with a risky challenge. In fact, if the "world of reason" (that is, everything that is not merely *natural*) is somehow "produced" by the recognitive activity of the "I," what about the "I" *itself*?

It is easy to adopt a *realist* conception of the "I." Historically, such a realist conception of the "I" was supported by the "left Hegelians," such as David Strauss and Ludwig Feuerbach, whose thought featured fundamentally realist commitments to humans' essential properties. These commitments, however, imply a regression into the philosophical realism that post-Kantian idealism had circumvented.[51] Hegel was not a realist regarding the human spirit. Being an idealist regarding the "I" signifies, therefore, the recognition of its intrinsic relational structure; Hegel's strategy in avoiding the subjective account of the "I" without embracing the realist drift consists in conceiving the "I" in *relational* terms. The trinitarian account of God thus provides the model for this Hegelian conception of the "I."

The similarities between Hegel's approach to the Trinity and to the "I" are striking, beginning with the identification of the same enemy, that is, subjectivism: *theological* subjectivism and *philosophical* subjectivism, respectively. Theological subjectivism reduces God to a reflection of the finite mind, whereas philosophical subjectivism reduces the world to a reflection of the "I," which alone is regarded as real. In fact, the two conceptions are complementary—in the Enlightenment, for example, or in the thought of Fichte. As Hodgson states, this type of approach "ends with an abstract and empty self-identity over against the equally empty beyond."[52]

Hegel's goal is to overcome theological and philosophical subjectivism by restoring *content* to both God and the "I." In this respect, it is clearer why Hegel is so fascinated by Böhme, despite the "barbaric" nature of his thought. For Böhme, the second moment of the Trinity is *das Ich*, the "I," or selfhood.[53] The emergence of God's individuality is an important step, a clear advance over the previous Aristotelian conception of God, but it is also a critical moment, as it introduces difference into the previous undifferentiated unity and thus requires a new moment, a moment that permits the unity to be won back without the regression represented by a potential loss of the achieved individuality. Similarly, the modern conception of the "I"—the "I" as subjectivity, to use Hegel's terminology—is an important step, but it must be overcome to avoid the risk of solipsism. In this respect, the two tasks of overcoming theological and philosophical subjectivism are one and the same. Hegel uses the same strategy, that is, his theory of recognition, exemplified by the famous Hegelian definition of freedom as "being at home with oneself in one's other" (E I, 8:84/60) (Hegel regards the overcoming of subjectivism as an essential step in achieving a fully developed self-consciousness: in turn, only the achievement of such a self-consciousness makes a human being really *free*).

The relation between the concept of the Trinity and the self has previously been alluded to by Jaeschke, who has clarified that, for Hegel, this concept is not restricted to the philosophy of religion but must be regarded as the solution of a "fundamental problem of speculative philosophy," that of conceiving "the relation to self as a relation to an other."[54] In turn, Williams has praised Jaeschke for having highlighted this relation, which (Williams claims) addresses "the fundamental intersubjective and speculative problem, namely self-recognition in other."[55] In this respect, Jaeschke and Williams consider the otherness to be preserved in the human–divine relationship, unlike other interpreters, such as Desmond and Wendte, who consider Hegel unable to preserve the otherness of God.[56]

Williams sees the Trinity as the Hegelian successful alternative to the "dyadic subject-object identity," which was the inadequate response to modern subjectivism advanced by previous forms of idealism, such as those of Fichte and Schelling. Williams argues that, for Hegel, the idea of reconciliation is possible only when God is conceived as triune, that is, as reproducing the dynamics of mutual recognition within Godself.[57] "The triad," Williams writes, "signifies the achievement of equivalence between being-for-self and being-for-other."[58] Spirit (*Geist*) can be described with this equivalence, which represents the reestablishment of unity.[59]

Jaeschke's connection and Williams's argument can be further strengthened through a deeper consideration, first of the Trinity as the solution to the "fundamental problem of speculative philosophy," and then of the second moment of the Trinity considered as the prototype of the "I."

Regarding the former consideration, one can indeed consider the Trinity as the (Hegelian) solution to the fundamental problem of philosophy, and one might even find a connection between the immanent and economic Trinity on the one hand and alternative forms of (German) idealism on the other. The immanent Trinity might be considered to be mirroring the three principles of Fichte's *subjective* idealism: the immanent Father is pure self-identity (I = I); the Son corresponds to the Fichtean "principle of opposition" (*Satz des Gegensetzens*), that is, the positing of something other than the self; and the Holy Spirit can be regarded as Fichte's "grounding principle," that is, the required internal mediation and reconciliation between the first two principles. God is complete as the immanent Trinity; likewise, the "Fichtean" account of the "I" is in itself "complete." The problem, in Hegel's view, is that such an "I" is self-contained, that is, it does not grant its objects independence.[60] As for the immanent Trinity, for the Fichtean "I," too, the "show of finitude" seems not to have occurred yet.[61] No real "other" is given to the Fichtean "immanent" "I," and therefore, the "I" is its own other. The Fichtean "I" is an "unsatisfied" "I," and, for Hegel, the only object that can "satisfy" the "I" is *another* "I," another self-consciousness.[62] In trinitarian language, the economic Trinity is the *diremption* of the immanent Trinity, when the Father confronts his creation in the incarnation. We have seen that in the context of the economic Trinity, God the Father is regarded by Hegel as subsuming in himself the logical stance of the immanent Trinity as an entirety. In addition, the Father of the economic Trinity, as opposed to the Son who has become human in Christ, can be considered as mirroring the stance of Schelling's *objective* idealism, insofar as it expresses the idea of an original ground preceding the separation of the "I" and the world. However, without any *distinction*, Schelling's absolute "I" is no more than the famous night in which "all cows are black" (PG, 3:22/9). The unity of the "I" and the world must be achieved through a preliminary separation. Thus, the Son of the economic Trinity represents simultaneously the "eternal Son," or self-differentiation, and the God who renounces his absoluteness to engage with the world in the incarnation.

As previously argued, the second moment of the Trinity can be regarded as the prototype of the "I."[63] Hence, like God, the "I" always has a relational structure, and, as previously mentioned, the "I" itself is its first own "other"; but, like God, the "I" requires this internal relationality to be externalized and concretized. In this respect, Christ represents both the type of "subjective" account of the "I" that dominated the seventeenth and eighteenth centuries *and* its overcoming—first in *love*, and second in *community*. The overcoming of abstract subjectivism consists, therefore, in a process that starts with the "I's" encounter with another "I." The dynamics of recognition are exemplified by the practices of forgiveness and reconciliation. In these speech acts, in fact, the "I" acknowledges that the reason why it cannot achieve independence (that is, the reason why it is "unsatisfied") is that it must relinquish its absoluteness (epistemologically expressed by the phrase "God's-eye view") and recognize itself as finite—as I have already mentioned in chapter 2, this dynamic is depicted in the *Phenomenology of Spirit* through the episode of the "hard-hearted judge" acknowledging his being contingent and eventually forgiving the "beautiful soul" (PG, 3:488–94/403–9). This moment is dramatic for the "I's" self-development, as the acknowledgment of one's finitude implies the acceptance of one's vulnerability and fallibility—and eventually, of one's death. Again, if the first moment of love consists in an openness to the other, then the second moment of love consists in a renewed self-discovery *in* the other. "The truth of personality," Hegel writes, "is found precisely in winning it back through this immersion, this being immersed in the other" (Rel III, 211/286). In other words, the "I" renounces something of its abstract identity to win that identity back as concrete within a community.[64]

Thus, spirit—the "configuration of mutually recognising individual subjects" whose existence as subjects depends upon a joint act of recognition[65]—represents the final overcoming of subjectivism. Here, the relation between the third hypostasis of the Trinity (the Holy Spirit) and the reestablished identity and unity of the "I" within the community surpasses a simple analogy. From Hegel's perspective, the divine spirit *is* the community of humans contributing to the divine personality, and this community *is* the plurality of the individual "selves" that contributes to the spirit (*Geist*) through the process of mutual recognition.

Hegel's notion of the Trinity is usually considered a *Vorstellung*: a picture-thinking, or a memory-like image, which is perceived as external by the consciousness. Considered in its "childlike" form of a God constituted by three persons, the Trinity is undoubtedly, for Hegel, a *Vorstellung*. However, after Hegel's *philosophical* analysis of the Trinity has been considered, even briefly (as in the previous section), the Trinity clearly becomes, in Hegel's view, *anything but* external to consciousness. Hegel considers the Trinity in an unorthodox manner—not as three persons, as is common in the Christian orthodox doctrine, but as "*one* person in a trinity of personifications or gestalts."[66] Considered thus, the Trinity is not merely a *Vorstellung*, that is, a *representational* model of the "I." *Vorstellung* is, in fact, the product of the activity of ordinary consciousness; as such, it is static (the English translation of *Vorstellung* as "picture-thinking" is useful here, as it captures the static nature of the products of such activity). Insofar as the triune God is utterly concrete selfhood and thus exhibits recognitive relational structure in its perfection, the Trinity should be considered a *Darstellung*. This term, usually translated into English as "exposition," "display," or "presentation," is rather an account of something in its peculiar *movement*, and it is the exhibition or presentation of content that is presented in proper philosophy as a concept (*Begriff*); however, given that, for Hegel, the development of truth cannot be grasped independently of cultural presentations within which humans see themselves reflected, *Darstellungen* are the authentic modalities in which philosophy unpacks its content. Famously, Hegel claims that his *Science of Logic* represents the "exposition of God" (*die Darstellung Gottes*); another instance of Hegel's use of *Darstellung* is represented by the history of Jesus, which, "understood retrospectively from the vantage point of the first congregation [. . .] appears as a *Darstellung* of the divine idea."[67] Similarly, the Trinity is the presentation of a conception of relationality that goes beyond ordinary consciousness to reach the level of "mediated objectivity," which can only be brought about by *Darstellungen*, that is, presentations of an idea in its organic unity (*Gestalt*). The Trinity can, therefore, be regarded as the "I's" *Darstellung*, presenting the "I's" relational structure and exhibiting its self-development.

I have argued that Hegel's idealism can be read as an attempt to overcome the subjective account of the "I" that modern philosophers inherited from Descartes, and to which even Kant was not immune. An essential component of Hegel's answer to the question of subjectivism is his theory of recognition. I have also argued that the Trinity represents the presentation or exhibition (*Darstellung*) of a conception of the "I" in a way that overcomes the modern "subjectivist" account of the "I." I will come back to Hegel's conception of the "I" in chapter 7: but we can already note that a line of interpretation that combines Hegel's theory of recognition and his conception of the Trinity is useful for showing that Hegel's idealism can be conceived as a type of philosophical expression of a self-conception as an "I," which considers the role of intersubjective acts of mutual recognition. In other words, the Hegelian conception of the "I" should be considered as avoiding the subjectivist account (the "I" conceived as nothing more than the succession of various contents) and the realist drift (the position maintaining that everything is "I"-dependent, *except for the "I"*), and as advancing an alternative conception, which conceives the existence of the "I" as dependent on the intersubjective activity of recognition.

The connection between the Hegelian account of the Trinity and Hegel's conception of the "I" that has been suggested here is not immune to objections. One objection might concern how the Trinity can be the prototypical presentation of the "I" if the Trinity is itself a cultural product, that is, a result of individuals' recognitive activity. Another objection might argue that if the Trinity is a cultural product of the "I," does this fact indicate that there was no "I" before the Christian affirmation of the doctrine of the Trinity? Moreover, if it was possible to be an "I" before the affirmation of such a doctrine, might this possibility imply that the Trinity serves no purpose?

These objections are, to some extent, understandable if they are posed *outside* the context of Hegel's philosophy, and the philosophical problems and priorities established by post-Kantian idealist thinkers. Nevertheless, if considered *within* the context of Hegel's philosophy, these objections simply miss the point. In fact, from Hegel's point of view, the prototypical presentation of the "I," insofar as it is a *Darstellung*, must necessarily be a cultural product (given that a natural object could never be the prototypical model or representation for the development of a self-conscious "I"). However, the "I" *itself* is, for Hegel, a cultural product; therefore, the Christian Trinity is the favored model because it is considered as more accurately representing the modern form of the "I"—in other words, the contemporary form of the "I," that is, an "I" conceived in a way that circumvents modern subjectivism.

Another objection might concern the parallel readings of Hegel's conception of the Trinity and his conception of the mind/world relation, arguing that it is possible to have parallel readings merely because both relate to Hegel's more fundamental conception of the triadic structure of the concept (*Begriff*), and so such conception can be regarded as structuring both. And there is no doubt that, as recalled at the beginning of this chapter, Hegel has a preference for triadic arrangements. But it would be a mistake to consider this preference as merely an idiosyncrasy and the triadic structure of the "I" as a mere reflection of the triadic structure of the concept in general. Rather, the "I" is triadic because, to really be an "I," it is constitutively required to be self-identity, self-differentiation, and self-return. By the same token, God has to be thought of as trinitarian, because God is the utterly concrete selfhood.

Contrary to popular (and sometimes widespread) opinion, Hegel does not require his philosophy (or even philosophy *tout court*) to exhaustively explain everything. The mysterious idea of three "personifications" in one divine "personhood," with its dialectic of self-identity, self-differentiation, and self-return, remains inexhaustible[68]—as does the idea of a God who *dies*.

# 6

# The Death of God and Recognition of the Self

The expression "death of God" is usually associated with the philosophy of Friedrich Nietzsche, who, in his 1882 work *The Gay Science*, depicts a madman who announces the death of God.[1] Nietzsche refers to the modern mistrust of metaphysical values, which humans no longer regard as objects of belief. As such, Nietzsche's parable is consistent with a standard humanistic narrative according to which the affirmation of human reason corresponds to a loss of faith in transcendence and a decline of old religious values and beliefs.[2]

Nietzsche was not, however, the first Western thinker to philosophically confront the death of God, as Hegel referred to this idea in several of his works. Hegel's use of this expression is not as famous as that of Nietzsche—most likely because it is less clear what Hegel actually meant by using this expression. Hegel's death of God has sometimes been interpreted as an early acknowledgment of the end of religion: is not Hegel, after all, the inspiring mentor of nontheistic philosophers such as Feuerbach and Marx?[3] At the other extreme of the interpretative spectrum, the relevance of Hegel's expression has sometimes been downplayed, rather emphasizing the theistic commitment of his philosophy. This interpretative opposition is as old as the history of Hegel scholarship itself, which soon after Hegel's death witnessed the split between the "atheistic" ("left Hegelians") and the "theistic" ("right Hegelians") factions of his followers. Still today, the debate about Hegel's view on God is far from settled.

In order to appreciate the relevance of Hegel's view on the death of God, the question needs to be contextualized both historically and theoretically beyond any simplistic and ideological reading. In particular, the aforementioned "humanistic" narrative needs to be refined, and the process of secularization of thought that happens in the history of modern philosophy from Descartes to Nietzsche, rather than being conceived as a progressive affirmation of "human reason," should be reevaluated against the relative weight of the ideas of God[4] and the "I." Descartes appealed to God as the guarantor that things are as they appear—so that we can have "clear and distinct ideas." Kant removed the role of God from the realm of theoretical reason; with this move, however, we lose the guarantee that things really are as they appear to us. The I-think plays, to some extent, the role of guarantor: we can trust our knowledge, provided we admit that we know things as they appear to us (*phenomena*) and not the things in themselves (*noumena*), which can never be known.[5]

The relevance of a reference to Kant in this context is confirmed by the centrality that the role of Kant's philosophy has in the current debate on Hegel's philosophy, especially in the opposition between the post-Kantian/revisionist interpretation of Hegel, which largely considers Hegel's thought as an extension of Kant's transcendental philosophy (with the conditions of human rationality not limited to mental formal structures, but including historically and socially determined conditions), and the revised metaphysical/conceptual realist interpretation of Hegel, which rejects any transcendental interpretation of Hegel and tends to consider Hegel as building on the critical aspect of Kant's philosophy. Significantly, Robert Williams—a Hegel scholar who, because of his distinctive approach, cannot easily be regarded as fully belonging to either of the interpretative trends mentioned earlier—has recently emphasized the centrality of the theme of the death of God in Hegel's philosophy in his book *Tragedy, Recognition, and the Death of God*.

In the last two chapters, I have argued that Hegel's philosophy of religion, as well as its implications for Hegel's idealist metaphysics, can be appreciated in terms of the equilibrium between the ideas of God and the "I" in forging a normative framework for the use of reason. This chapter aims to show that the notion of the death of God is, in the context of Hegel's philosophy, the expression of a mutual dependence between the idea of God and the idea of the self, and that, if properly reconstructed, the death of God constitutes an integral part of Hegel's project of a recognition-based idealist metaphysics.

I will first analyze the passages where Hegel refers to the death of God, considering the various interpretations of these passages provided by

Hegel scholars and evaluating their strengths and weaknesses. Then, I will focus on the question of the "reality status" of the death of God (that is, to what extent God really *dies*, for Hegel) by considering the most relevant accounts of Hegel's notion of the death of God. I will argue that for Hegel it is essential to think of God as effectively dying as an abstract being in order to reconceptualize God in modernity. Finally, in the conclusion, I will contend that such reconceptualization of God is coessential with the establishment of the modern self, and that therefore unpacking the significance of the death of God is crucial in understanding the requirements that an idealistic philosophy must meet.

## The Death of God

Hegel's first use of the expression "death of God" is in the 1802 work *Faith and Knowledge*, originally published as an article in the *Critical Journal of Philosophy*:

> [. . .] the pure concept or infinity as the abyss of nothingness in which all being is engulfed, must signify the infinite grief [of the finite] purely as a moment of the supreme Idea, and no more than a moment. Formerly, the infinite grief only existed historically in the formative process of culture. It existed as the feeling that "God Himself is dead," upon which the religion of more recent times rests [. . .]. By marking this feeling as a moment of the supreme Idea, the pure concept must give philosophical existence to what used to be either the moral precept that we must sacrifice the empirical being [*Wesen*], or the concept of formal abstraction [e.g., the categorical imperative]. (GW, 2:432/190)

It is quite clear, and in fact it has been almost unanimously remarked by commentators, that Hegel here is criticizing abstract traditional metaphysics and theology: the death of God is the death of the old, absolutely transcendent, abstract God.[6] Hegel also quite clearly associates the death of God with Kant's philosophy.[7] Why?

Let us take a step back and consider the cultural climate of the late eighteenth century. In the age of Enlightenment, we witness the emergence of deism as an attempt to reconcile faith with reason. In this context, Kant's Copernican revolution is a groundbreaking moment. For Kant maintains that God cannot be known (that is, God cannot be the object of theoretical reason) but should rather be regarded as a moral postulate. However, as Jaeschke points out while commenting on this passage, "A God who is not known Hegel declares to be a dead God for a God about whom nothing more can be said has no further significance, whether for life or for philosophy."[8] But philosophy needs the idea of God, according to Hegel.

Hegel returns to the issue of the death of God in the *Phenomenology of Spirit* with a passage that might seem confusing in the light of what he said in *Faith and Knowledge*, but whose meaning, if properly reconstructed, actually helps us to understand the trajectory that Hegel intends to follow. Hegel writes: "The unhappy consciousness [. . .] is [. . .] the tragic fate of the certainty of self that aims to be absolute. It is the consciousness of the loss of all essential being in this certainty of itself, and of the loss even of this knowledge about itself—the loss of substance [*Substanz*] as well as of the self, it is the grief which expresses itself in the harsh saying that 'God is dead'" (PG, 3:547/455). As I have already mentioned in chapter 2, the main feature of the unhappy consciousness is the renunciation or surrender (*Aufgeben*) "first of its right to decide for itself, then of its property and enjoyment" (PG, 3:175/137). The outcome of this process, which is regarded as already starting in the late ancient world (with Stoicism and skepticism) is, for the consciousness, the certainty of having truly emptied itself of its "I," of its self-sufficiency. This certainty seems to have been achieved with Christianity: thus, the "death of God" mentioned in the passage of the *Phenomenology* "reflects the Christian appropriation and transformation of the unhappy consciousness."[9] And here is the apparent confusion: in *Faith and Knowledge*, Hegel connects the death of God with the Enlightenment's critique of traditional metaphysics and theology, and even with Kant's philosophy; in the *Phenomenology*, the death of God is rather identified with Christianity and with the central speculative moment of Christianity, that is, the incarnation (God accepting finitude in the incarnation up to death). How can the death of God express at the same time both the establishment of Christianity *and* what seems to be the most powerful *attack* against Christian theism—that is, the Enlightenment's critique and the "reflective philosophy of subjectivity"?

In the light of a deeper analysis, there is actually no contradiction. After the crucifixion (and before the resurrection), Christ's disciples found themselves in a tragic situation: they had lost their old faith in the coming of a powerful Messiah, *and* their personal faith in Jesus: the world was "godless," "absurd," "meaningless."[10] Even the descent of the Holy Spirit (at Pentecost) did not completely dissolve that feeling: the abstract God—the legislator—was gone, and human beings were left alone to construct their own normativity (with the help of the Spirit). This is actually what the church is about, according to Hegel: an institution that facilitates the ethical freedom of its members. In this sense, Christianity facilitates the process of formation of the modern self[11]—in other words, it is Christianity that allows the process of secularization that culminates in the Enlightenment. The Enlightenment pursues the emancipation of the self that Christianity had initiated: this is the merit of the Enlightenment. However, as often happens in Hegel's system, the Enlightenment contains the reasons for its being overcome in itself. Accomplishing intellectual liberation from the abstract God of traditional metaphysics and theology (which is the death of the Cartesian divine guarantor), the Enlightenment represents the peak of the crisis in normativity. Here one can think of Kant's repeated claim that one must listen to moral commands as if they were spoken by the voice of God—an attempted solution to safeguard normativity that shows all its intrinsic weakness soon enough and results in the "reflective philosophy of subjectivity." Like Christ's disciples after the crucifixion, human beings now experience grief in a godless and meaningless world. However, this grief has some value: the intellectual death of the abstract God is not "a misleading delusion, but the achievement of maturity." Burbidge makes an important point when he stresses that the "secular experience" of the Enlightenment cannot be properly understood without the "integration of God and man" represented by Christianity: "Once Feuerbach and others divorce man's maturity from that which constitutes it, their assertions become finite and positivistic claims, not negatively comprehensive self-knowledge."[12] In the general framework that I have been suggesting, this means that for Hegel the maturity and freedom of the modern self can be appreciated fully only if the self is thought of in relation to the idea of (the Christian) God and divine history (most importantly, God's death). I will come back to this point later in this chapter. For now, it is sufficient to state that, as pointed out by Jaeschke, to designate Hegel's insight as a mere "diagnosis" of the death of God would be "an inadequate, one-sided understanding," for "what characterizes it is rather the simultaneous appearance of diagnosis and therapy."[13] And the therapy, as Jaeschke maintains, consists in elaborating "a philosophy that rectifies the false premises that led the Enlightenment to renounce" the knowledge of God "not by stepping back behind the Enlightenment," but by stepping "beyond the Enlightenment, to a deeper insight into the conditions and possibilities of an improved philosophical knowledge."[14] The most relevant of the "false premises" of the Enlightenment is, in my reading, precisely the idea that it is possible to think of the self disjoined from an idea of normativity of the kind once provided by God: thus, that "deeper insight" is possible only if the integration of human being and God (finite and infinite, in the idealist jargon) is thought of as possible. But Kant seems to have closed the doors to such integration by arguing for the intrinsic finitude of the human being and for the impossibility for her to step out of her finite view of the world (which is limited by her a priori cognitive constraints). Isn't Hegel's attempt a desperate move? And yet, once again, the answer to the shortcomings of Kant's philosophy can be found, at least incipiently, in Kant's philosophy itself. This becomes apparent if we consider Kant's philosophical enterprise as a whole. Kant, in fact, reintroduced God as a necessary postulate in the *Critique of Practical Reason*, and then, in the *Religion*, he defended the use of symbolic religious representations to make moral commands applicable to the world, the most important of which is, Kant maintains, the prototype of pure moral disposition—that is, Christ. Being divine and human at the same time—God incarnate—Christ is the symbol of pure moral perfection.[15] But then, his role of mediation between the finite and the infinite is downplayed by Kant in favor of his *legal* function, thus regressing to the monarchical metaphor alluded to earlier. As I previously argued, this is precisely one of the reasons behind Hegel's dissatisfaction with Kant's conception.

In other words, in Hegel's view, Kant had failed to appreciate the implications of the symbol of Christ considered as a mediator (*Mittler*). Significantly, this is precisely the name Hegel uses for Christ in the second passage of the *Phenomenology* that features the expression "death of God," a passage that needs to be considered in full to understand the centrality of this image in Hegel's philosophy and—even more importantly—its implications for Hegel's metaphysics: "The death of the Mediator [*Tod des Mittlers*] as grasped by the self is the sublation [*Aufheben*] of his objectivity [*Gegenständlichkeit*],[16] that is, of his particular being-for-self [*Fürsichseins*]: this particular being-for self has become universal self-consciousness. On the other side, and precisely as a result, the universal has become self-consciousness, and the pure, that is, the non-actual spirit [*Geist*] of mere thinking has become actual" (PG, 3:571/476). Christ is the mediator (that is, the middle term) because he is the representation (*Vorstellung*) of the unity between the self and God. If the appearance of this representation is relevant, the *death* of this representation is even more relevant. What is of particular interest to Hegel is that this death needs to be *thought*; and in thinking this representation, its concreteness is sublated (into thought).[17] This is the reason why Hegel claims that the death of the mediator is the universalization of self-consciousness:[18] once the concrete representation of the mediator is gone (that is, once Christ has died), Christians need to *conceptualize* his death. Hegel continues:

> The death of the mediator is the death not only of his natural aspect, that is, of his particular being-for-self, not only of the dead shell from which the essence [*Wesen*] has already departed, but of the abstraction of the divine essence as well. For the mediator, in so far as his death has not yet completed the reconciliation [*Versöhnung*], is the one-sidedness that knows the simple thought as *essence* in contrast to actuality; this extreme of the self is not yet of equivalent value with the essence; it is only as spirit that the self has that value. The death of this representational thought [*Vorstellung*] contains at the same time the death of the abstraction of the divine essence that has not yet been posited as a self. That death is the painful [*schmerzliche*] feeling of the unhappy consciousness that God himself has died. This harsh expression is the expression of innermost simple self-knowledge, the return of consciousness into the depth of the night of the "I = I," which no longer distinguishes or knows outside of it. This feeling thus is in fact the loss of *substance* and of the substance taking a stance against consciousness [. . .] (PG, 3:571/476)

The death of the mediator expresses not only the death of Christ in its concrete objectivity but also the death of the abstract God. But with his death, and with the *conceptualization* of his death, the human self is alone—again. Despite appearances, Hegel is not using "imagistic" or "evocative" jargon here. The concept of God is the highest expression of normativity, first perceived as completely external ("abstract"), then united with the self (in the incarnation), and then lost again (with the death of Christ). At a conceptual level, the human self is "left alone to create its own world"[19]—in my interpretative framework, this means that it is left alone to create its own normativity. As Burbidge rightly remarks, "These are the claims of humanism."[20] The use of the word *schmerzliche*—meaning "painful" or even "agonizing"—implies a thinly veiled criticism of the common humanist triumphalism in addressing the process of secularization and the loss of normativity—a process that, in Hegel's account, is also tragic. Hegel concludes this long paragraph as follows:

> [. . .] but at the same time it [the feeling of the death of God] is the pure *subjectivity* [*Subjektivität*] of substance, that is, the pure certainty of its own self that it lacked as concrete object [*Gegenstände*, "what stands over against"], conceived as immediate, or as pure essence. This knowledge is therefore *spiritualization*, as a result of which substance [*Substanz*] becomes subject [*Subjekt*], its abstraction and lifelessness have died, and substance has become *actual*, simple, and universal self-consciousness. (PG, 3:571/476)

The death of God grants humans modern subjectivity, namely, that "certainty of the self" that was lacking in the concrete representation of God (Jesus during his earthly life) and in his purely abstract conception. The knowledge of the death of God (its conceptualization) is *spiritualization*, that is, a process through which the abstract God dies, and the union between God and the self is achieved, in a twofold way: God has now assumed (human) finitude, and the (human) self is now actually able to contribute to the establishment of normativity. Hegel's claim that "substance becomes subject" is central to understanding his entire idealist project; I will, therefore, come back to this claim later in this chapter, after going through all the passages where Hegel addresses the death of God, and after a more comprehensive interpretation of the issue.

To recapitulate: in the *Phenomenology*, Hegel reaffirms the point he had already made in *Faith and Knowledge* about the death of God, that is, that it first represents the death of the abstract, indifferent, not-knowable God of deism; in addition, he argues that it is the death of the middle point between that abstraction and human finitude; and with its disappearance, humans are traumatically forced to realize a union with the divine.[21] Once again, it is important to stress that there is nothing "mystical" in this line of reasoning; in less representational and more conceptual language, it might be said that normativity must become relational and relationality must become normative. And the religious representation of relationality is, for Hegel, the Christian doctrine of the Trinity. The set of connections that link the death of God, the notion of divine self-divestment, and the

Trinity is in fact the focus of some relevant passages of the *Lectures on the Philosophy of Religion*, which therefore ideally complete Hegel's account of the death of God.

The death of God is a moment in the development of the economic or worldly (as opposed to the immanent, or pre-worldly) Trinity: God giving up God's divinity and absoluteness to accept all human limits (including death) in the incarnation. And it is in this context that we find the first reference to the death of God in the lectures, in the 1821 lecture manuscript: "The highest divestment [*Entäußerung*] of the divine idea—as divestment of itself, i.e., [the idea that] is in addition this divestment—is expressed as follows: 'God has died, God himself is dead.' [This] is a monstrous, fearful representational thought [*Vorstellung*],[22] which brings before the imagination the deepest abyss of cleavage" (Rel III, 60/125). In common with the account in the *Phenomenology*, this passage has the description of the death of God as a *Vorstellung*, and the qualification of this *Vorstellung* as painful. Here, however, the death of God is explicitly referred to as the outcome of God's self-sacrifice—the divestment of the divine Idea. This point is further developed in the following pages of the 1821 lecture manuscript, thus showing that such connection is regarded by Hegel as absolutely essential:

> But although [it is] a natural death, [this is] the death of God, and now its relevance for us, how we are placed in relation to it, [must be considered]: this death is one that makes satisfaction for us because it presents the absolute history of the divine idea as a history that has taken place in itself and happens eternally. [. . .]
>
> It is not an extrinsic sacrifice that is performed, nor a matter of someone else [being] punished so that punishment might be rendered, (nor of life [being] negated and other-being sublated,) [as in the case of] natural death. [. . .]
>
> That which is represented as the lowest and which the state uses as an instrument of dishonor is here converted into what is highest. [. . .] We find here the direct expression of a complete revolution against all that is established and regarded as valuable. (Rel III, 62–65/127–29)

In the incarnation, we witness a divestment of the divine: the infinite becomes finite. Here Hegel opposes once again any "legal" or "monarchical" interpretation of the incarnation: the death of Christ is not a "required punishment" but rather an act of love: "That is the deepest anguish, this the highest love" (Rel III, 67/131).[23]

The connection of the death of God with divestment and love remained constant in the philosophy of religion courses that Hegel taught in 1827 and 1831. In the 1827 lectures, the topic was introduced by a reference to a hymn written by the Lutheran Pastor Johann Rist:[24] "'God himself is dead,' it says in a Lutheran hymn, expressing an awareness that the human, the finite, the fragile, the weak, the negative are themselves a moment of the divine, that they are within God himself, that finitude, negativity, otherness are not outside of God and do not, as otherness, hinder unity with God" (Rel III, 250/326). Here Hegel is even more explicit: God suffers, and there is *negation* in God. Traditional (philosophical and theological) conceptions of God considered perfection and the absence of any negativity as essential aspects of the divinity: conversely, Hegel maintains that the death of Christ on the cross tells us that another conception of God is possible—one that includes the negative as well; the presence of the negative in God, far from preventing the unity of the divine and the human, actually constitutes its presupposition. The death of Christ is defined by Hegel as "the consummation of externality in deepest cleavage, in conscious negation" (Rel III, 68–69/132), and this claim can be taken as evidence that (as remarked by Williams) the suffering of God is not "necessary" for Hegel but rather "gratuitous"—"for the sake of an other."[25] It is not possible to take seriously these passages from the *Lectures on the Philosophy of Religion* and then argue that Hegel's God is simply the expression of logical necessity, for this would not explain the gratuitousness of the self-divestment. This formulation is—to use Hodgson's expression[26]—"pushed" even further in the 1831 *Lectures on the Philosophy of Religion*:

> *God has died, God is dead*—this is the most frightful of all thoughts, that everything eternal and true *is not*, that negation itself is found in God. The deepest anguish, the feeling of complete irretrievability, the annulling of everything that is elevated, are bound up with this thought. However, the process does not come to a halt at this point; rather, a reversal [*Umkehrung*] takes place: God, that is to say, maintains himself in this process, and the latter is only the death of death. God rises again to life, and thus things are reversed. The resurrec-

tion is something that belongs just as essentially to faith [as the crucifixion]. (Rel III, 246/323n)

Negation itself is found in God: this is what the death of God shows. But then "a reversal takes place": the resurrection. "What does this reversal mean?" Williams wonders, and continues: "Does it signal a return to the metaphysics of light [. . .]? Does it imply a vindication of onto-theology and metaphysics that suppresses the tragic and suffering [. . .]?"[27] Williams's answer to this question is a negative one, and rightly so: if stopping at the death of God would mean endorsing the claim of humanism that it is possible to think of the self as disjoined from the idea of normativity once provided by God, regressing to the old idea of an immutable God as the transcendent source of normativity would equally be a mistake. Death is the way in which the unity of the divine and the human is realized: as Hegel had anticipated in the *Phenomenology*, "This death is, therefore, its resurrection as Spirit" (PG, 3:566/471). God is resurrected "in the spirit that lives in the community of believers":[28] the self is now free to contribute to the production of a normativity that is not the reflection of the old, legal conception of the divine but that constitutes the essence of the idealist project.

## Which death? Which god?

In the previous section, I considered the most significant passages in Hegel's work that address the theme of the death of God. A connection between divine self-divestment (kenosis) and the death of God emerged. Hegel's lifelong commitment to a kenotic reading of the death of God appeared as early as the Jena period (1802–1807); in an aphorism he wrote: "God sacrifices himself [*opfert sich auf*], surrenders himself [*gibt sich hin*] to destruction. God himself is dead [*Gott selbst ist todt*]: the supreme despair of complete abandonment by God."[29] Several Hegel scholars have remarked on the relevance of this approach for Hegel's account of God (and beyond). Hans Küng defines Hegel's notion of incarnation as "renunciation on the part of the Absolute itself" and as God "emptying himself into the world";[30] O'Regan makes the connection even more explicit, arguing that the death of God renders for Hegel "a complex phenomenon, centering around a double divestment or kenosis (*Entäußerung*)";[31] Hodgson defines sacrifice as that "divine love that divests itself for the sake of reconciliation with its other" and argues for the "necessity" of sacrifice;[32] conversely, Williams emphasizes the "gratuitousness"[33] of the self-divestment, conceived as "the self-abandonment of the divine to its other finitude to the point of death" and "the supreme exemplification of releasement (*Gelassenheit*),"[34] which he later connects with God's loving nature—one that "cannot remain indifferent to God's other."[35] Williams is probably the interpreter who has insisted most on the death of God as a manifestation of God's self-divestment. Williams's reading of Hegel's account is succinctly and yet efficaciously expressed by the following statement: "The death of God involves a double divestment or kenosis. This double divestment includes the death of the mediator and the death of abstract immutable substance that is devoid of self."[36] Thus, according to Williams, the two key elements of the death of God (conceived as a double divestment) are the death of Christ conceived as the "mediator" (*Mittler*) between the finite and the infinite, and the death of the conception of God as an immutable, abstract substance. This is effectively consistent with the analysis that we carried out in the previous section. Nevertheless, two questions remain open: (1) How should the death of the mediator be interpreted? How *real* is the death of God? (2) Hegel claims that as a result of the death of God the "substance" (which, Williams rightly points out, is "devoid of self") becomes "subject" (PG, 3:571/476). What does it mean that the resulting subject is no longer "devoid of self"? I will analyze these two questions in the present and following sections, respectively.

When Hegel talks about the "death of God," how literally should we take this expression? Clearly, each and every serious interpretative attempt entails an (at least implicit) answer to this question (call it the *reality of the death of God problem*). It is possible to provide a taxonomy of the various answers to this question, by distributing them along a graduated scale from the weakest to the strongest reality status.

At one extreme of the scale, we find the position according to which the death of God is merely a "slogan"; the supporters of this answer, such as Thielicke, argue that the claim "cannot be meant literally since it involves a logical contradiction." Their argument is simple: either God effectively dies—but if he can die, he never really was God (as God cannot really die, by definition) and Feuerbach was right (God lived only in our imagination, and now that imagined God has disappeared); or it is only a *specific* experience or belief in God that dies, and not God Godself—but in that case, God Godself is not really dead.[37]

Beiser too dismisses the "Feuerbachian" reading of Hegel's claim of the death of God—that is, "the irrelevance of faith in a more secular culture"; but, unlike Thielicke, he defines the expression "death of God" as a "metaphor" for the life of the spirit. Although Beiser does not address this issue directly, "metaphor" seems to be more than Thielicke's "slogan," as "it expresses the fact that we must lose and discover ourselves in the experience of love and in the development of reason."[38] Beiser's definition must be read in the context of his general interpretation of Hegel's philosophy of religion, which he regards as a rationalization of the concept of God and as the negation "of its supernatural status," thus "making it immanent in the world."[39]

Pinkard does not use the term "metaphor" but defines the expression "death of God" as a "representational intuition"[40] of Hegel's account, according to which—Pinkard argues—we worship "the divine principle within ourselves" rather than "some transcendent entity beyond human life and concerns."[41] Thus, even assuming that the *vorstellung*-ish status of a "representational intuition" confers more reality to the death of God than that conferred by Beiser's "metaphor," both Beiser and Pinkard seem to agree that the death of God for Hegel is a symbolic expression of the speculative movement from a transcendent to an immanent conception of God.

Williams has the most sophisticated account of the death of God among those presented here. He refrains from categorically defining the expression, but from his criticism of Beiser's definition of it as "metaphor" it is clear that he holds a more "realist" position. Interestingly, Williams is not sympathetic to Pinkard's reading of Hegel, and yet he seems to agree with Pinkard (and Redding[42]) that the Christological theme of the "death of God" implies a critique of divine immutability and impassibility. He regards Hegel, however, as having a more realist position about God; therefore, the death of God is real, but it is "not final"—it is "a moment within a transition wherein the power of being overcomes non-being."[43]

At the other extreme of the scale, we have the "radical realist" position of Altizer, who argues that God truly died: with the incarnation, "God himself has ceased to exist in his original mode as transcendent or disincarnate Spirit":[44] so after the death of Christ, affirming belief in a transcendent God is no longer possible.

Let us consider the aforementioned graduated scale. The first conclusion that can be drawn from it is that the interpreters have very different conceptions of God; thus, it is effectively not possible to assess Hegel's notion of the death of God per se, because it depends on the conception of God that is in use. From this angle, therefore, such a "scale of realism" can be considered as a "litmus test," as it were, to understand the conception of God at work each time.

On the basis of the analysis carried out in the previous section, which is the most appropriate reading of the death of God? First, we can quickly exclude the "radical realist" position—Altizer's account might be an interesting theological position, but as an interpretation of Hegel it is mistaken, as Hegel puts a strong emphasis on the "reversal" (*Umkehrung*) and says explicitly that "God maintains himself in this process" (Rel III, 246/323n). We can also exclude the other extreme of the scale, that is, Thielicke's "weak" view, according to which the death of God is only a "slogan" and it is merely a specific experience or belief in God that dies—but if this were true, why should this death be such an "agonizing" (*schmerzliche*) and devastating experience for us? As for the "metaphorical" reading advanced by Beiser, I agree with Williams that it does not give enough consideration to the metaphysical implications of Hegel's philosophy of religion: Hegel's insistence on the death of God would be odd if it were merely a "metaphor." Williams does not address Pinkard's position directly (his polemical target being mostly Pippin); however, Pinkard's definition of the death of God as a "representational intuition" does not seem to be incompatible with Williams's account. The question is whether the status of "representational intuition" exhausts the meaning of the expression "death of God" or—as Williams seems to suggest—the expression should be given a more realist interpretation beyond his representational (*vorstellung*-ish) status. In short, I think that both Pinkard's and Williams's reading best capture Hegel's account of the death of God—but here an important qualification needs to be made.

Christianity represents a *reconceptualization* of God—that is, a new conception of God must emerge after the death of Jesus. This process of reconceptualization is long and largely coincides with the history of modernity: it therefore includes transitional phases such as those represented by the Enlightenment and Kant—that is, it has to go through a complete *separation* of thought and being and of the finite and the infinite. When Hegel reacts against Kant's separation of the unity of thinking and being (as he does, for instance, by rejecting Kant's critique of the ontological argument), he does not deny the necessity of such separation but asks for this separation to be overcome. This is the meaning of the reversal of the death of God: humans now have to learn how to bridge that disjunction between being and thought and between finite and infinite, through recognitive reconciliation (that is, spirit).[45]

Assuming the preceding qualification is correct, one might object that the death of God, thus conceived, is merely a symbolic representation of *our* way of conceiving God—that is, it says something about *us*, but it does not say much about *God*. Such an explanation might possibly satisfy Pinkard, but it would still look wanting to Williams and to all those who are not completely satisfied by a reading of Hegel's philosophy of religion that sounds too "anthropological."[46] We are dealing, once again, with the question addressed in chapter 3—that is, whether the death of God happens only in the history of thought and culture (that is, it is a process through which, to use Pinkard's words, we learn how to worship the divine within us rather than a transcendent divine) or the death of God has an *ontic* status. We can, therefore, apply the answer provided there to the "reality of the death of God problem." Once again, the question, put in these terms, is misleading, as it is presented in *pre-critical* (pre-Kantian) terms: God is not absolutely transcendent and separated from humans, and God's properties cannot be discussed regardless of our thinking of it.

To some, it might appear that the answer sketched earlier avoids the question, but actually for Hegel there is no other way to put it. The death of God is clearly a *Vorstellung*, but its conceptual translation (that is, the way that our conception of God has been changing thanks to the "long wave" of Christianity) does not mean to dismiss such a *Vorstellung* as a mere "metaphor." God really died, and his death is as real as, say, our mindedness can be: from an ontological point of view, God and the self are, as it were, on the same level. An individual subject will surely take the fact of its own mindedness to be as real as anything could be. But Hegel's recognitive account of spirit argues that it is a necessary condition of one's being minded that one exist within relations of recognition and that others recognize one as so minded. That God Godself exists within those sorts of relations (i.e., within spirit) makes God no less real. It is this argument that rules out both the traditional metaphysical interpretation of God as radically self-sufficient and independent of God's relationality to human beings (a traditional "substance") and the antithetical "anthropological" interpretation in which God is regarded as a mere creation of human beings.

The "death of the mediator" is the death of the abstraction of the divine being,[47] which calls for a reconceptualization of God—but it is also the death of the *mediator*, of that middle term that guaranteed a normative unity between the finite and the infinite; his death therefore marks the need for a normativity that includes the divine and does not see it as external.

## "Substance Becomes Subject"

Once the answer to the *reality of the death of God problem* sketched in the previous section is assumed, one major interpretative problem regarding Hegel's account of the death of God still needs to be addressed. Hegel claims that as a result of the death of God "substance becomes subject" (PG, 3:571/476). We have already addressed this passage from the *Phenomenology of Spirit* in chapter 2: God, for Hegel, is a subject, and Christianity eminently captures this through emphasis on the death of Christ. God is *alive*. Only something that is alive can, in fact, *die*. This is a representational way of capturing something of the idea of God that is expressed in philosophical terms by the definition of God as a "concept." Hegel here is addressing the process of the transformation of God as an absolute idea ("the depth of the night of the 'I = I,'" PG, 3:571/476), which is the culmination of Hegel's *Logic*,[48] into something that is both self-conscious and self-realizing. This explains why "concept" is, for Hegel, associated with subject, and thus with the "I." This association entails a withdrawal from absoluteness, a withdrawal represented by the incarnation—which is also mediation, that is, recognition of the other. Hence, it is a kenotic and recognitive process.

In his analysis of the death of God, Williams captures several aspects of this process: God's self-divestment, the death of God as signifying a criticism of abstract transcendence, and the process of mediation with the other in order to become a subject. On these grounds, Williams defines Hegel's theory of self-divestment as a "deconstructive critique of metaphysical theology or substance metaphysics," which is criticized "for conceiving God as actual apart from relation" (as in Aristotle and Spinoza) "and when in relation, as absolute non-reciprocal Master," as in Kant's "monarchical" conception.[49] Then Williams (appropriately) wonders: "can there be nonfoundational discourse about God that does not lapse into foundationalist anthropology, i.e., into Feuerbach's inversion of Hegel?"[50]

Williams believes there can be such nonfoundational discourse for Hegel, and I agree with him. In chapter 2, I identified both a theological *and* a philosophical justification for such nonfoundational discourse, which—as it should be expected from Hegel—are interconnected and can be considered two perspectives on the same question. Williams particularly focuses on the theological justification. Hegel's alternative to traditional ontotheology and the reversed anthropo-ontology is, Williams argues, a "holistic triadic conception of God," for "such a concept articulates the constitutive otherness that underlies the possibility of freedom and suffering."[51] The incarnation, which marks the passage from the immanent (pre-worldly) Trinity and the economic (worldly) Trinity, provides a model for the development of the subject as spirit: it expresses, in other words, the recognitive dynamic that is religiously expressed by the reconciliation between God and humanity. A claim by Hegel from the *Berliner Schriften* seems to confirm Williams's account: "There is the sharpest of contrasts with Lutheran faith and with overall Christian faith, when today professional theologians wish to be still committed to the Christian doctrine of reconciliation [*Versöhnungslehre*] and at the same time deny that the doctrine of the Trinity is the foundation [*die Grundlage*] of the doctrine of reconciliation. Without this objective foundation [*objektive Grundlage*] the doctrine of reconciliation can have only a subjective [*subjektiven*] sense" (W, 11:315).[52]

According to Williams, the justified possibility of a nonfoundational discourse on God resides, therefore, in Hegel's account of "divine self-emptying or kenosis," in the "union of God with death in the anguish of infinite love": God suffers because God "cannot remain indifferent to God's other."[53] From a religious (theological) perspective, this answer exhausts Hegel's account, and it is very convincing, in the sense that it looks consistent with an exegesis of Hegel's works. The question I am interested in here is: what are the implications of such a religious justification for Hegel's philosophy more broadly? In the aforementioned passage from the *Berliner Schriften*, Hegel defines the Trinity as the objective foundation of the doctrine of reconciliation. What does the use of the term "objective" tell us? It clearly suggests that any anthropological reading, such as that suggested by the left Hegelians (according to which notions such as those of the Trinity and the death of God are merely metaphors that have no significant value once they are translated into philosophical, conceptual terms) is clearly mistaken (it would merely have a subjective sense, Hegel warns). But does this mean that we have to regress to a traditional metaphysical (right Hegelian) reading of such claims, where "objective" means "independent of the (human) subject"? This would contradict the transformation of substance into subject, which, as previously argued, cannot happen *outside* of the relation between God and humanity. This impasse seems to require us either to accept metaphysics in order to safeguard the objective meaning of the Trinity and the death of God—and ultimately, of God Godself—or to reject metaphysics and resign ourselves to the consideration of such religious notions as mere metaphors.

This apparent opposition derives from the mistaken assumption that Christianity and (traditional, ontotheological) metaphysics are inseparable, so that one has to either accept both or reject both.[54] Can a rational philosophical thought support a conception of God that entails an objective (that is, nonmetaphorical) understanding of notions of the Trinity and of the death of God without being foundationalist (in a pre-Kantian sense)?

The answer to this question is to be a philosophical one, although—as previously anticipated—it is not unrelated to the theological justification for Hegel's nonfoundational stance outlined earlier, and the two actually are two sides of the same coin (that is, the same question considered from two perspectives). The figural interpretation that we pursued in chapter 3 has provided us with the conceptual instruments required to overcome the impasse, and to affirm—with Hegel—that rational philosophical thought can indeed support a conception of God that entails a mediately objective understanding of the Trinity and of the death of God. God becomes actual in the relation with God's creation: this is Hegel's theological (heterodox) position. In a strictly philosophical sense (that is, insofar as the *concept* of God is concerned), the same state of affairs can be addressed by arguing that the concept of God becomes actual only in the thought of human agents (subjective sprits, in Hegel's jargon). Such a claim disposes of any traditional (pre-Kantian) metaphysical conception of God, according to which the concept of God was nothing but the logical reproduction of an entity existing "outside there." But—and our analysis of Hegel's treatment of the ontological argument in chapter 4 has been helpful in this respect—the claim that the concept of God becomes actual only in the thought of human agents does not mean that God is left without any independent existence. God has an independent existence, but thinking of that existence in empirical terms, as Kant does in his confutation of the ontological argument, is a mistake, according to Hegel. The existence of God, insofar as we can think of it, is the existence of a self-realizing concept. Once again, and despite Hegel's undeniable obscurity, there is nothing mystical or magical in this conception, once it is properly reconstructed. The concept of God cannot be thought *outside* the relation with humans. *Contra* Feuerbach, we do not "create" the concept of God, but God self-actualizes *in* the human-divine relationship.

On these grounds, it is now possible to appreciate why the theological-kenotic perspective and the philosophical post-Kantian perspective are indeed coessential. I have used the term "post-Kantian" here to refer to a position that is acutely aware that, while God's existence is independent of us, God's concept cannot be thought independently of the relation in which that very concept self-actualizes. This position opposes the traditional, pre-Kantian metaphysics, but it is clearly not anti-metaphysical per se. An interpretation that considers the recognition-theoretic approach as Hegel's fundamental "hermeneutic scheme,"[55] which values the historical, cultural, and social conditions determining the development of concepts, and which acknowledges the self-actualizing nature of concepts, is not only compatible with the conception of God previously outlined, but it is even coessential with it.

This is what is to be learned from this analysis about the difference between Hegel's philosophy of religion and atheism, deism, and historical constructivism. *First*, Hegel's claim mentioned in the previous chapter, that God cannot exist only "as something posited by us, produced by us" (VBD, 382/66) rules out atheism. *Second*, Hegel's philosophy of religion is not a form of deism, because his God is a *subject*. Qua subject, God is free, and God's kenotic act of withdrawal is gratuitous. Williams mentions Jüngel's claim that "God chooses suffering in absolute freedom"[56] to remark that "what 'dies,' that is, what God renounces and divests, is precisely exclusive *fürsichsein*, relationless abstract substance, the impassible divine being."[57] This is indeed an important point; and it also explains the importance that Hegel attributes to Christianity, both epistemically and historically, for the emergence of the modern conception of freedom as a full acceptance of otherness. *Third*, Hegel is not a historical constructivist either. By "historical constructivism" here I mean the view that changes that occur in an idea's historical and cultural context also change its meaning. It is true that Hegel connected the conception of recognition with that of normativity, in the sense that the generation of norms is dependent on recognition. However—and this is the point—recognition is, in turn, modeled on the divine giving-up, or withdrawal: God's kenotic act has a *normative* value, or, to use Williams's words, "If the divine were abstract impassible substance, or fate, then no finding of self in other, and no reconciliation would be possible."[58] To be a historical constructivist about God in the aforementioned sense, one should first consider God merely as a product of the mind (as an object), but God is not merely a product of the mind for Hegel: God is also a subject. If our conception of God changes, it is because the relationship between God and human beings changes. Thus, as God dies in his corporeal form to become Spirit *for* the world, similarly the "I" renounces something of itself in the recognition of the other within a community to become spirit *in* the world—that is, a "configuration of mutually recognising individual subjects" whose existence as subjects depends upon a joint act of recognition (according to Redding's definition mentioned in the previous chapter[59]). Furthermore, the death of the abstract conception of God (whose concept is the highest expression of normativity) allows human beings (subjective spirits) to contribute to the construction of a nonheteronomous normativity grounded on recognitive relationality among themselves *and* with the divine Spirit.

If the argument here was that, in dying, God recognizes humanity and withdraws so that the "I," conceived as the individual self, can construct its own independent normativity, this conclusion would make Hegel indistinguishable from, say, Nietzsche or Sartre. Hegel's argument, however, goes in the *opposite* direction: the death of God is in fact not only a representation (*Vorstellung*) of recognition, but it also captures a distinct historical phenomenon—that is, the overcoming of the Enlightenment's idea that the "I" can be thought of as disjoined from the idea of normativity of the kind once provided by God. Actually, Kant already represented an exception in the context of the Enlightenment, because, as I emphasized in chapter 1, Kant's conception of the archetype responded precisely to the need to acknowledge an indissoluble connection between one's (moral) identity and God as the source of normativity. Hegel effectively radicalizes Kant's position: the Hegelian "I," in fact, is not the individual self, but already the result of a process of mutual recognition with other selves: as such, it cannot exist in isolation. Its existence is entirely normative, as it is grounded on recognitive relationality. From a religious standpoint, that recognitive relationality finds its "objective foundation" in the doctrine of the Trinity, which—in its expression of the economic Trinity—also includes the death of God, that is, Christ's gratuitous act of sacrifice, which is the prototype of all those acts of mutual recognition and forgiveness that bring about reconciliation.[60] God's kenotic act, being gratuitous, is completely nonfoundational and, as such, must be thought of as beyond immanence. It is not surprising then that the ideas of God and of the "I" are in mutual equilibrium in forging the normative framework for the use of reason. The death of God does not result, for Hegel, in a strict negativity but rather permits the emergence of the full revelation of God: Absolute consciousness.[61]

In this chapter we have seen that Hegel viewed the crisis in normativity (the death of the abstract God, the Cartesian divine guarantor) as strictly linked to the conception of the self. Kant's critique of traditional metaphysics also entailed the reduction of the idea of God to a regulative idea, thus regarded as unknowable. This move led to what Hegel calls the "reflective philosophy of subjectivity," that is, a subjectivist drift in religion and theology that conceived God in a direct and unconceptualized way by grounding God in feeling. Theological subjectivism, taken to its extreme, eventually reduces God to a reflection of the finite mind. Hegel reacts against subjectivism, and he maintains that it is possible to build on Kant's critique of traditional metaphysics while at the same time maintaining that it is possible to have a conceptual knowledge of God (that is, to restore *content* to God). However, an idealist conceptual knowledge of God does not regress to pre-Kantian metaphysics, because an idealist philosophy is very well aware that God cannot be properly thought of apart from God's relation with the human "I." The incarnation and death of God objectively represent, for Hegel, the overcoming of theological subjectivism and of the subject/object opposition in the human–divine relationship. Now, however, the self is exposed to the opposite risk, that is, the establishment of a normativity apart from the relation with God and the world. This risk finds historical realization in the Enlightenment and in the thought of Fichte—and, later on, in left Hegelianism. This is why Hegel's struggle against theological subjectivism is not complete without a corresponding critique of *philosophical* subjectivism, which reduces the world and God to a reflection of the "I," which alone is regarded as real. The overcoming of subjectivism in the concept of God always implies, therefore, a corresponding overcoming of subjectivism in the "I," so that content can be restored to both God and the "I" in their mutual relationship, and an autonomous normativity can be established.

# 7

# Beyond Subjectivism

## The Subjectivism of the "I"

Throughout the history of philosophy, the development of the concept of the "I" has been a constant concern. The Cartesian conception of the "I" as a *thinking* subject gave modern philosophy its peculiar *subjectivistic* twist. This subjective account of the "I" is effectively characteristic of modernity and, as observed by Malpas, indissolubly connected with "the way in which modernity also seizes upon, and thematizes, the objective." In other words, "the attempt at a purely 'objective' understanding of the world (the prioritization of physical science)" is strictly related to subjectivism ("the prioritization of the *'cogito'*").[1]

A further, revolutionary step was Kant's reversal of the Aristotelian conception, such that the way of being of things for us must itself be conceived as a reflection of our ways of judging; thus, our ways of being must be bound up with how we feature in the structure of our judgments (Kant's "Copernican" revolution). However, as already remarked upon in chapter 2, even Kant was not immune from this subjective account. According to Kant, experiences are held together in a unity of consciousness—the transcendental unity of apperception, or I-think. As noted by Beatrice Longuenesse, "Kant shares Descartes' conviction of the foundational role of the proposition 'I think' on the one hand, of the concept of God on the other hand, in framing all cognitive use of reason."[2] As I argued in the previous chapter, the entire history of modern philosophy from Descartes to Nietzsche can be evaluated against the relative weight and equilibrium of these two ideas (the "I" and God) in forging the normative framework for the use of reason, thus identifying a general trend according to which the weakening of the normative use of the idea of God corresponds to a strengthening of the normative use of the "I." The I-think plays, for Kant, the role of guarantor in epistemology: we can trust our knowledge, which is, however, knowledge of appearances, not of things-in-themselves. This principle also applies to the self—we know ourselves as we phenomenally appear to ourselves (not as "things in themselves"). In other words, objectivity for Kant does not mean extra-subjectivity but universal and necessary subjectivity.

The Kantian notion of the thing-in-itself quickly became a subject of dispute. Fichte questioned its very existence—after all, if we cannot know the things in themselves, they might also not exist. The rejection of the thing-in-itself turned Fichte's philosophy into a form of subjectivism (the Kantian intellectual intuition becomes creative, and reality may even be conceived as a creation of the human mind).[3] In his radicalization of the Kantian "I-think," however, Fichte built on the Kantian idea that the I-think is self-consciousness (not only "I know," but also "I become conscious that I know") to argue that the "I" must be self-positing and self-determining. Thus, if, on one hand, Fichte's account of the "I" shares a fundamental subjectivistic twist with Descartes's conception of the ego, on the other hand it puts into jeopardy the very distinction between subject and object on which the entirety of Cartesian and post-Cartesian metaphysics is based. In fact, Fichte's second principle (the "principle of opposition") claims that "the positing of something other than the self depends on the self doing that positing, and that self just is the process of self-positing."[4]

Much contemporary debate over the concept of the self continues to be characterized by a *polarization* between subjectivity and objectivity. That is, some philosophical definitions of the self are expressed in the first person, as with Descartes, Locke, and Hume, while other approaches tend to provide a third-person definition that does not refer to specific mental qualia (subjective qualities of conscious experience) but instead strives for a quasi-naturalistic objectivity[5] or operationalism (which regards the "I" as a "fuzzy concept" whose content, value, and boundaries of application vary with specific conditions). As such, these debates situate subjectivist and objectivist readings of the "I" in irreconcilably opposed camps. However, both readings assume a fundamental distinction between subject and object, a distinction on which the possibility of conceiving a "subjectivist" or "objectivist" position is grounded. Indeed, it is on this distinction that most of the contemporary theories of the self still rely.

In the last chapter, I pointed out that Hegel viewed the crisis in normativity (the death of the Cartesian divine guarantor) as strictly linked to the conception of the self. Moreover, in the previous chapters, we saw how, in his discussion of religion and God, Hegel employs a conception of the "I" that overcomes Cartesian subjectivism and bypasses traditional oppositions between subjectivist and objectivist accounts of the self. In other words, the overcoming of subjectivism in thinking about God and the overcoming of subjectivism in thinking about the "I" are complementary. In the rest of this chapter, I will therefore address Hegel's strategy in dealing with the overcoming of subjectivism with respect to the "I." It is not possible to pay attention to Hegel's execution of the arguments, as this would lead to a different work from the one that we have pursued in this book. I will therefore sketch Hegel's general trajectory with respect to an analysis of the "I" and leave its in-depth consideration (something that definitely deserves to be pursued) to further research.

Hegel's idealism can be conceived as a type of philosophical expression of a self-conception as an "I"—that is, as a competent user of the morpheme. It is also an attempt to make explicit what every language user "knows" about what it is to be an "I," where such knowledge is the practical knowledge underlying the use of that word. Put differently, it can be argued that one of the main concerns of Hegel's idealism was what our conception of the "I" (*das Ich*) must be like in order to be consistent with how we conceptualize our activity as thinkers and moral agents[6]—including, in a prominent position, our activity of thinking about God.

A starting point for an analysis of Hegel's concept of the self is Kant's notion of the "I," since, in the context of Hegel scholarship, there is now almost general agreement that Hegel's philosophy cannot be viewed as a *regression* to pre-Kantian metaphysics and that Hegel builds on some aspects of Kant's philosophy—although various approaches differ in their assessment of the extent to which Hegel builds on Kant and in their interpretation of which aspects of Kant's philosophy Hegel builds on.

As is known, it was Descartes who placed the "I" at the center of philosophical debate.[7] For Descartes, the "ego" is the *res cogitans*, the "thinking thing" whose existence can be ascertained through methodical doubt once the reality of the external world has been suspended. The *Cogito* relies heavily on the subject/object distinction. As I stressed in chapter 2, Kant's "Copernican revolution" was an important step in questioning this model. In the preface to the second edition of the *Critique of Pure Reason*, Kant famously writes:

> Up to now it has been assumed that all our cognition must conform to the objects; but all attempts to find out something about them a priori through concepts that would extend our cognition have, on this presupposition, come to nothing. Hence let us once try whether we do not get farther with the problems of metaphysics by assuming that the object must conform to our cognition.[8]

Kant's novel idea consists in the suggestion that the "I" actively contributes something to all objects of knowledge—their "form." The I-think, Kant argues, must be able to accompany all our representations (*Vorstellungen*). This is indeed a revolutionary step, but in Hegel's view, as I previously stressed, the Kantian approach to experience might lead to a conception of the "I" still marked with subjectivism. An oft-cited quote from the *Encyclopedia* illustrates the point:

> [. . .] the Kantian objectivity of thinking itself is in turn only subjective insofar as thoughts, despite being universal and necessary categories, are, according to Kant, merely our thoughts and distinguished from what the thing is in itself by an insurmountable gulf. By contrast, the true objectivity of thinking consists in this: that thoughts are not merely our thoughts but at the same time the in itself [*das Ansich*] of things and of the object-world [*des Gegenständlichen*] in general. (E I, 8:116/85)[9]

This is undoubtedly a strong attack on Kant's subjectivism. Indeed, despite the Copernican revolution, Kant continued to maintain the existence of "things in themselves"—things certainly unknowable to us because we can only know phenomena (that is, things as they appear to us, as they are subsumed by the I-think) but (qua things in themselves) nevertheless posited as existing independently of the "I." As long as the subject/object opposition is maintained (in Hegelian language, as long as "the Idea has been posited in absolute opposition to Being," VSF, 2:11/81), knowledge is not possible;[10] we remain prisoners of the fundamental subject/object opposition. There is general agreement among Hegel scholars that Hegel wanted to overcome the (Kantian) opposition between subject and object. However, if the *negative* aspect of Hegel's critique of Kant seems (apparently) clear, the *constructive* aspect of it is much more controversial. Some scholars interpret Hegel's claim that "thoughts are not merely our thoughts but at the same time the in itself [*das Ansich*] of things" in a *conceptual realist* way, that is, as suggesting that Hegelian metaphysics is an inquiry into fundamental "features" or "structures" of the world itself (independently of the "I"). In chapter 3, I mentioned Stern's claim that "the characteristic feature of Hegel's absolute idealism is his freeing of the Idea from Mind and from the thinking subject."[11] This idea that, in Hegel's view, "human thought reflects the nature of reality itself, not its own subjectivity," is shared by Guyer, for whom Hegel's philosophy is a form of idealism (rather than absolute realism or materialism) because "the deepest fact about the nature of reality is that it is a product of God."[12]

While Kant regarded thoughts as imposed by us on things, Hegel regards them as constituting the essences of things—there is no doubt about that.[13] However, as I argued in chapter 5, in the context of an idealist metaphysics an object cannot be sharply distinguished from what that object is *to us*, from the object *as it is thought* by us. Stern interprets Hegel as criticizing Kant for being unable to distinguish between "idea" and "mind"; but what if Hegel's critique of Kant was effectively the *opposite*, that is, what if he were criticizing Kant for being unable to *unite* subject and object?[14] After all, in *The Difference between Fichte's and Schelling's System of Philosophy*, Hegel writes:

> The Kantian philosophy needed to have its spirit distinguished from its letter, and to have its purely speculative principle lifted out of the remainder [. . .]. In the principle of the deduction of the categories Kant's philosophy is authentic idealism; and it is this principle that Fichte extracted in a purer, stricter form and called the spirit of Kantian philosophy. But the things in themselves—which are nothing but an objective expression of the empty form of opposition—had been hypostasized anew by Kant, and posited as absolute objectivity *like the things of the dogmatic philosophers* [*die Dinge des Dogmatikers*]. [. . .] All this springs at best from the form of the Kantian deduction of the categories, not from its principle or spirit. (VSF, 2:79–80/9–10)[15]

Let us consider Kant's inability to unite subject and object as our working hypothesis. It might be argued that, in Hegel's view, Kant's problem is the conservation of *noumena* considered as objective "features" or "structures" of the world itself and thus as analogous to the "things" of pre-Kantian dogmatic thinkers—a move that is not, according to Hegel, consistent with the "spirit" of Kantian philosophy. Fichte is then seen as trying to rectify the situation and turn Kant's philosophy into a "genuine idealism" by "lifting out" its "speculative principle"—the self-positing "I." However, this interpretation could, prima facie, be considered counterintuitive. If this reading of Kant is correct, it might be objected: does not the unity of subject (Mind) and object (Idea) lead to *more* rather than *less* subjectivism? Attributing intellectual intuition to the self-positing "I," is not Fichte's philosophy the most radical example of subjectivism?

Before answering this objection, let us briefly consider Fichte's solution and the way Kant's project is transformed in the context of Fichtean subjectivism. Fichte clearly believes that Kant's problem consists in the retention of the thing-in-itself. In light of our working hypothesis, the retention of the thing-in-itself is connected with Kant's inability to overcome the distinction between subject and object. As Fichte puts it in the Jena *Wissenschaftslehre*, there are only two options: either one maintains the notion of the "thing-in-itself" and believes that the ground of experience resides in a world of "merely given" objects that exist independently of the "I" (dogmatism), or one accepts the idea that the self-positing "I" is the ground of all possible experience (idealism).[16] Fichte clearly advocates the latter position.

Therefore, Fichte's "I" is pure self-identity (I = I), an undifferentiated "I"—an "I," we might say, using Hegel's language, prior to any *diremption*. In more ordinary language, we might say that Fichte's "I" precedes any distinction from other I's and from nature; self-consciousness is also rooted in this self-identity, and therefore the "I" is self-positing—it exists because it is aware of itself.[17] With no more "things-in-themselves" in existence, only the "I" now exists "anyway." It is inevitable, therefore, that in Fichte's philosophy, the "I" is opposed to the world of its objects—after all, one cannot think *absolutely* but one must always think *of something*; and the presence of something other than the "I" (the object) contrasts with the absoluteness of the self-positing "I" (the subject). The opposition between subject and object is, in Fichte's view, posited by the "I" *itself*; the "I" and the world (subject and object) are, nonetheless, still opposed.

Now, let us consider Hegel's position vis-à-vis Fichte's account. Hegel agrees with Fichte that the Kantian retention of the "thing-in-itself" is a metaphysical residue that should be rejected in light of the true spirit of Kant's "Copernican revolution." Fichte's diagnosis of the problem is, therefore, correct in Hegel's view. Fichte is also right, according to Hegel, to look to the "I" to find a solution to this problem. Hegel clearly regards the "I" as supremely important, as self-consciousness itself is rooted in this ability to "abstract from all one's determinate features and concentrate one's existence into a bare point of being-for-self."[18] Thus, if Fichte is *right* in looking to the "I" to resolve the Kantian problem, what is *wrong*, in Hegel's view, with his attempted solution?

*First*, Fichte's "I" is, for Hegel, *too abstract* and *immediate*.[19] It is not enough to say, as Fichte does, that either one must accept the idea that the world is made of "merely given" objects that exist independently of the "I," or one must agree that the self-positing "I" is the ground of all possible experience. In fact, Fichte's suggested solution—that is, the coincidence between the subject and an immediately self-aware absolute "I"—inevitably leads to subjectivism (therefore, the answer to the question we asked earlier is a positive one: Fichte's philosophy *is* an instance of subjectivism). *Second*, and as an implication of the previous point, subject and object are still opposed in Fichte's (subjective) idealism, and Fichte is therefore unable to overcome the problem of subjectivism. If our working hypothesis is correct, Hegel therefore wants to unite subject and object—that is, he wants to close the Kantian "impassable gulf" between thought and thing—but he also wants this unity to be realized not *a parte subjecti*, that is, subjectively (which is Fichte's way: the opposition between subject and object is posited by the subject), but *a parte objecti*, that is, objectively.

This may appear to be a desperate move. How can Hegel ask for a unity of subject and object and demand *objective validity* for this unity (the "the true objectivity of thinking" of the *Encyclopedia*)? Is Hegel not trying, so to speak, to have his cake and eat it, too?

## Overcoming the Subjectivism of the "I"

Let us examine how Hegel proposes to overcome the problem of Fichte's subjectivism. Fichte's "I," we remarked, is too *abstract*. Therefore, the first move should be to return concreteness to the "I." Fichte has already done the preliminary work in this regard by emphasizing that one should "switch from awareness of objects to awareness of the self."[20] This is Fichte's notion of *Streben* (the moral striving or endeavor of activity), an idea that was already present, in a less discursive way, in another thinker who was influential for Hegel: the German mystic Jacob Böhme, who, in one of his works, claimed, "Without contrariety [*Widerwärtigkeit*] no thing can become manifest to itself"—a quote that Hegel himself mentions (VGP,

9:83/3:125). This "switching" from awareness of objects to awareness of the self is generated, in Hegel's view, by the *desire* to alter the world to bring it "into accord with the subject's wishes."[21] However, it is not always easy to satisfy our desires, as the world has an annoying tendency to resist them. It is this resistance that makes me aware of *myself desiring*—which is, therefore, the original source of self-consciousness.[22] The idea of desire returns concreteness to the "I."

Second, Fichte's "I" is too *immediate*. Fichte's absolute "I" arises from a process of abstraction: in Fichte's account, the "I" is precisely the bare self, that is, what remains once everything else has been abstracted from the "I." "But the identity of the Ego = Ego," Hegel writes, "is no pure identity, that is, it does not arise through reflective abstraction" (VSF, 2:56/122). In Fichte's account the "I," precisely because it is what remains once everything else has been abstracted, is absolutely immediate. For Hegel, however, this is a naïve assumption. The "I" cannot be immediate: the desire is the source of the I-awareness (awareness of one's bare self-identity), but "I-awareness is only the beginning of self-consciousness and of spirit."[23] The process of the development of the "I" is far from being complete. As a consequence, the "I = I" principle, Hegel writes, "remains only the rule whose infinite fulfillment is postulated but not constructed in the system" (VSF, 2:61/126). Conceiving this "I" as already "fulfilled," albeit infinitely, is equivalent to considering it as "given"—as something that is there prior to any *mediation*. For Hegel, this is not the case: the "I" must be thought of as (as Schmidt puts it) a "mediated and achieved identity, which is realized through the process that Hegel calls 'World-history'"[24]—that is, it is a historical product.

Historical determination is completely absent from the way Fichte thinks of the arising of the "I," which is also why Fichte's infinite strife (*ein unendliches Streben*) produces, in Hegel's view, an *unsatisfied* "I." We have already touched on this issue in chapter 5: to be satisfied, the "I" needs another "I." In other words, "full self-consciousness requires awareness of oneself as one inhabitant among others of a world informed by spirit."[25] For Hegel, "subject" (*Subjekt*) and "I" (*das Ich*) are not equivalent or interchangeable. "Subject" is a much broader notion than the "I" and has, for Hegel, different meanings, depending on the context in which the term is used. Conversely, the "I" is the human subject, which is associated with the concept (*Begriff*). This association between the human subject and (its) concept is not a natural process but a historical one that is, in Hegel's view, driven by the process of *recognition* (*Anerkennung*)—a notion that was indeed introduced by Fichte in the context of his legal philosophy. Only the encounter with another "I" and the process of mutual recognition (two human subjects recognizing each other as "I's") can make the "I" consistent with its concept—which is Hegel's way of expressing the idea that, properly speaking, there is no "I" prior to this process of recognition. The "I" cannot be said to exist as such *independently* of the social practices involving its recognition. In this context, Hegel's *absolute* idealism can be conceived as an attempt to approach the "I" from a perspective that takes into account the role of intersubjective acts of mutual *recognition* for the genesis of self-conscious thought and of human culture (the realm of Hegel's absolute spirit).

Therefore, Hegel's "I" is not opposed to a world composed of "merely given" objects that exist independently of the "I" (dogmatism), but neither is it solipsistically and egotistically conceived as positing a world opposed to itself (Fichte's subjective idealism). Of course, natural objects exist independently of the "I." However, at the very moment that the "I" enters into a relation with any object—that is, when an object becomes "an object of thought"—it is *mediated*, that is, conceptualized.[26] It might be objected that Hegel's idealism, described in such a way, does not appear to significantly differ from Kant's transcendental idealism. Recall, however, that the key point of discussion here, and indeed our starting point, is the question of the retention of the "thing-in-itself." Kant himself had suggested that, despite significant ambiguity on the topic, metaphysics could and should be reconceived from a practical point of view.[27] Fichte followed Kant's lead, eliminated the "thing-in-itself," and established the primacy of practical over theoretical reason through the activity of the self-positing "I." Hegel took the self-positing "I" as the model or prototype of his conception of "concept,"[28] which is the object of his idealistic metaphysics (the realm of absolute spirit): neither something merely given nor something merely posited by an absolute "I" but collectively generated through intersubjective acts of mutual recognition. The choice of the "I" as model is not arbitrary, nor is it simply determined by the fact that it was already developed, to some degree, by Fichte. The point here is that the "I" cannot exist without thought.[29] After all, what am I without my thoughts? And how can there be a thought without someone thinking it? Thought cannot be thought of as *separate* from the objects *that are thought*. Therefore, the opposition between subject and object was a false problem from the very beginning. By the same token, it was wrong, on Fichte's part, to view this opposition as posited by an absolute "I," considered as an immediate starting point. The development of the "I" requires both mediation (conceptual thought) and mutual recognition (recognition by another "I"). Only the combination of these two aspects can generate an identity between the subject (the bare self-aware "I," which is not properly an "I" for Hegel) and the (Absolute) "I" (the human subject associated with its concept). The absolute "I" is, therefore, not the starting point but the *final* point of the human enterprise—which is why "Hegel tends to equate the absolute I and its development with God."[30]

Assuming that this brief sketch represents, in a nutshell, Hegel's strategy to overcome the opposition between subject and object, and the subjectivism to which it gives rise, it might be objected that Hegel does not take us much beyond Fichte, if Hegel's introduction of recognition is merely an effort to conceive of the activity of the constitution of "idealities" (Hegel's self-positing concepts) as distributed over the species rather than as the prerogative of the (Fichtean) single absolute "I." This might lead one to conclude that Hegel's concepts (idealities) are *merely* cultural and social reflections.[31] But has Hegel not already clarified that the "true objectivity of thinking" implies that thoughts, far from being merely ours, must also be the real essences of things? Does not the overcoming of the subject/object opposition, which relies on recognition, look suspiciously similar to Kant's universal subjectivity—with the only difference being that we now have historically determined and super-individual, rather than universal and individual, "transcendental forms"?

Once again, Hegel might reply that, as close as this account may seem to his own, the key distinction resides in the preliminary assumption of an opposition between subject and object. Kant's transcendental idealism still maintains this opposition as one of its fundamental presuppositions (Kant's self-described Copernicanism is based on a conception of the object conforming to the subject, thus inverting the traditional metaphysical position), and we have seen how Fichte merely shifts the problem by conceiving of this opposition as posited by the "I." In both cases, something is regarded as "merely given," that is, as completely independent of the subject—Kant's "thing-in-itself" and Fichte's "I." From the point of view of Hegel's recognitive-theoretic approach, however, *nothing is merely "given"—not even the subject (the "I")*. This consideration can appear counterintuitive, but this happens because at a certain cognitive level—the level of, say, our everyday experience—everything is experienced as "given," empirical objects (a table, a mountain) as well as "institutional facts" (I am married, I am a citizen). We then capture these "states of affairs" that are perceived as "given" in *representations* (*Vorstellungen*). The activity of "picture-thinking" effectively provides us with manageable mental tools (representations) that, precisely because they are considered as "given" and independent of each other and of our consciousness, can subsequently be employed to carry on the everyday tasks we are all familiar with. However, as soon as one starts to rationally analyze a *specific* state of affairs represented in a *Vorstellung* and its connections, one recognizes that it is mediated—that is, that it cannot be thought without thinking of it in relation to the "I" *and* other objects and "states of affairs."[32]

Put differently, the mind is not conceivable without the world, and the world is not conceivable without the mind—or, as Hegel puts it, "Whoever looks at the world rationally sees it as rational too; the two exist in a reciprocal relationship" (VPW, 143/81). Moreover, it is this perfect and inextricable fusion between mind and world that constitutes Hegel's "true objectivity," which is objective not in the sense that the "things of the dogmatic thinkers" are objective but *idealistically* objective. It is not a given objectivity but a mediated, *achieved* objectivity—achieved through recognition. For Hegel, "true objectivity" is—as I have already stressed in chapter 5—"the agreement of a content with itself" (E I, 8:86/62), which is the task of spirit: to make a representation consistent with its content, thus generating a concept. Additionally, one should not forget that the "I" is, in turn, a representation made consistent with its content.

The last consideration is far from being a secondary aspect of Hegel's philosophy, as, on close inspection, this aspect of Hegelian thought has not been properly interpreted by either of the two factions of Hegel's followers that split after his death—that is, the right and left Hegelians. While right Hegelians have tended to interpret Hegel's philosophy in a pre-Kantian way, supporting a regression to traditional metaphysics in which the role of the "I" is greatly reduced, left Hegelians have strongly emphasized the "I" but interpreted it in a metaphysically realist way. Here, one thinks of such Hegelians as David Strauss and Ludwig Feuerbach, whose thought featured fundamentally realist commitments to the essential properties of humans—conceived as existing "anyway," that is, independently of any intersubjective links. As a consequence, the conception of an "I" that takes into account the role of intersubjective acts of mutual recognition (which, in the interpretation advanced here, Hegel's absolute idealism was intended to achieve) was almost forgotten and certainly not developed.

Hegel sought to establish a conception of the "I" based on the unity of subject and object while at the same time demanding that this unity have objective validity. He sought to reach that goal through a dialectic of recognition,[33] which can be regarded as an attempt to overcome the subjectivism of modern philosophy. Hegel's position is not properly an anti-subjectivist one, as, to be anti-subjectivist properly, one must subscribe to a prior opposition between subject and object—which is precisely the view that Hegel wished to challenge. As stressed by Gadamer, "Hegel's dialectical mediation had already accomplished the overcoming of modern subjectivism." Gadamer concludes: "We need look no further than the Hegelian notion of objective spirit for eloquent witness to this."[34]

Hegel's theory of recognition is seminal in the development of a more comprehensive account of the "I" by virtue of its emphasis on an intersubjective component, according to which the "other" is someone faced in a recognitive relationship rather than someone who is simply "on my side." The philosophical goal of such an operation is to conceive of *objectivity* without falling into *objectivism* and of *subjectivity* without falling into *subjectivism*.

As mentioned earlier, much contemporary debate over the concept of the self continues to be characterized by a radical opposition between subjectivity and objectivity. Such opposition, from a Hegelian perspective, implies a philosophically misleading conception of the "I" that conceives of the "I" as an entity that can be thought of independently of intersubjective acts of mutual recognition and of the network of relations determining it. Hegel's idealist metaphysics provides a new sense in which the "I" can be regarded as (idealistically, that is, mediately) "objective." The main idea here is that the world is neither "always already there" nor merely a projection of the "I," but both the "I" and the world come into existence through the interaction of the "I" with other "I's" and with the world.

At the end of chapter 2, we considered the hypothesis that the reconceptualization of God that Hegel regarded as the revolutionary aspect of Christianity—that is, a conception of God not separated from the human agent, but as indissolubly connected with her, at the point that a proper notion of what it means to be "human" cannot be thought in isolation from that conception of God—has consequences for an understanding of metaphysics conceived as the realm of self-realizing and self-correcting norms. An analysis of this process of reconceptualization—which brought us to consider the figural interpretations of religious representation, a redefinition of the concept of God, the transition from that concept to existence, its intersubjective structure, and the consequences of that reconceptualization on normativity—has confirmed that hypothesis; but in carrying on that analysis, we also came to realize that the overcoming of religious subjectivism is possible only if not only God but also the human "I" is reconceptualized beyond the subject/object opposition. In this chapter, therefore, we have sketched the determination of the formal conditions of a complete overcoming of (both religious and philosophical) subjectivism. If we now look back over our journey, we notice that the very idea of a "philosophy of religion" needs to be reconsidered in light of that overcoming. Even more importantly, we notice that the philosophy of religion can no longer be conceived (both in the context of Hegel studies and in the context of post-Kantian philosophy more broadly) as a subdiscipline or as a secondary form of philosophy, because it addresses questions and problems that are crucial for the way we think of ourselves as cognitive and moral agents and has therefore practical implications for a variety of contemporary issues. Our work would not be complete, therefore, without a brief consideration of the Hegelian legacy vis-à-vis contemporary philosophy of religion, and of its potential contribution to thinking through solutions to contemporary problems.

# 8

# The Relevance of Hegel's Philosophy of Religion Today

## The Human God

Central to Hegel's overall philosophy of religion is the idea of a *human God*, but for this idea not to be misunderstood, it has to be evaluated against the background of a set of qualifications that largely coincide with the essential steps of this study. Let us recapitulate those fundamental points; this will also help us to appreciate to what extent Hegel's approach to religion is still relevant for the discipline of philosophy of religion today, and more broadly for our understanding of religion and its implications in the contemporary world.

At the beginning of this study we looked at Kant's theory of conversion and grace, the pivotal point of which is the conception of the prototype of pure morality (Christ) regarded as an embodied ideal. If we "make room" for this archetype, conversion becomes possible; we can therefore hope to appear as justified before God, but we can never be completely sure. We thus considered two important implications of Kant's theory of conversion and grace, namely, the distinction between truth and truthfulness, and the fact that Kant's theory still needs an external divine and judging standpoint from which the moral subject can be condemned or absolved but not forgiven. Despite the absence of a theory of forgiveness, and despite the fact that Christ is still treated by Kant as an external symbol, there is already, in Kant's theory of conversion, an emphasis on the need for the subject's participation in the divine life (specifically, Christ's incarnation and sacrifice) that can be considered as the starting point of the process of humanization of the idea of God—a process that, however, could be developed in various directions.

After Kant, two approaches to God seem to be feasible: an abstract approach (God as a regulative idea that cannot be properly known) or an unconceptualized approach (faith identified with feeling). In both cases, the outcome is a form of *subjectivism*. It is against this subjectivistic drift that Hegel develops his project centered on a *reconceptualization* of God: subjectivism can be avoided, and content can be restored to religion, only to the extent that God is understood in God's relation to human beings, and human beings are understood in their relation to God, so that God appears in God's "humanity" and the human subject appears in her "divinity." Kant had already put the question of the subject/object relation at the center of the philosophical scene and had tried to solve it through an attempted unification of subject and object *in the subject alone*. From a cognitive point of view, God was considered merely as an object—specifically, an object that could not be known, because it could not be subsumed by the transcendental forms (categories) of a finite mind. Of course, God cannot be "known" in the way natural objects are known; Kant, however, neglects to take into consideration the knowledge of metaphysical objects ("concepts," in Hegel's jargon), whose knowledge requires a deeper understanding of the relation between subject and object.

Thus, from a Hegelian point of view, Kant's form of "negative theology," which culminates in his refutation of the ontological argument, is the consequence of his inability to pursue his own project to the end, and to wonder—to paraphrase Kant himself—whether we do not get farther with the problem of metaphysics by assuming not only that the objects must conform to our cognition but also that subject and object are *not* in original opposition. Our mind does not contribute only the form of knowledge but also some of its content; properly speaking, we cannot distinguish the contribution that comes from the subject and the contribution that comes from the object, because there is no (metaphysical) world prior to self-consciousness and no self-consciousness prior to the encounter between the subject and the world; as I put it before, our gaze is always already part of reality, and reality is such because it includes our gaze.

If subject and object are not in original opposition, then the task of reason becomes to retrieve and consciously realize the unification between subject and object, which constitutes a *mediated* objectivity. Reason therefore plays a normative role, and metaphysics itself is conceived as entirely normative; objectivity can then be defined as the coincidence (for concepts) of their existence with the normative status they are meant to express. This is essentially a redetermination of perspective: the traditional metaphysical illusion of an immediate objectivity (the "God's-eye view") is overcome in favor of an idealist, *mediated* standpoint that acknowledges the intrinsic and unavoidable circularity of knowledge.

All of this is very relevant to Hegel's reconceptualization of God. God is the source of normativity or, which is the same, the norm or norms. Hegel regards Christianity as the "consummate religion" because Christianity, through the incarnation and the death of God, allows for this kenotic reconceptualization of God—a God who renounces the God's-eye view and, in becoming human, becomes properly God. However, Christianity *itself* requires that it be approached as mediately objective. Thus, the "truth" of the story of Jesus is to be identified neither merely with the historical events of his life, nor merely with the spiritual meaning that they might signify, but in the *relation* between them: the "mediated objectivity" of the incarnation of Christ results, in other words, from the ongoing process of mediation between subject and object, which is always already in place.

Understanding how mediation works is the task of philosophy, and understanding how mediation works for religion is the task of the *philosophy of religion*. This process requires being able to distinguish between images, concepts, and ideas—terms that, as I previously remarked, Hegel employs with a very specific meaning. In particular, "concept" is not, for Hegel, a mental representation but an entity that has the capacity to fulfill its normative status: concepts are, in other words, self-realizing.[1] The self-realization of concepts, however, does not happen in isolation: being the result of a process of mediation, a concept is always inevitably intertwined with other concepts to form a system. Because the relative relevance of each specific concept is determined by its degree of self-consciousness, it should not come as a surprise that the two concepts that possess self-consciousness in the highest degree—the human being and God—are indissolubly connected to each other. Therefore, we cannot know God without knowing ourselves, but at the same time we cannot know ourselves without knowing God; and this knowledge is possible only in the context of an epistemological openness (perspectivism) and practical openness (recognition). It is this openness that made God human in the incarnation, and it is this openness that makes us human. If our world is intrinsically relational—something that Hegel captures through his account of the Christian Trinity—the proper way to know it and to live in it is to embrace this relationality and overcome the subject/object distinction. This is the ultimate meaning of Hegel's account of God as "the whole of wholes."[2]

Moreover, with his analysis of religion, Hegel also captures a historical phenomenon, which is typical of modernity: namely, the general trend according to which the weakening of the normative use of the idea of God corresponds to a strengthening of the normative use of the "I." On one hand, the strengthening of the normative use of the "I" is a huge step forward from the old metaphysical account of the God's-eye view (and its associated practical implications, which are still at work in the "monarchical" conception that features in Kant's treatment of grace). On the other hand, however, modern philosophy from Descartes onward has embraced a normative use of the "I" *in isolation*, that is, as disjoined from the recognition of other selves and from the idea of God. For Hegel, this is highly problematic for at least two reasons. First, the attribution of normative capacity to an "I" in isolation substantially reproduces the opposition of subject and object and inevitably leads to subjectivism. Second, the complete disconnection of the "I" from the idea of God makes it very hard (not to say impossible) for the human "I" to aim at that mediated objectivity, which is the necessary precondition for any epistemological and practical openness: as I previously put it, humans cannot be extricated from their relation to God and properly *be* humans. Thus, when Hegel addresses the divestment (*Entäußerung*) of God in the world, he is neither merely using a religious representation, nor is he simply providing a philosophical account of the process that is at the center of Christianity, but he is arguing that the only way to overcome the old metaphysical account of the God's-eye view without falling into the subjectivism of the "I" is to think of God as a human God, that is, a God indissolubly connected with human beings.

It is clear, then, that the reconceptualization of God has important consequences *for* the understanding of metaphysics (conceived as the realm of self-realizing and self-correcting norms); consistently, the issues that Hegel deals with in that context are not exclusively "religious." Philosophy of religion addresses questions and problems that are crucial for the way we think of ourselves as cognitive and moral agents.

## Philosophy of Religion Today

To what extent is Hegel's approach to religion still relevant for the discipline of philosophy of religion today? To answer this question, it is useful to briefly consider the current status of the discipline. Of course, an exhaustive analysis of all the approaches, methodologies, and trends currently employed in the discipline of the philosophy of religion would deserve a study in itself, and any attempt at such an analysis in the context of the conclusive chapter of a book on Hegel's philosophy of religion would be absurd. Rather, in an admittedly Hegelian fashion, I will focus here on two extreme positions that have become very popular in the last few years. Even the briefest consideration of these positions will help us understand why and to what extent Hegel's philosophy of religion is still relevant today.

The two positions I am referring to are the following. On one hand, outspoken atheists reject religion in the name of reason and science. On the other hand, we witness an increase in scholarship sympathetic to natural philosophy that welcomes rational proofs for the existence of a personal God and supernatural/religious explanations for scientific phenomena. For the sake of simplicity, I will use the term "new atheists" to refer to the former approach, and the term "new theists" to refer to the latter.

"New atheists" is a label that has become usual for identifying some thinkers such as Richard Dawkins, Sam Harris, and Quentin Smith. Atheism being a general term, a more detailed specification is necessary. The distinguishing feature of the "new atheism" seems to be a kind of "scientific atheism." To borrow Dixon's definition, scientific atheism involves belief in three central doctrines.[3] The first is anti-theism. The second is scientism, conceived as the belief that "science, especially natural science," is "the most valuable part of human learning" because it is "the most authoritative, or serious, or beneficial."[4] Third, scientific atheists "recognise the need to develop an alternative worldview to replace supernaturalism and theism, in which to ground their interpretation of the results of natural science, their understanding of the origins and meaning of human life, and their ethical discourse."[5]

Providing a precise account of the "new theism" is more difficult. Although it is true that some scholars explicitly profess Evangelicalism, or at least some of its characteristics as identified by Bebbington (including: conversionism, biblicism, activism, crucicentrism),[6] and hence are often referred to as "Evangelical Christians," the term is only partly accurate, both because not all of them profess all these beliefs, and because the movement embraces a wider range of philosophical expressions. Sometimes they are referred to as "Christian nationalists," but this label is even less accurate, because it implies an emphasis on the political dimension of their philosophical activity, which, even assuming this as their ultimate goal, does not represent the philosophical justification for their reasoning. Rather, the distinguishing feature of what I call "new theism" seems to be a revived natural philosophy that welcomes rational proofs for the existence of a personal God and supernatural/religious explanations for scientific phenomena. This philosophical attitude is exemplified by (but not limited to) the theory of intelligent design. Intelligent design is the claim that "certain features of the universe and of living things are best explained by an intelligent cause, not an undirected process such as natural selection."[7]

Despite the frontal opposition that could lead one to think that these two positions have nothing in common, the standpoint of new theists and the standpoint of the new atheists mirror each other. They *have* something in common. They both assume that *religion is a theory*. They assume that philosophy can and/or should consider religion as a system of theoretical propositions—so that it is possible, for instance, to increase the rationality of a specific claim regarding the existence of God. More specifically: they assume that religion is a theory that can be evaluated *in isolation*, that is, as a closed system.

The assumption that religion is a theory seems to be based on a kind of meta-naturalism. Atheist philosophers profess a methodological naturalism (which might or might not entail metaphysical naturalism[8]), conceived as that approach that considers supernatural phenomena as nonexistent or as not inherently different from natural hypotheses. On the other hand, the new theists profess a natural philosophy that welcomes supernatural explanations of natural phenomena. In both cases, religion is considered as a theory, the propositional content of which is then rejected (for it expresses something that does not exist, or that can be explained naturally) or assumed (for it is taken as the ground of natural phenomena).

A good (although inevitably partial) account of this approach to religion can be found in Quentin Smith's article "The Metaphilosophy of Naturalism."[9] Smith complains about the consideration of atheism as a "subfield of the philosophy of religion": "atheism is usually classified as a body of counter-arguments against the cosmological, teleological and ontological arguments, and counter-arguments against the arguments from religious experience." Conversely, Smith argues, "Atheism should be considered as a defense of naturalism against skeptical attacks, and thereby to play a foundational role in justifying the presuppositions of positive naturalist philosophy." On this account theism should be considered as a "subfield of naturalism, namely, as a skepticism about the basic principles of naturalism." As the final consequence of this "reclassification move," "'[p]hilosophy of religion' disappears, to be replaced by a new subfield of naturalism, namely, 'skepticism about naturalism,' with skeptical arguments being put forth and argued against, with the aim in mind of further developing the argumentative foundations of the naturalist world-view."[10] The position of the new theists could be expressed by the same words, by just inverting the terms "atheism" and "theism": theism should be considered as a defense of natural philosophy (expressing supernatural explanations of natural phenomena) against skeptical attacks. Even in this case, philosophy of religion ultimately disappears, to be replaced by a subfield of theology, namely, apologetics (defense of theist positions against atheist attacks).

What kind of opinion would Hegel have of the "new atheists" and the "new theists"? Hardly a positive one. First, their approach to religion is characterized by an epistemological arrogance to "speak the truth" and to know the world in a directly objective way—an attitude that reminds one of the so-called "friends" of Job. And to the possible objection that Hegel too has the ambition to "speak the truth" and retrieve objectivity, it should be replied that for Hegel the correspondence theory, which is clearly the model of truth to which both the new atheists and the new theists conform, does not exhaust a comprehensive theory of truth, and it would be highly reductive to use that model of truth to deal with religion. For Hegel truth is, as I have already mentioned, "the agreement of content with itself" (E I, 8:86/62); it is not a direct objectivity, but a mediated objectivity resulting from the ongoing process of mediation between subject and object.

Second, as an implication of the previous point, the view of the new atheists, and that of the new theists, is disconnected from history. The new atheists appeal to the history of religions only to argue, at best, for a form of historical constructivism; so that showing the historical transformation of a concept (say, the Christian Trinity) is taken as evidence of its total lack of validity. What they fail to understand, from a Hegelian standpoint, is that the history of concepts is also the life of concepts: concepts, in other words, are alive and cannot be disconnected from culture and history. Even the new theists, from a Hegelian point of view, can hardly be said to restore content to religion: their epistemology of religion is abstract, and their arguments (consider, for example, the recent flurry of new formulations of the ontological proof) almost never make reference to the Christian context. Conversely, as I argued, for Hegel the ontological argument can work only if it is considered in that context—or, we might say using a more contemporary philosophical vocabulary, from a specific hermeneutic horizon.

The new atheists and the new theists are extreme instances (extreme insofar as they represent the most radical and opposite points of the spectrum) of an attitude quite common within contemporary philosophy of religion, one that—to quote Jaeschke—completely abandons "the prospect of securing a deeper meaning of religion."[11] And the first step to secure a deeper meaning of religion is, first of all, to realize that religion is *not* a theory. There is not, and there cannot be, any direct epistemology of God. If what is at stake is the existence of God conceived as a natural object, then no rational argument is adequate to justify the commitment required by theism or atheism. This is why the lack of rational or empirical proofs is compensated for by believers with faith, a nonrational component that provides the believer with the required degree of commitment. By analogy, it could be argued that what compensates for the lack of rational and empirical proofs for the atheist is faith in the nonexistence of God. In other words, personal belief in the existence or nonexistence of God as a separate entity is, and remains, a matter of choice. As such, it is a matter for *religion*—but not for the *philosophy* of religion. This does not mean that philosophy of religion should be indifferent to the question of the existence of God or—even worse—that it should become an empty container for any argument that somehow deals with religion. It rather means that, being *philosophy*, it should approach the issues *of religion* from the point of view of reason—which, for Hegel, means the life of the concepts and everything that that entails. When Smith claims that "atheism should be considered as a defense of naturalism against skeptical attacks," he clearly considers God only insofar as God's existence is meant to provide a supernatural explanation for natural phenomena; this is because he embraces a form of metaphysical naturalism. However, if an *idealist* standpoint is adopted, then one realizes that the idea of God cannot be easily expelled. When Hegel points out that animals do not make the transition "from the finite towards the infinite," but they "stop short at sensory sensation and intuition [*sinnlichen Empfindung und Anschauung*], and for this reason they have no religion" (E I, 8:131/97), he is not only making the somehow obvious argument that, since animals are incapable of abstract thought, they cannot have religion. Hegel's main point is that "this transitioning is nothing but thinking [*dies Übergehen ist nur Denken*]" (E I, 8:131/97). In Hegel's view, proper thinking *requires* the thought of God.

The conception of rational thought requiring the thought of God might be, in principle, compatible with a form of philosophical deism, but we already know that Hegel is also critical of deism. As he writes in the *Encyclopedia Logic*, "the definition of God put forward by so-called deism, is the concept of God insofar as it is a mere concept of the understanding, while by contrast the Christian religion, knowing [*wissen*] God as the triune God, contains the rational concept of God" (E I, 8:334/255–56).[12] This is a shocking move for our contemporary (secularized) tastes; and if his rejection of a direct epistemology of God makes Hegel's view incompatible with the analytic philosophy of religion, an outspoken identification of the "rational concept of God" with the Christian triune God makes his view much less palatable for most of current "Continental" philosophy of religion. However, it is precisely by reading these two claims together that we can make sense of Hegel's philosophical preference for Christianity. If, in fact, there cannot be a direct epistemology of God and, as I have previously remarked, it is not possible to approach religion in general, and the concept of God in particular, outside its historical and cultural context, it follows that even *our* discourse on God is situated within the same context. Put differently, and to paraphrase a claim we have previously stated, our gaze is already part of God, and God is such because God includes our gaze. In more prosaic terms, this means that our knowledge of God is also inevitably knowledge of our *experience of* God. Christianity is a central moment in our experience of God, one that—Hegel believes—has significantly shaped modern self-consciousness. Again, Jaeschke has argued that the death of God, conceived as that moment when any self-evident recourse to a belief in God had forfeited its indubitability, has played an important role in the internal constitution of modern philosophy of religion; however, Hegel wants philosophy of religion to be more than a mere consideration of religion as a cultural phenomenon.[13] Jaeschke expresses Hegel's project by arguing that Hegel wants philosophy of religion to be also a form of post–death of God philosophical theology, but there is another, broader way to describe Hegel's project: Hegel aims at establishing a *post-critical* and *hermeneutic* philosophy of religion.

The reason why Hegel's philosophy of religion is *post-critical* is obvious, in the light of our previous analysis: as I have repeated innumerable times throughout this book, Hegel endorses the Kantian turn that rejects any direct epistemology of God, but at the same time Hegel thinks that content must be restored to religion. If the knowledge of God is mediated, *tradition* becomes a legitimate source for philosophy to elaborate on; philosophy, however, does not stop at the content of tradition but puts that tradition *in perspective*. "Absolute knowledge," which is the final goal of reason, can therefore be conceived as the collection of different, and even contrasting, ways of seeing the world, none of which can alone be taken as directly true in its own right. This conception is not far from that expressed through Heidegger's notion of *Geworfenheit*: the human mind is "thrown" into situations without being able to reflect on them first—the movement of reflection is therefore a movement of mediation, which reinterprets the situation (with all its legacy of tradition). This dialectical process of reinterpretation, however, is not merely and externally *applied* to a content but also contributes *shape* to that content: a dialectic interpretation in fact is aimed at clarifying all the connections among the concepts that are involved in a situation, and through this clarification it permits the "truth" of that situation to be discovered. This is the reason why Hegel's philosophy of religion can also be described as *hermeneutic*.[14]

The human mind neither passively knows a world that is already there "anyway" nor creates a world that was not there prior to the encounter with the mind; what we call the (metaphysical) world is born (and is constantly renewed) *in* the encounter between the mind and the situation it finds itself "thrown in" (to use the Heideggerian expression). This also applies to religion. Therefore, the metaphysical world is inevitably, to some extent, also the reflection of how one *wants* the world to be.

At this point, one might wonder "what else" there is to God besides or beyond "our gaze," that is, human consciousness. To some extent, we have already addressed such a question at the end of chapter 3, when we reached the conclusion that, for Hegel, conceiving God in a direct and unconceptualized way is simply impossible and that, therefore, we need to conceive God as necessarily intertwined with the human self through the recognitive activity of the community and as a commitment that one necessarily undertakes when thinking of norms. The commitment to a belief in the independent existence of a supernatural being that we refer to as God (its ontic status) can only be an act of faith (*Glaube*); however, as Hegel had already argued in *Faith and Knowledge*, thus drawing a trajectory of thought to which he remained substantially faithful for the rest of his life, reason requires the acknowledgment of the internal relations that connect all the entities in the world among them *and* with human consciousness. Therefore, once we adopt the standpoint of reason, we are inevitably led to consider God as connected with everything else and as approached through (human) consciousness—our "gaze." That which was a limit for Kant (the world being accessible exclusively through transcendental forms, and the "things in themselves" as inaccessible and unknowable) is thus transformed by Hegel and turned into the entry point to metaphysical reality—not an independently objective one, but a mediately objective one—and hence to God.

Hegel's philosophy of religion, considered in this way, constitutes an important perspective on the nature of religious representations, concepts, and norms, which however has often been ignored in the subsequent history of philosophy because of misunderstanding. Even philosophers of the "Continental" tradition have only partially grasped the groundbreaking nature of Hegel's move. For instance, Paul Ricoeur shows a great understanding of the subject/object relation when he writes: "The first declaration of hermeneutics is to say that the problematic of objectivity presupposes a prior relation of inclusion that encompasses the allegedly autonomous subject and the allegedly adverse object"[15]—a claim that might follow quite easily from our account of Hegel's strategy. Then, however, he adds that "hermeneutics seeks precisely to radicalize the Husserlian thesis of the discontinuity between transcendental foundation and epistemological grounding."[16] The entire set of implications of this claim is too complex and labyrinthine to be more than alluded to here; it is, however, interesting to note that here Ricoeur sees hermeneutics as building on a Husserlian discontinuity—that between transcendental foundation and epistemological grounding, which, in turn, is, once reduced to its basic constituents, the result of a Kantian approach, which sees the transcendental and the epistemological as fundamentally distinct. From a Hegelian perspective, stating the discontinuity is not wrong: what is wrong is to stop at the discontinuity, insofar as for Hegel a much more productive philosophical attitude (and indeed the only one that can do justice to the "world") consists in overcoming that discontinuity, looking for the connections between the transcendental and the epistemological, to form a new, mediated objectivity. Without this move, contemporary philosophy remains stuck in the process according to which the weakening of the normative use of the idea of God corresponds to a strengthening of the normative use of the "I," but the *opposition* between the "I" and God (and religion in general) is *not* overcome.

Looking at the status of philosophy of religion as a discipline nowadays, it is hard not to conclude that we are still stuck in the middle of that process. This can also explain the overemphasis on *symbols*, which is common in much contemporary Continental philosophy, particularly hermeneutics. The (religious) symbol, in fact, conceived (according to Ricoeur's famous definition) as a sign able to transmit a meaning, seems capable of expressing the relation between the interpreting "I" and religion. The main characteristic of a symbol, however, is its opacity, which can be penetrated but, according to Ricoeur, never solved in perfect transparency. Nevertheless, this conception seems to adopt, albeit negatively, the same idea of "direct objectivity" ("transparency") typical of traditional metaphysics. Hegel's hypothetical response to Ricoeur would probably be much like his response to Kant: Ricoeur is right in claiming that a direct rationalization of religion and (just to mention an important religious question, and one to which Ricoeur devotes a significant amount of philosophical effort) of the question of evil ends up in the abstract dissolution of the meaning of religious experience itself. But it is a mistake, from a Hegelian perspective, to develop from this claim the conclusion that we should, therefore, stop at the opacity of the symbol and (to use Ricoeur's expression) "undo the concept." What needs to be "undone" is not the concept, but the myth of direct objectivity, so that not only its positive use (employed by traditional metaphysics) but also its negative use (which Ricoeur employs) can definitely be dismissed. The work of reflective mediation then, performed by reason, can show that the "opacity" of symbol is not, as it were, a sight impediment but the foveal blind spot that makes seeing possible. It is by relying on this conceptual and dialectical work that Hegel thinks it is possible to establish a philosophy of religion that can address the transformation of religious symbols into concepts beyond the subject/object opposition.

## Why It Matters

There is still one question that needs to be addressed. Assuming that the account of Hegel's philosophy of religion provided in this book is correct, and also assuming that this account presents some advantages over other approaches, what significance does this work have, if any, beyond the discipline of the philosophy of religion, and for our world today?

Both Hegel's metaphysics and his philosophy of religion allow a new sense in which religious symbols, concepts, and norms can be regarded as objective while avoiding the quasi-naturalistic account of religion found in most contemporary philosophy of religion. Hegel's idealistic metaphysics develops a mode of philosophizing about religion that goes beyond the *existential commitment* of religious claims and focuses on religion's *significance* for the self-constitution of human beings as free and rational. Moreover, it develops the idea of a continuity between religion and philosophy in that the latter, like the former, relies on a type of normative commitment that goes beyond rationally based *belief*—in this case, an "ungroundable" commitment to rationality itself.

As I tried to show in the brief analysis carried on in the previous section, in many ways, most contemporary philosophical and popular debates on religious issues resemble those of the eighteenth century. Now as then, atheists dismiss religion as they consider supernatural phenomena as nonexistent. Conversely, theists welcome supernatural explanations of natural phenomena. Religion is often still considered as a theory about independent reality, the propositional contents of which have to be rejected or assumed. At a "high-cultural" level, dogmatic atheism and dogmatic theism legitimate intolerant behaviors toward, respectively, religious beliefs and non-religious-based moral codes. At the popular level, similarly, lifestyles directed to the pursuit of materialistic and individual gratification or to the embrace of traditional religious values and mores are often presented as the only alternatives of personal choice.

Members of modern communities that are crossed by distinctions between believers and nonbelievers, and by creedal distinctions *among* believers, need access to a wider spectrum of ways of thinking about religion. A reinterpretation and revaluation of Hegel's approach to religion, such as the one pursued in this work, is primarily directed to the philosophical community, because this is the context within which ideas can be critically shaped, but the problem being addressed is far from being narrowly "philosophical." An important perspective on the nature of religious symbols, concepts, and norms has been excluded from consideration for more than a century, and the resources of the idealist tradition have been ignored because of misunderstanding. The reestablishment and development within philosophical culture of the orientation advocated here is a first but necessary step in a process of contesting, or complementing, existing perspectives.

Hegel's approach to religion, as depicted here, also presents some additional and specific benefits for our contemporary world. *First*, one of the prominent advantages of an idealistic/mediated approach to religion is its intrinsic cognitive humility (which does not mean that it is not, at the same time, highly ambitious). If I embrace this approach, whatever my personal creed, I remain aware that I do not have access to any direct objectivity: the system of my religious (or nonreligious) beliefs will always be regarded by me as being also the "precipitate," as it were, of historically changing notions and narratives, *and* the reflection of how I want the world to be. Also, if I embrace such an approach, I am constantly warned against the danger of subjectivism. To anyone, the practical (sociopolitical) implications of religious subjectivism can, prima facie, appear as much less dangerous than the implications of religious dogmatism. This is true, however, only to a limited extent. Subjectivism produces a lack of normativity that, in turn, generates the process according to which the weakening of the normative use of the idea of God corresponds to a strengthening of the normative use of the "I." However, the "I" cannot be disconnected from the idea of God; even the most atheistic and subjectivistic standpoint implies, albeit negatively, a reference to a certain idea of God. To put things in a more concrete light: it is often assumed that religious commitment poses problems for democracy when conceived of along "deliberative" lines. On an idealist account, however, the issue may not be *specifically* about doctrinal belief, as a secular community could be just as riven by disagreements that operate *independently* of espoused religious belief, but rather at the level of presupposed "ideas of God." For example, even overtly *atheistic* societies, such as the former Soviet Union, presuppose particular *ideas* of God—ideas of God entertained, we might say, in the mode of *disbelief*;[17] as such, they have philosophical theologies open to reflection and criticism, and which can have social and political implications as dangerous as religiously dogmatic ones. Therefore, the disjunction of the "I" from the idea of God can never be completely accomplished but can only lead to a relation where the idea of God is thought negatively, and the "I" ascribes to itself all normative power; this extreme form of subjectivism, however, can dialectically lead to the emergence of the other extreme, namely, a form of religious radicalism. This is a dynamic with which today we are sadly familiar; and indeed, much of the propaganda of any religious extremism, once conceptually analyzed, can be shown to rely on a critique of subjectivism, regarded as "weak," "relativist," and "untruthful," to which a strong, objective, religiously dogmatic truth is opposed. To put things in a harsh and nonetheless probably accurate way, we might say that a certain radically subjectivist Enlightenment, which is still very much alive today, is indirectly responsible for religious radicalism.

*Second*, an idealist/mediated approach to religion also has the advantage of avoiding an immediate or unconceptualized approach to religion. If our mind contributes to the shaping of the content of religion, then all the content of religion is, to some extent, already mediated; it is mediated because it is always the result of a cultural and historical mediation, and this mediation is an ongoing process—one that, as it were, is happening as we speak. Such an idealist philosophy of religion that separates commitment to certain "ideas of God" from the question of *doctrinal belief or nonbelief* is relevant to pressing practical issues such as the role of religion in politics. If we look at public debates over the most divisive issues, we see that most of the time they are polarized into the appeal to a doctrinal (unmediated) belief on one side, and into the appeal to an allegedly neutral conception of rationality on the other. From an idealist angle, the point is that every belief is always already mediated, *as is rationality* itself. Such an idealist standpoint, considered so broadly, clearly does not solve any of the dilemmas involved in those divisive issues, but at least it provides a framework within which dialogue becomes possible.

*Third*, an idealist/mediated approach to religion can also provide useful conceptual instruments to understand several religious phenomena. For example, the rise of forms of religious extremism, of which nowadays we are witnessing some incredibly violent and inhumane expressions, has come as a shock for a Western (mostly secularized) world, which had come to believe that certain forms of dogmatic extremism were a thing of the past. Why this certainty, which is now proven incorrect? Because we were (and we still are) under the influence of the old paradigm that saw the "I" and the world in opposition. If, as I previously claimed, our gaze is always already part of the world, and the world is such because it includes our gaze, we need to realize that our world is such because *we see it* as such—but then, this applies also for those religious extremists whose view we consider so appalling. Of course, this does not mean that all views are equally valid: nothing is farther from idealism in general, and Hegel's thought in particular, than relativism. A genuine form of idealism is confident of human rational faculties and is committed to establishing objectivity—but the only accessible form of objectivity is a mediated objectivity. In other words, the point is that not only at the level of historical happenings, but also at the level of ideas, we are all intertwined in organic systems (*Gestalten*, to use Hegel's term) within which concepts are indissolubly connected with each other, so that a movement of thought dialectically responds to another movement of thought—but thoughts always have, we should remember, practical implications. Therefore, an idealist approach to religion does not justify the commitment resulting from a specific view; but it provides the conceptual instruments to understand the processes and dynamics that lead to its rise.

Clearly, the idealist approach cannot "fix" the huge problems that have been alluded to in this final section. No philosophy book and no philosophical approach can. And yet, ideas can and do have an impact on our world. Philosophy, then, has the duty to investigate ideas; but it also has, even more importantly, the duty to be committed to the question of meaning. Regardless of one's personal beliefs on the matter, religion is an expression of such a quest for meaning. Hegel's philosophy provides an important perspective on religion, which therefore deserves full recognition.

# Notes

## Introduction

1. Cyril O'Regan, *The Heterodox Hegel* (Albany: State University of New York Press, 1994), 25.

2. Robert R. Williams, *Tragedy, Recognition, and the Death of God: Studies in Hegel and Nietzsche* (Oxford: Oxford University Press, 2012), 16–21.

3. Frederick Beiser, "Dark Days: Anglophone Scholarship since the 1960s," in *German Idealism: Contemporary Perspectives*, ed. E. Hammer (London and New York: Routledge, 2007), 70.

4. Robert Pippin, *Hegel's Practical Philosophy: Rational Agency as Ethical Life* (Cambridge: Cambridge University Press, 2008), 33. Pippin explicitly refers to Beiser as providing "voluminous paraphrases" of German thinkers, and to Robert M. Wallace's *Hegel's Philosophy of Reality, Freedom, and God* (Cambridge: Cambridge University Press, 2005) as providing paraphrases that often produce "impenetrable Hegelese" (33n34).

5. Pippin, *Hegel's Practical Philosophy*, 33.

6. Williams, *Tragedy, Recognition, and the Death of God*, 17; the emphasis is mine.

7. Ibid., 20.

8. Ibid., 16. Cf. Beiser, "Dark Days," 70. Beiser states that he owes this anecdote to Bonnie Kent, a student of Paul Kristeller.

9. Hans-Georg Gadamer, *Truth and Method*, trans. J. Weinsheimer and D. G. Marshall (New York: Continuum, 1997), 302.

10. Hans-Georg Gadamer, *Philosophical Hermeneutics*, trans. and ed. D. E. Linge (Berkeley: University of California Press, 1976), 55, 112. Gadamer links Hegel's notion of absolute spirit with the Cartesian/Enlightenment philosophy of reflection (which Hegel himself explicitly criticizes), maintaining that Hegel's absolute knowledge eventually aims at a dull completion and transparency. See Kristin Gjesdal, *Gadamer and the Legacy of German Idealism* (Cambridge: Cambridge University Press, 2009), 154ff. I tend to agree with Gjesdal that Gadamer somehow

"misread" Hegel on this point, by failing to address Hegel's own reflection on historical work.

11. Paul Redding, "Georg Wilhelm Friedrich Hegel," in *The Stanford Encyclopedia of Philosophy*, ed. Edward N. Zalta, Spring 2014 ed., http://plato.stanford.edu/archives/spr2014/entries/hegel/.

12. Ibid. See Charles Taylor, *Hegel* (Cambridge: Cambridge University Press, 1975); Frederick C. Beiser, *Hegel* (New York and London: Routledge, 2005); Rolf-Peter Horstmann, *Wahrheit aus dem Begriff: eine Einführung in Hegel* (Frankfurt am Main: Hain, 1990).

13. Redding, "Georg Wilhelm Friedrich Hegel."

14. Robert B. Pippin, *Hegel's Idealism: The Satisfactions of Self-Consciousness* (Cambridge: Cambridge University Press, 1989); *Idealism as Modernism: Hegelian Variations* (Cambridge: Cambridge University Press, 1997); *Hegel's Practical Philosophy*.

15. Terry Pinkard, *Hegel's Phenomenology: The Sociality of Reason* (Cambridge: Cambridge University Press, 1994); *Hegel: A Biography* (Cambridge: Cambridge University Press, 2000).

16. Robert Brandom, *Tales of the Mighty Dead: Historical Essays in the Metaphysics of Intentionality* (Cambridge: Harvard University Press, 2002).

17. See Robert Stern, *Hegelian Metaphysics* (Oxford: Oxford University Press, 2009); Kenneth Westphal, *Hegel's Epistemology: A Philosophical Introduction to the "Phenomenology of Spirit"* (Indianapolis: Hackett, 2003); James Kreines, "Hegel: Metaphysics without Pre-Critical Monism," *Bulletin of the Hegel Society of Great Britain*, nos. 57/58 (2008): 48–70.

18. Williams, *Tragedy, Recognition, and the Death of God*, 16.

19. William Desmond, "Religion and the Poverty of Philosophy," in *Philosophy and Religion in German Idealism*, ed. W. Desmond, E.-O. Onnasch, and P. Cruysberghs (New York: Kluwer Academic, 2004), 153.

20. Beiser, "Dark Days," 81.

21. Williams, *Tragedy, Recognition, and the Death of God*, 17.

22. Redding, "Georg Wilhelm Friedrich Hegel." "The very idea of an 'Hegelian metaphysics,'" Redding argues, "is in no way straightforwardly incompatible with the project of a post-Kantian 'completion' of Kant's critical program." For an expanded version of this argument, see Paul Redding, "Kantian Origins: One Possible Path from Transcendental Idealism to a Post-Kantian Theology," in *Religion after Kant: God and Culture in the Idealist Era*, ed. P. D. Bubbio and P. Redding (Cambridge: Cambridge Scholars, 2012), 1–21.

23. Klaus Hartmann, "Hegel: A Non-Metaphysical View," in *Hegel: A Collection of Critical Essays*, ed. A. MacIntyre (Notre Dame: University of Notre Dame Press, 1976), 101–24.

24. Pippin, *Hegel's Idealism*, 178.

25. Paul Redding, "Mind of God, Point of View of Man, or Spirit of the World? Platonism and Organicism in the Thought of Kant and Hegel" (conference

paper, Von Kant bis Hegel IV: Naturalism and Naturphilosophie, Concordia University, Montreal, October 11–12, 2008), http://www-personal.usyd.edu.au/~pred 9095/Redding_Platonism-Organicism-Kant-Hegel.pdf, accessed May 8, 2015.

26. Beatrice Longuenesse, *Hegel's Critique of Metaphysics* (Cambridge: Cambridge University Press, 2007), xvii.

27. The expression "mediated objectivity" was previously used by Jere O'Neill Surber, Introduction, in *Hegel and Language*, ed. J. O. Surber (Albany: State University of New York Press, 2006), 17, to refer to Reid's argument that "all concepts are already mediations between thought and being" (Jeffrey Reid, "Objective Language and Scientific Truth in Hegel," in Surber, ed., *Hegel and Language*, 95–110). This is a *linguistically* mediated objectivity; I employ the term in a stronger sense, which goes beyond linguistic mediation.

28. On perspectivism, see Paul Redding, *Continental Idealism: Leibniz to Nietzsche* (London and New York: Routledge, 2009), 145ff., and "Some Metaphysical Implications of Hegel's Theology," *European Journal for Philosophy of Religion* 4, no. 1 (2012): 129–50.

29. Paul Redding, "Hegel, Idealism and God: Philosophy as the Self-Correcting Appropriation of the Norms of Life and Thought," *Cosmos and History: The Journal of Natural and Social Philosophy* 3, no. 2–3 (2007): 16–31; "The Metaphysical and Theological Commitments of Idealism: Kant, Hegel, Hegelianism," in *Politics, Religion, and Art: Hegelian Debates*, ed. D. Moggach (Evanston: Northwestern University Press, 2011), 47–65; and "Some Metaphysical Implications of Hegel's Theology." From a slightly different perspective, similar work has been done by Thomas Lewis, *Religion, Modernity, and Politics in Hegel* (Oxford: Oxford University Press, 2011).

30. Paolo Diego Bubbio, *Sacrifice in the Post-Kantian Tradition: Perspectivism, Intersubjectivity, and Recognition* (Albany: State University of New York Press, 2014).

31. Michel Foucault, "The Discourse on Language," appendix to *The Archeology of Knowledge*, trans. A. M. Sheridan Smith (New York: Pantheon Books, 1972), 235.

## Chapter 1. Christ as Symbol in Kant's Religion

1. Immanuel Kant, *Der Streit der Fakultäten / The Conflict of the Faculties*, trans. and ed. A. W. Wood and G. di Giovanni, in *Religion and Natural Theology* (Cambridge: Cambridge University Press, 1996), 7:63/283, and *Die Religion innerhalb der Grenzen der bloßen Vernunft / Religion within the Bounds of Bare Reason*, trans. Werner S. Pluhar, ed. Stephen R. Palmquist (Indianapolis: Hackett, 2009), 6:87/124. For all Kant's works cited in the current book, the number/s immediately before the slash refer/s to the pagination in the standard German edition of Kant's works, *Kants Gesammelte Schriften*, edited by the Royal Prussian—later

German—Academy of Sciences (Berlin: Georg Reimer, later Walter de Gruyter, 1900–). The number/s after the slash refer/s to the corresponding pagination in the English translation that is cited.

2. For a comprehensive account of the debate, as well as an in-depth analysis of Kant's notion of grace, see Stephen R. Palmquist, "Kant's Ethics of Grace," *The Journal of Religion* 90, no. 4 (2010): 530–53.

3. Kant, *Religion*, 6:47/54.

4. Ibid., 6:47/54 and 6:48/55.

5. Ibid., 6:166n/182n152.

6. Ibid., 6:74/82.

7. Ibid., 6:47/54 and 6:74/82.

8. Immanuel Kant, *Anthropologie in pragmatischer Hinsicht / Anthropology from a Pragmatic Point of View*, trans. R. B. Louden, ed. M. Kuehn (Cambridge: Cambridge University Press, 2006), 7:294/194.

9. Patrick R. Frierson, *Freedom and Anthropology in Kant's Moral Philosophy* (Cambridge: Cambridge University Press, 2003), 122.

10. Ibid., 128.

11. Kant, *Anthropology*, 7:294/194.

12. Kant, *Religion*, 6:48/54–55.

13. Frierson, *Freedom and Anthropology in Kant's Moral Philosophy*, 128.

14. Allen W. Wood, *Kant's Moral Religion* (Ithaca and London: Cornell University Press, 1970), 229.

15. John E. Hare, *The Moral Gap: Kantian Ethics, Human Limits, and God's Assistance* (Oxford: Oxford University Press, 1966), 58.

16. Kant, *Religion*, 6:47/53.

17. Michelle Kosch, *Freedom and Reason in Kant, Schelling, and Kierkegaard* (Oxford: Oxford University Press, 2006), 58n34.

18. Kant, *Religion*, 6:48/54.

19. Cf. Wood, *Kant's Moral Religion*, 229.

20. This expression and argument are used by Gordon E. Michalson, Jr., "Kant, the Bible, and the Recovery from Radical Evil," in *Kant's Anatomy of Evil*, ed. S. Anderson-Gold and P. Muchnik (Cambridge: Cambridge University Press, 2009), 58.

21. See Alenka Zupančič, *Ethics of the Real: Kant, Lacan* (London and New York: Verso, 2000), 11.

22. Cf. Frierson, *Freedom and Anthropology in Kant's Moral Philosophy*, 122.

23. Kant, *Conflict of the Faculties*, 7:9/17; emphasis mine.

24. Ibid., 7:54/97.

25. Immanuel Kant, *Grundlegung zur Metaphysik der Sitten / Groundwork of the Metaphysics of Morals*, trans. M. Gregor (Cambridge: Cambridge University Press, 1997), 4:409/21.

26. Immanuel Kant, *Kritik der praktischen Vernunft / Critique of Practical Reason*, trans. M. J. Gregor (New York: Macmillan, 1996), 5:68/59.

27. Cf. Redding, *Continental Idealism*, 96ff.; Robert B. Louden, "Making the Law Visible: The Role of Examples in Kant's Ethics," in *Kant's Groundwork of the Metaphysics of Morals: A Critical Guide*, ed. J. Timmermann (Cambridge: Cambridge University Press, 2009), 72; Bubbio, *Sacrifice in the Post-Kantian Tradition*, 32–37.

28. Immanuel Kant, *Kritik der Urteilskraft / Critique of Judgment*, trans. W. S. Pluhar (Indianapolis: Hackett, 1987), 5:408/277.

29. Immanuel Kant, *Metaphysik / Lectures on Metaphysics*, trans. and ed. K. Ameriks and S. Naragon (Cambridge: Cambridge University Press, 1997), 28:577/340.

30. As noted by Palmquist, English translations often use "archetype" for both *Urbild* and *Vorbild*, thus creating confusion. Cf. Stephen Palmquist, *Comprehensive Commentary on Kant's Religion within the Bounds of Bare Reason* (Chichester: Wiley-Blackwell, 2015), 163n49.

31. Immanuel Kant, *Kritik der reinen Vernunft / Critique of Pure Reason*, trans. and ed. P. Guyer and A. W. Wood (Cambridge: Cambridge University Press, 1998), A569–B597/552. For an overview of Kant's use of the notion of archetype across his writings, see Howard Caygill, *A Kant Dictionary* (London: Blackwell, 2000), 83–84.

32. Cf. Jeanine Grenberg, *Kant and the Ethics of Humility: A Story of Dependence, Corruption, and Virtue* (Cambridge: Cambridge University Press, 2005), 203.

33. Palmquist, *Commentary*, 168.

34. Cf. Curtis H. Peters, *Kant's Philosophy of Hope* (New York: Peter Lang, 1993), 87; Predrag Cicovacki, *Between Truth and Illusion: Kant at the Crossroads of Modernity* (Lanham: Rowman & Littlefield, 2002), 95.

35. Michalson realizes that Kant "is not simply appealing to Christ as an illustrative figure who is easily interchangeable with other religious or moral figures" and claims that "there is an important, intrinsic connection for Kant between the figure of Christ and what he at one point calls the 'breaking' of the 'power' of radical evil to hold rational beings under its spell." Gordon E. Michalson, Jr., *Fallen Freedom: Kant on Radical Evil and Moral Regeneration* (Cambridge: Cambridge University Press, 1990), 109. Here, however, I try to give more emphasis to an aspect that, in my view, is underplayed in Michalson's account, that is, the relevance of Christ as prototype in the context of Kant's perspectivism.

36. Kant, *Groundwork*, 4:409/21.

37. Cf. Pamela Sue Anderson and Jordan Bell, *Kant and Theology* (London and New York: Continuum, 2010), 33. For an in-depth analysis of the question of the divinity of Christ in Kant's religion, see Stephen R. Palmquist, "Could Kant's Jesus Be God?," *International Philosophical Quarterly* 52, no. 4 (2012): 421–37.

38. Kant, *Religion*, 6:64/70–71.

39. Ibid., 65/73.

40. Kant, *Critique of Practical Reason*, 5:155–56/128.
41. Kant, *Groundwork*, section II, 4:406–8/19–21.
42. Ibid., 4:408/21.
43. Ibid.
44. Some Kant scholars argue that the archetype cannot be identified with Christ. For instance, Seung claims that "this archetype [. . .] cannot be identified with Jesus Christ himself. He is only an instance or example, while the archetype resides only in pure reason." However, Seung seems to miss—at least here—the distinction between the *archetype* and the *prototype*. It is true that it is the *archetype* (and not the *prototype*) that Kant regards as always being in us; and yet it is difficult to reject some kind of identification, or at least proximity, between Christ and the *archetype*, especially in light of those passages in *Religion* to which Seung himself points: "one can do better by saying that this archetype [*urbild*] has *come down* to us from heaven, that it has assumed humanity (for it is not equally possible to conceive how the *human being*, *evil* by nature, would on his own cast off evil and *elevate* himself to the ideal of holiness, as it is that this ideal [*das Letztere*] would assume *humanity*—which by itself is not evil—and *lower* itself to it)" (Kant, *Religion*, 6:61/67). Cf. T. K. Seung, *Kant: A Guide for the Perplexed* (London: Continuum, 2007), 134.
45. Kant, *Lectures on Metaphysics*, 28:577/340.
46. "The revolution of the will" is an expression used by Hare, *The Moral Gap*, 61.
47. Kant, *Lectures on Metaphysics*, 28:577/340; emphasis mine.
48. Kant, *Religion*, 6:61/67.
49. Ibid.
50. Kant, *Religion*, 6:61/68.
51. The first difficulty is concerned with the lack of absolute purity in any specific given time; Kant's solution is based on the distinction between timeless (divine) and temporal (finite) points of view on a subject's moral status. The second difficulty deals with the degree to which a moral subject can be confident of being on the path toward moral perfection (as total confidence might imply laziness, and a complete lack of confidence might lead to despair); Kant's solution consists in a moderate confidence. For an overview of the three difficulties and their implication, see Stephen R. Palmquist, Introduction to Kant, *Religion*, xxxff.
52. Kant, *Religion*, 6:74/83.
53. Cf. Allen W. Wood, "Kant's Life and Works," in *A Companion to Kant*, ed. G. Bird (London: Blackwell, 2006), 26.
54. Instances of this misleading (in my view) conception are Clement C. J. Webb, *Kant's Philosophy of Religion* (Oxford: Oxford University Press, 1926), 122, and Bernard M. G. Reardon, *Kant as Philosophical Theologian* (Totowa: Barnes and Noble Books, 1988), 115.
55. Kant, *Religion*, 6:74/84.

56. Ibid., 6:74/83.

57. Gary Banham, *Kant's Practical Philosophy: From Critique to Doctrine* (Houndmills: Palgrave, 2003), 144.

58. "He judges us as a completed whole 'through a purely intellectual intuition.' Intellectual intuition, in Kant's doctrine, is productive. God does not passively receive what he sees; he makes it. When he sees us as 'essentially well-pleasing to him,' he makes us so. In Lutheran terms, justification is constitutive. God is not, as it were, counting us as righteous *because* of the infinite progress towards holiness which he sees all at once. Rather, as the Lutheran Formula of Concord puts it, '[he] bestows and imputes to us the righteousness of the obedience of Christ; for the sake of that righteousness we are received by God into favor and accounted righteous.'" Hare, *The Moral Gap*, 54.

59. Ibid., 58.

60. David Sussman, "'Unforgivable Sins': Revolution and Reconciliation in Kant," in Anderson-Gold and Muchnik, eds., *Kant's Anatomy of Evil*, 233.

61. Christopher McCammon, "Overcoming Deism: Hope Incarnate in Kant's Rational Religion," in *Kant and the New Philosophy of Religion*, ed. Chris L. Firestone and Stephen R. Palmquist (Bloomington and Indianapolis: Indiana University Press, 2006), 84.

62. Kant, *Conflict of the Faculties*, 7:59/107.

63. For an interpretation of this issue, see Philip L. Quinn, "Christian Atonement and Kantian Justification," *Faith and Philosophy* 3, no. 4 (1986): 440–62, esp. 450ff.

64. Frierson, *Freedom and Anthropology in Kant's Moral Philosophy*, 193.

65. Banham seems to suggest something along these lines when he writes: "The new person arises from the sacrifice of the old and this sacrifice of the old person is the punishment of that person for what they did and the maxims on which they acted. This sacrifice of the old person in the birth of the new marks a continuity between them but the revision of the denial of transmissible liability is contained in the figurative notion of the Son of God" (Banham, *Kant's Practical Philosophy*, 144). As I explained earlier in this section, I do not agree with Banham's view that Kant is merely revising the classic theory of transmissible liability.

66. In a note entitled "The I," written sometime between 1785 and 1788, Kant comes back to the question of moral identity, significantly emphasizing the continuity of the self and adding: "Of course this cannot happen with humans as judges. Likewise one refers evil to one's childhood (Rousseau: the story about the ribbon) or also what we have done when drunk. Yet improvement is an experience that the character in us is not so entirely evil." Immanuel Kant, *Handschriftlicher Nachlaß / Notes and Fragments*, trans. C. Bowman, P. Guyer, and F. Rauscher, ed. Paul Guyer (Cambridge: Cambridge University Press, 2005), 18:295/277.

67. Reardon, *Kant as Philosophical Theologian*, 116. The main flaw of Reardon's approach is, in my view, that he wants to read Kant as a theologian and

then he finds him wanting as such; thus, Reardon ends by making claims such as this one: "For all its elevated ingenuity Kant's argument is unable to conceal the vital difference between an abstract moral ideal and its living embodiment in the reality of an historical personage." Kant's (transcendental) idealism and perspectivism are entirely missed here.

68. Kant could not be clearer than this: "Here is the question: whether someone can adhere to the *purest* virtue, by which many gratifications of this life must be sacrificed, without belief in God and another world. Such is wholly impossible." Kant, *Lectures on Metaphysics*, 29:778/134.

69. Kant, *Religion*, 6:74/83.

70. Michalson, *Fallen Freedom*, 117.

71. Ibid., 119.

72. Ibid.

73. Ibid., 120.

74. Cf. George di Giovanni, *Freedom and Religion in Kant and His Immediate Successors: The Vocation of Humankind, 1774–1800* (Cambridge: Cambridge University Press, 2005), 197. However, di Giovanni somehow downplays the role of the sacrifice of Christ by saying that it is a *figurative* representation of the expiation "accomplished once and for all by the Son of God dying on the cross," whose value consists in the "consolation" one can take "in the thought of an already extant surplus of merit from which everyone can draw as one would from a gift benevolently put at one's disposal (grace)."

75. Wood, *Kant's Moral Religion*, 235.

76. Among Kant's commentators, Anderson and Bell have grasped the relevance of this aspect: "The sinner also has to do something substantial, namely, to accept the forgiveness represented by Christ who, as prototype, enables us to recognize that we have fallen short of 'the archetype of the good moral disposition,' and this makes it possible to repent of our wrong-doing, and to hope to perform a radical, yet mysteriously conceived 'change of heart'" (Anderson and Bell, *Kant and Theology*, 68). Unfortunately, this intuition remains, in their book, somewhat underdeveloped.

77. "Christian doctrine has another, more familiar way to describe Christ's sacrifice: not that we offer Christ's sacrifice, but that he offers it. He is both sacrificial victim and priest. This becomes a continuing motif in the Fathers." Hare, *The Moral Gap*, 245.

78. Stephen R. Palmquist, *Kant's Critical Religion* (Aldershot: Ashgate, 2000), 159. See also Chris L. Firestone and Nathan Jacobs, *In Defense of Kant's Religion* (Bloomington: Indiana University Press, 2008), 27.

79. Christ, "though he was in the form [μορφῇ] of God, did not count equality with God a thing to be grasped, but emptied [ἐκένωσε] himself, by taking the form of a servant, [a] being born in the likeness of men" (Philippians

2:6–7, English Standard Version). Kant uses the term *Erniedrigung* (abasement), which captures well the significance of the kenotic experience.

80. Hare, *The Moral Gap*, 59.

81. Kant, *Religion*, 6:48/54. Cf. Palmquist, *Kant's Critical Religion*, 132.

82. Kant, *Religion*, 6:62/68.

83. Ibid.

84. Palmquist argues that Kant treats "the idea of Christ, the God-man, as the highest principle of transcendental philosophy." Palmquist, *Kant's Critical Religion*, 259.

85. Immanuel Kant, *Über das Mißlingen aller philosophischen Versuche in der Theodicee / On the Miscarriage of All Philosophical Trials in Theodicy*, trans. G. di Giovanni, in *Religion and Rational Theology* (Cambridge: Cambridge University Press, 1996), 8:265/32.

86. Ibid., 8:268/34.

87. "To be *truthful* is the greatest virtue in the world, on which all the remaining ones are grounded, and without truthfulness all the remaining virtues are in fact nothing but pretenses." Immanuel Kant, *Logik / Lectures on Logic*, trans. and ed. J. M. Young (Cambridge: Cambridge University Press, 1992), 14:62/45.

88. Kant, *Notes and Fragments*, 19:145/432.

89. Zupančič, *Ethics of the Real*, 47.

90. Immanuel Kant, *Über ein vermeintes Recht aus Menschenliebe zu lügen / On a Supposed Right to Lie from Philanthropy*, trans. and ed. M. J. Gregor, in *Practical Philosophy* (Cambridge: Cambridge University Press, 1996), 8:426/611.

91. Mark Larrimore, "Autonomy and the Invention of Theodicy," in *New Essays on the History of Autonomy*, ed. N. Brender and L. Krasnoff (Cambridge: Cambridge University Press, 2004), 81.

92. Robert Hanna, *Kant, Science, and Human Nature* (Oxford: Oxford University Press, 2006), 255.

93. Ibid., 285.

94. Kant, *On the Miscarriage of All Philosophical Trials in Theodicy*, 8:270–71/36.

95. On this point, cf. Larrimore, "Autonomy and the Invention of Theodicy," 83.

96. Ibid., 81.

97. "The authentic interpretation of the world is 'made by the law-giver himself,' and it tells us that the universe is ordered but not in a way we will ever understand. We are but one of its many purposes. We have met this God before. It is not the God we are enjoined to postulate by practical reason, but the 'all-sufficient' God of the *Only Possible Argument*, creator of a world in which all aims are achieved together." Ibid., 82.

98. Peter Byrne, *Kant on God* (Aldershot: Ashgate, 2007), 150.

99. Kant, *Religion*, 6:154/168–69.

100. Byrne, *Kant on God*, 150.
101. Kant, *Conflict of the Faculties*, 7:59/107.
102. Firestone and Jacobs, *In Defense of Kant's Religion*, 17.
103. Reardon, *Kant as Philosophical Theologian*, 116.
104. Kant, *Religion*, 6:171/190.
105. Cf. Webb, *Kant's Philosophy of Religion*, 81.
106. Kant, *Religion*, 6:141/157.
107. Wood, *Kant's Moral Religion*, 239.
108. Hare, *The Moral Gap*, 55.

## Chapter 2. Hegel's Conception of God

1. Frederick C. Beiser, "Moral Faith and the Highest Good," in *The Cambridge Companion to Kant and Modern Philosophy*, ed. P. Guyer (Cambridge: Cambridge University Press, 2007), 591.
2. Quoted in Emil Fackenheim, "Kant and Radical Evil," *University of Toronto Quarterly* 23 (1954): 340.
3. See Pinkard, *Hegel: A Biography*, 35.
4. See Henry S. Harris, "The Young Hegel and the Postulates of Practical Reason," in *Hegel and the Philosophy of Religion: The Wofford Symposium*, ed. D. E. Christensen (The Hague: Nijhoff, 1970), 65ff.
5. Gottlob Christian Storr, *Annotationes quaedam theologicae ad philosophicam Kantii de religione doctrinam* (Tübingen: J. G. Cotta, 1793); German translation by Friedrich Gottlieb Süskind, *Bemerkungen über Kants philosophische Religionslehre* (Tübingen: J. G. Cotta, 1794; reprint: Brussels: Culture et civilisation, 1968).
6. "I do propose to respond to these judgments, but I dare not promise it, because of the afflictions with which old age opposes primarily work with abstract ideas" (Kant, *Religion*, 6:13/13). Stephen Palmquist recently argued that Storr's book had an influence on Kant's decision to write a second edition, and that Kant's "pure rationalism" was an attempt to mediate between Storr's "pure supernaturalism" and Fichte's naturalistic rationalism (Fichte's book *Attempt at a Critique of All Revelation* had appeared anonymously in 1792 and was initially mistakenly attributed to Kant). See Palmquist, *Commentary*, 389ff.
7. See Harris, "The Young Hegel and the Postulates of Practical Reason," 66.
8. Dieter Henrich, "Some Historical Presuppositions of Hegel's System," in Christensen, ed., *Hegel and the Philosophy of Religion*, 37.
9. See Lewis, *Religion, Modernity, and Politics in Hegel*, 24.
10. See Henrich, "Some Historical Presuppositions of Hegel's System," 37.
11. In Rel I, 40/123, Hegel writes: "The most sharply opposed views are exegetically demonstrated by theologians on the basis of scripture, and in this way so-called holy scripture has been made into a wax nose." "Wax nose" was

an expression used by Lessing in his polemic against Goeze, and Hegel mentions it again in VGP, 9:13/3:30. In Rel III, 185/258, Hegel argues: "[T]here are in fact many people who are very religious and hold exclusively to the Bible, who do nothing but read the Bible, cite passages from it, and in this way lead a very pious, religious life. Theologians, however, they are not; such an attitude has nothing of a scientific, theological character"; and a comment by Hegel, not included in the main text but mentioned in several sources, reads: "Goeze, the Lutheran zealot [*Zelot*], had a celebrated collection of Bibles; the Devil quotes the Bible too, but that by no means makes the theologian."

12. See Pinkard, *Hegel: A Biography*, 37.
13. Quoted in Lewis, *Religion, Modernity, and Politics in Hegel*, 24.
14. *Hegels theologische Jugendschriften*, ed. Herman Nohl (Tübingen: J. C. B. Mohr, 1907), quoted in Henrich, "Some Historical Presuppositions of Hegel's System," 37.
15. Cf. Harris, "The Young Hegel and the Postulates of Practical Reason," 66.
16. George di Giovanni, Introduction to George W. F. Hegel, *The Science of Logic* (Cambridge: Cambridge University Press, 2010), xlix.
17. Ibid., xlix.
18. Moors refers to this move as "a Christology in the function of schematism": "Indeed, for sake of the restoring to the original predisposition's power to the good, Kant has philosophically called upon a moral Christo-centered religion. Finitude, displayed in the tension between '*Denkungsart*' and '*Sinnesart*,' with regard to the necessary restoration, will thus have opened again a proper locus for religion. By the same token, to this moral Christo-centered religion is assigned the role of a schematic mediation." Martin Moors, "Kant on Religion in the Role of Moral Schematism," in Desmond, Onnasch, and Cruysberghs, eds., *Philosophy and Religion in German Idealism*, 32.
19. Kant, *Religion*, 6:141/157.
20. I borrow this expression from Robert R. Williams, "Theology and Tragedy," in *New Perspectives on Hegel's Philosophy of Religion*, ed. David Kolb (Albany: State University of New York Press, 1992), 49.
21. "Christ bore the sin of the world and slew it. This conflicts with [the theory of] juridical (= moral) imputation, which requires that each of us must take the stand for him- or herself." Rel III, 287/371.
22. Kant, *Religion*, Second Piece, Section One, Subsection C. Cf. Robert R. Williams, "The Inseparability of Love and Anguish: Hegel's Theological Critique of Modernity," in *Hegel on Religion and Politics*, ed. Angelica Nuzzo (Albany: State University of New York Press, 2013), 135.
23. Cf. Peter Dews, *The Idea of Evil* (Malden: Blackwell, 2008), 106.
24. Cf. Eric von der Luft, "Sources of Nietzsche's 'God is dead!' and Its Meaning for Heidegger," *Journal of the History of Ideas* 45, no. 2 (1984): 269.
25. Kant, *Critique of Pure Reason*, B421–22/452–53.

26. See Beiser, *Hegel*, 65.

27. Graham Bird, *The Revolutionary Kant: A Commentary on the Critique of Pure Reason* (Chicago and La Salle: Open Court, 2006), 39.

28. Frederick C. Beiser, *German Idealism: The Struggle against Subjectivism, 1781–1801* (Cambridge: Harvard University Press, 2002), viii.

29. "The major philosophers of the German Idealist period are all very much oriented against, rather than toward, 'subjectivism' as it is ordinarily understood in English—for example, in the sense of any reduction of ontology to a set of mental states." Karl Ameriks, *Kant and the Historical Turn: Philosophy as Critical Interpretation* (Oxford: Oxford University Press, 2006), 257.

30. Kant, *Critique of Pure Reason*, Bxvi/110.

31. An interpretation along similar lines is suggested by Adams: "Hegel interprets Kant's transcendental idealism as one which opposes subject to object, and which resolves this opposition on the side of the subject. Kant is to be applauded for insisting that philosophy must be an account of the relation of subject to object, rather than only of the object (transcendental realism) or only of the subject (empirical idealism). [. . .] Kant was right to critique this, in Hegel's view. But Kant's solution was to divide the conditions for knowledge into sensible intuitions (the objective) and concepts (the subjective) which are then united in judgment. The intention to unite 'two' in 'one' (two 'conditions' in one 'judgment') is sound. But judgment is firmly on the side of the subjective, rather than reflecting a genuine relation between subject and object. And the effect of this is to say that we know 'phenomena' and cannot know 'noumena.' We can cognize appearances, but we cannot cognize things in themselves." Nicholas Adams, *Eclipse of Grace: Divine and Human Action in Hegel* (Malden: Wiley-Blackwell, 2013), 22.

32. Cf. Deland S. Anderson, *Hegel's Speculative Good Friday: The Death of God in Philosophical Perspective* (Atlanta: Scholars Press, 1996), 151.

33. Cf. Pinkard, *Hegel's Phenomenology*, 269.

34. Cf. Anderson, *Hegel's Speculative Good Friday*, 139n.

35. Cf. Pippin, *Hegel's Idealism*, 92–93: "Kant and Fichte reenact a Christian, religious tragedy of human finitude; they insist on a fundamental, eternal difference between the human and divine perspectives, and ascribe to the latter the only genuine, absolute knowledge of things in themselves."

36. Interestingly, Robert Stern makes a similar point, but he emphasizes the divinization of the human rather than the humanization of God—which I believe is related to his understanding of Hegel's attitude toward the subject/object opposition (more on this in the next chapter): "There are clear parallels here between what Hegel says of us, and what Kant says of the holy will—so if in one sense Kant's anthropocentrism represents the divinisation of the human in making us and not God the legislators of the moral law, Hegel may be said to take this a step further, in freeing us from subjection to any law at all, not by

setting us outside the ethical, but by seeing us as fundamentally capable of aligning our desires and characters on the one hand and what it is right for us to do on the other, much as Kant sees the situation for God, and God alone." Robert Stern, "Freedom, Self-Legislation and Morality in Kant and Hegel: Constructivist vs. Realist Accounts," in Hammer, ed., *German Idealism*, 256.

37. Cf. Paul Redding, *Analytic Philosophy and the Return of Hegelian Thought* (Cambridge: Cambridge University Press, 2007), 222.

38. Terry Pinkard, *Hegel's Naturalism: Mind, Nature, and the Final Ends of Life* (Oxford: Oxford University Press, 2011), 142.

39. Cf. Paul Redding, "Hegel, Fichte and the Pragmatic Contexts of Moral Judgment," in Hammer, ed., *German Idealism*, 235.

40. "As we know, Hegel understands God to be absolute reason, not to be an infinite, self-conscious personality who exercises reason, and it is evident that reason cannot grant forgiveness as we normally understand it. Only human beings filled with divine love can actually forgive one another; indeed, they are, for Hegel, the effective agents of divine forgiveness." Stephen Houlgate, "Religion, Morality and Forgiveness in Hegel's Philosophy," in Desmond, Onnasch, and Cruysberghs, eds., *Philosophy and Religion in German Idealism*, 105. On God not being a "personality" for Hegel, I have a slightly different view, which will be explained in the next chapter.

41. David Walsh, *The Modern Philosophical Revolution: The Luminosity of Existence* (Cambridge: Cambridge University Press, 2008), 104.

42. Cf. Bubbio, *Sacrifice in the Post-Kantian Tradition*, 37–38.

43. Cf. Dews, *The Idea of Evil*, 106.

44. Henry S. Harris, *Hegel's Ladder* (Indianapolis: Hackett, 1997), II, 503. Cf. also Allen Speight, *Hegel, Literature and the Problem of Agency* (Cambridge: Cambridge University Press, 2001), 118.

45. Miller translates *darstellt* here as "exhibit."

46. Terry Pinkard, *German Philosophy 1760–1860: The Legacy of Idealism* (Cambridge: Cambridge University Press, 2002), 242.

47. See Bubbio, *Sacrifice in the Post-Kantian Tradition*, 62ff.

48. Cf. Robert R. Williams, *Hegel's Ethics of Recognition* (Berkeley: University of California Press, 1997), 69.

49. Pinkard, *Hegel's Phenomenology*, 77.

50. Harris, *Hegel's Ladder*, II, 190.

51. Cf. Peter C. Hodgson, *Hegel and Christian Theology: A Reading of the Lectures on the Philosophy of Religion* (Oxford and New York: Oxford University Press, 2005), 39.

52. Hegel describes Böhme as "the first German philosopher"; it is "through him," Hegel claims, "that philosophy of a distinctive character first emerged in Germany" (VGP, 80/3:120). The importance of the notion of kenosis in Hegel's

thought, as well as Böhme's influence in this respect, has already been stressed in previous literature, most notably by Cyril O'Regan in his *The Heterodox Hegel*, 216–31.

53. See Bubbio, *Sacrifice in the Post-Kantian Tradition*, 78ff.
54. Williams, "The Inseparability of Love and Anguish," 135.
55. Williams, "Theology and Tragedy," 53.
56. Ibid. See also Houlgate, "Religion, Morality and Forgiveness in Hegel's Philosophy," 92.
57. Williams, "Theology and Tragedy," 53.
58. "There is never any rational necessity that one person forgive another; there is a radical gratuitousness about the act of forgiveness." William Desmond, "Evil and Dialectic," in Kolb, ed., *New Perspectives on Hegel's Philosophy of Religion*, 175.
59. Cf. Raymond Keith Williamson, *Introduction to Hegel's Philosophy of Religion* (Albany: State University of New York Press, 1984), 82.
60. Pippin, *Hegel's Practical Philosophy*, 233n.
61. Ibid.
62. For this interpretation, I am indebted to Redding, "Hegel, Idealism and God," 29.
63. Cf. Redding, *Analytic Philosophy and the Return of Hegelian Thought*, 228.
64. Pinkard, *Hegel's Phenomenology*, 219.
65. Pinkard, *Hegel's Naturalism*, 186.
66. Redding, *Analytic Philosophy and the Return of Hegelian Thought*, 229.
67. Williams has beautifully underlined the role of the Trinity as the logical structure of Hegel's kenotic thought: "At the logical level Hegel's alternative to foundationalist ontotheology and anthropo-ontology is a holistic triadic conception of God. For only such a concept articulates the constitutive otherness that underlies the possibility of freedom and suffering" (Williams, "Theology and Tragedy," 53). See chapter 5 for further elaboration on this point.

## Chapter 3. The Reality of Religion in Hegel's Idealist Metaphysics

1. See, for example, Beiser, *Hegel*, 310: "These religious and political controversies within the Hegelian school were not so easily resolvable because they involved an apparently intractable problem in the interpretation of Hegel's metaphysics."
2. See Robert Stern, *Routledge Philosophy Guidebook to Hegel and the Phenomenology of Spirit* (London: Routledge, 2002), and *Hegelian Metaphysics*; Westphal, *Hegel's Epistemology*; James Kreines, "Hegel's Metaphysics: Changing the Debate," *Philosophy Compass* 1, no. 5 (2006): 466–80, and "Hegel: Metaphysics without

Pre-Critical Monism." Another important strand of metaphysically oriented Hegel interpretation is represented by Houlgate, who has, however, a distinctive approach, especially in relation to the question of Hegel's relation to Kant.

3. Robert Stern, *Hegel, Kant, and the Structure of the Object* (London: Routledge: 1990), 115.

4. "So Hegel's *Begriffe*, including initially natural kinds governed by universal laws, are not mind-dependent in the sense we would expect given the term 'concept': the reality and the real effective impact of laws governing natural kinds does not depend on their being represented by us. They are not mind-dependent, but they are accessible only to thought." James Kreines, "Between the Bounds of Experience and Divine Intellect: Kant's Epistemic Limits and Hegel's Ambitions," *Inquiry* 50, no. 3 (2007): 333. Kreines links his approach here to the interpretations of Kenneth Westphal and Robert Stern.

5. See Pippin, *Hegel's Idealism*, and *Modernism as a Philosophical Problem* (Cambridge: Cambridge University Press, 1991; 2nd ed. 1999); Pinkard, *Hegel's Phenomenology*, and *German Philosophy 1760–1860*.

6. This (quite accurate, in my view) description of Pippin's position is provided by Stern, *Hegelian Metaphysics*, 5. Stern is referring to Pippin, *Hegel's Idealism*, 33. Stern discusses and ultimately rejects Pippin's position.

7. In the last few decades, a number of philosophers have emphasized the importance of recognition (*Anerkennung*) in Hegel's philosophy. Robert Williams (*Hegel's Ethics of Recognition*), drawing upon the work of Ludwig Siep, *Anerkennung als Prinzip der praktischen Philosophie* (Munich: Alber, 1979), and of Andreas Wildt, *Autonomie und Anerkennung: Hegels Moralitätskritik im Lichte seiner Fichte-Rezeption* (Stuttgart: Klett-Cotta, 1982), has shown that the general pattern of Hegel's *Sittlichkeit* is constituted by his theory of recognition. The theory of recognition is also central in the post-Kantian/revisionist approach to Hegel (see Redding, *Continental Idealism*, 150).

8. Redding, "Kantian Origins," 16n38.

9. Hammer, Introduction, in Hammer, ed., *German Idealism*, 5.

10. Redding, "Mind of God, Point of View of Man, or Spirit of the World?"

11. Longuenesse, *Hegel's Critique of Metaphysics*, xvii.

12. See Redding, *Analytic Philosophy and the Return of Hegelian Thought*, and *Continental Idealism*. Since the publication of his first book (Paul Redding, *Hegel's Hermeneutics* [Ithaca: Cornell University Press, 1996]), the two major threads of Redding's distinctive reading can be identified in "the interpretation of recognition as a hermeneutic scheme and the emphasis of Hegel's reliance on 'immanentist' arguments." Jean-Paul Deranty, "Hegel's Metaphysics as Hermeneutics," *Parrhesia* 11 (2011): 80.

13. "Indeed, critics have charged that this line of interpretation cannot account for his treatment of religion." Lewis, *Religion, Modernity, and Politics in Hegel*, 12.

14. "It would be incorrect, however, to conclude from these statements that Hegel's philosophy is a metaphysics in exactly the sense proscribed by Kant." Beiser, *Hegel*, 55.

15. Williams, *Tragedy, Recognition, and the Death of God*, 18.

16. Beiser, *Hegel*, 145. Later on, Beiser adds: "Hegel accepts the Protestant doctrine only on a symbolic or metaphoric level" (146).

17. Williams, *Tragedy, Recognition, and the Death of God*, 20.

18. Pinkard, *Hegel: A Biography*, 219.

19. Thomas A. Lewis, "Beyond the Totalitarian: Ethics and the Philosophy of Religion in Recent Hegel Scholarship," *Religion Compass* 2, no. 4 (2008): 571.

20. Paul Redding, "G. W. F. Hegel," in *The History of Western Philosophy of Religion*, ed. G. Oppy and N. N. Trakakis, vol. IV, *Nineteenth Century Philosophy of Religion* (Oxford: Oxford University Press), 60.

21. Ibid.

22. See Redding, *Continental Idealism*, 63–69.

23. Redding continues: "This does not make selves unreal or fictional, it simply makes their reality, unlike that of nature, conditional upon their recognition by others" (Redding, "Hegel, Idealism and God," 27–28). The use of the term "organism" can be a bit misleading here, because in some sense "organism" is already a "concept" (insofar as an "organism" is a complex "thing" with properties normally associated with living beings—which leads us to wonder what defines "life," etc.). I think that a distinction should be more appropriately made between the external, sensible instantiation of an object ("empirical bio-mechanical agglomerate," rather than "organism"), and the metaphysical concept (the human being). The idea here is that the "empirical bio-mechanical agglomerate" has a "naturalistic" existence (it exists "anyway"), whereas a "human being" exists only as a metaphysical object, because its existence is based on recognition—it exists only insofar as we attribute to that empirical biomechanical agglomerate some properties, rights, and so forth, that form the concept "human being."

24. Redding, "Hegel, Idealism and God," 18.

25. Glenn Alexander Magee, *The Hegel Dictionary* (London: Continuum, 2010), 189.

26. "Picture-thinking" and "representation" are the most common translations of Hegel's *Vorstellung*, with some exceptions: for instance, Walter Jaeschke, "Philosophical Theology and Philosophy of Religion," in Kolb, ed., *New Perspectives on Hegel's Philosophy of Religion*, 1–18, translates *Vorstellung* as "picture," and Raymond Geuss, *Outside Ethics* (Princeton: Princeton University Press, 2005), 48n18, prefers the use of "representation" to translate *Darstellung*. I use "picture-thinking" to refer to the *activity* (that is, the conceiving of something in terms of representations) and "representation" to refer to the *product* of that activity in general.

27. Robert R. Williams, *Recognition: Fichte and Hegel on the Other* (Albany: State University of New York Press, 1992), 257.

28. Adams, *Eclipse of Grace*, 84.

29. Cf. Michael Inwood, *A Hegel Dictionary* (Oxford: Blackwell, 1992), 286.

30. There is no room here to address such an interesting debate. John Burbidge, *Hegel on Logic and Religion: The Reasonableness of Christianity* (Albany: State University of New York Press, 1992), has noted the relevance of Christian doctrines for Hegel's own philosophy of religion, and O'Regan, *The Heterodox Hegel*, has shown the relevance of the mystical tradition of thinkers such as Böhme, Eckhart, and Joachim de Fiore for the appreciation of Hegel's Christology.

31. O'Regan, *The Heterodox Hegel*, 360.

32. Williams, "Theology and Tragedy," 53.

33. According to Williams, the justified possibility of a nonfoundational discourse on God resides in Hegel's account of "divine self-emptying or kenosis," in that "union of God with death in the anguish of infinite love," which Williams does not hesitate to name "Hegel's fundamental speculative intuition": God suffers because God "cannot remain indifferent to God's other" (Williams, "The Inseparability of Love and Anguish," 137). Cf. also Williams, *Recognition*, 232, and *Tragedy, Recognition, and the Death of God*, 237.

34. Here one can think of Hegel's analysis of *cultus* in the *Phenomenology of Spirit* (PG, 3:523/434). Pinkard, *Hegel's Phenomenology*, 329, comments: "By making themselves into participants without whose participation the god could not appear, the members of the cult create the 'social space' in which it will be possible for them to acknowledge their own determining power in the way in which things are conceived. They no longer take themselves to know the divine immediately but only in terms of the shared activity between the divine letting itself come to presence before them and their activity of calling forth the divinity."

35. Paul Redding, "Idealism: A Love (of Sophia) That Dare Not Speak Its Name," *Arts: The Journal of the Sydney University Arts Association* 29 (2007): 71–94.

36. On this point, see also the interesting remarks by Tom Rockmore, "Hegel on Reason, Faith and Knowledge," in Desmond, Onnasch, and Cruysberghs, eds., *Philosophy and Religion in German Idealism*, 133.

37. Adams, *Eclipse of Grace*, 16. Adams calls the former "epic metaphysics" and the latter "dramatic metaphysics."

38. "Hegel's concept of *Geist* and its dialectic realization in history are fundamentally indebted to Kant's 'transcendental embodiment' even though they are presented as overcoming the formal subjectivism of the pure 'I think' (they are, to wit, its true *Aufhebung*)." Angelica Nuzzo, *Ideal Embodiment: Kant's Theory of Sensibility* (Bloomington: Indiana University Press, 2008), 322.

39. Karin de Boer, "Hegel's Account of Contradiction in the *Science of Logic* Reconsidered," *Journal of the History of Philosophy* 48, no. 3 (2010): 346n.

40. A world that "is there anyway" is one of the central images of philosophical realism: cf. Peter G. Railton and Gideon Rosen, "Realism," in *A Companion to Metaphysics*, ed. J. Kim and E. Sosa (Oxford: Blackwell, 1995), 433. "Read as

an 'absolute' idealist in a post-Kantian sense," Redding writes, "Hegel might be seen as extending such a non-realist approach to both the individual soul and to God" (Redding, "Hegel, Idealism and God," 18).

41. Erich Auerbach, *Scenes from the Drama of European Literature* (Minneapolis: University of Minnesota Press, 1984).

42. Charles S. Singleton, *"Commedia": Elements of Structure* (Cambridge: Harvard University Press, 1954).

43. Alan C. Charity, *Events and Their Afterlife: The Dialectics of Christian Typology in the Bible and Dante* (Cambridge: Cambridge University Press, 1966).

44. For instance, commenting on Genesis, Origen wrote: "For who that has understanding will suppose that the first, and second, and third day, and the evening and the morning, existed without a sun, and moon, and stars?" Origen, *De Principiis*, bk. IV, trans. F. Crombie, in *Ante-Nicene Fathers*, vol. 4, ed. A. Roberts, J. Donaldson, and A. Cleveland Coxe (Buffalo: Christian Literature, 1885).

45. Raffaele De Benedictis, "Dante's *Epistola a Can Grande*: Allegory, Discourse, and Their Semiotic Implications," *Quaderni d'italianistica* 31, no. 1 (2010): 14. Cf. Auerbach, *Scenes from the Drama of European Literature*, 36.

46. Auerbach, *Scenes from the Drama of European Literature*, 54: this and the following quote are taken from the essay "Figura," trans. by R. Manheim from the original German text in "Neue Dantestudien" (Istanbul: Horoz, 1944), 11–71.

47. Erich Auerbach, *Mimesis: The Representation of Reality in Western Literature*, trans. W. R. Trask (1953; Princeton: Princeton University Press, 2003), 196.

48. Auerbach, *Scenes from the Drama of European Literature*, 72.

49. Ibid., 73.

50. Ibid., 74.

51. Singleton, *"Commedia": Elements of Structure*, 89–90.

52. Auerbach, *Scenes from the Drama of European Literature*, 74.

53. William of Ockham, *Philosophical Writings: A Selection*, trans. P. Boehner (Indianapolis: Bobbs-Merrill, 1964), 36–37.

54. Ibid., 12–13. I am grateful to Damion Buterin for having drawn my attention to a number of relevant passages in Ockham's work.

55. Auerbach, *Mimesis*, 571.

56. Auerbach, *Scenes from the Drama of European Literature*, 71.

57. Cf. Paul Redding, "The Relevance of Hegel's 'Absolute Spirit' to Social Normativity," in *Recognition and Social Ontology*, ed. Heikki Ikäheimo and Arto Laitinen (Leiden and Boston: Brill, 2011), 226.

58. Cf. Hodgson, *Hegel and Christian Theology*, 113. Moggach remarks that "Hegel's lack of concern with the contrast between symbol and allegory may reflect the fact that these terms never became fixed in the contemporary debate. The Romantics themselves were not consistent in their usage, a lack of clarity that may be explained not only by the dependence of the concept of the

symbolic upon the intrinsically murky categories of the intuition but also by the fact that both symbols and allegories ultimately have a common identity as forms of sensuous imagery or as indirect representations of concepts by analogy." Douglas Moggach, *The New Hegelians: Politics and Philosophy in the Hegelian School* (Cambridge: Cambridge University Press, 2006), 74.

59. Redding explains: "A photograph of a gleaming new car can represent that particular car, or more generally, the model exemplified by that particular car, or, figuratively, abstract entities like wealth or a lavish lifestyle. But it can express these more general meanings because in the first place it can represent that car itself: as Freud purportedly claimed, 'sometimes a cigar is just a cigar.' In short, the distinction between literal and figurative is one that works within 'representation,' rather than between representation and thought." Redding, "Some Metaphysical Implications of Hegel's Theology," 142.

60. Hodgson translates *bildlich* as "figurative." I translated it as "metaphorical" here to mark the difference between "merely metaphorical" representations and representations that are also "historical" (which I take to be the properly "figurative" representations) that emerge from this passage.

61. Lewis suggests something similar, I think, when he writes: "Appreciating this distinction is essential to Hegel's entire approach to religion. The history represents these divine activities, so that these events are representations of the absolute activity." Lewis, *Religion, Modernity, and Politics in Hegel*, 153.

62. See, for instance, this claim by Vater: "Religion may announce truth, our Mephistopheles concedes, but it speaks in *Vorstellungen* and thus disfigures what it says." Michael Vater, "Religion, Worldliness, and *Sittlichkeit*," in Kolb, ed., *New Perspectives on Hegel's Philosophy of Religion*, 202.

63. Houlgate, "Religion, Morality and Forgiveness in Hegel's Philosophy," in Desmond, Onnasch, and Cruysberghs, eds., *Philosophy and Religion in German Idealism*, 99.

64. Lewis has a different but—I think—complementary way to put it: "The movement toward thought thus does not merely overcome the images and allegories typical of sensible representations. The fundamental issue is overcoming the appearance that the determinations stand independently over against each other—the aspect of representation placed in relief by the treatment of nonsensible representation." Lewis, *Religion, Modernity, and Politics in Hegel*, 161.

65. Angelica Nuzzo, *Memory, History, Justice in Hegel* (Basingstoke: Palgrave Macmillan, 2012), 25. To the best of my knowledge, Nuzzo is the only Hegel scholar to mention Auerbach's figural reading as a resource to interpret Hegel's philosophy (specifically, as a resource to clarify Hegel's philosophy of history).

66. Inwood, *A Hegel Dictionary*, 108.

67. Nuzzo, *Memory, History, Justice in Hegel*, 39.

68. Cf. Quentin Lauer, *Hegel's Concept of God* (Albany: State University of New York Press, 1982), 188. See also Hodgson, *Hegel and Christian Theology*,

31: "for religion there is no *Geist* without *Gestalt*, no spirit without sensible or intellectual configuration."

69. See Auerbach, *Scenes from the Drama of European Literature*, 72.

70. John David Dowson, *Christian Figural Reading and the Fashioning of Identity* (Berkeley: University of California Press, 2001), 83.

71. A similar point is raised by Hegel in VPW, 481/490–91.

72. Adams, *Eclipse of Grace*, 3.

73. In the English translation edited by Hodgson, *zu eigen gemacht* is translated as "made its own." Here I follow the translation suggested by Dews, *The Idea of Evil*, 105.

74. Cf. Hodgson, *Hegel and Christian Theology*, 137.

75. See Paul Redding and Paolo Diego Bubbio, "Hegel and the Ontological Argument for the Existence of God," *Religious Studies* 50, no. 4 (2014): 482.

76. From now on in the book, I will capitalize the initial letter of "Idea" when the term refers to the Hegelian notion in its specific meaning (*Idee*), as distinct from "image" (*Bild*), "representation" (*Vorstellung*), and "concept" (*Begriff*), to distinguish it from the common use of "idea" as generic "mental content."

77. Cf. Magee, *The Hegel Dictionary*, 112.

78. Damion Buterin, "Hegel, Recognition, and Religion," *Review of Metaphysics* 64, no. 4 (2011): 810–11.

79. See Redding, "Kantian Origins," 12.

80. See Redding, *Continental Idealism*, 150–60.

81. Cf. Peter C. Hodgson, Editorial Introduction to G. W. F. Hegel, *Lectures on the Philosophy of Religion*, vol. 3 (Berkeley and Los Angeles: University of California Press, 1985), 52.

82. "[. . .] this means that the boundary between oneself and the other shifts, so that the self includes a good deal of the social environment that was previously supposed to be other than oneself." Inwood, *A Hegel Dictionary*, 111.

## Chapter 4. Hegel's Version of the Ontological Argument for the Existence of God

1. Some recent review discussions of ontological arguments include: Gareth B. Matthews, "The Ontological Argument," in *The Blackwell Guide to the Philosophy of Religion*, ed. W. E. Mann (Oxford: Blackwell, 2005), 81–102; Brian Leftow, "The Ontological Argument," in *The Oxford Handbook of Philosophy of Religion*, ed. W. J. Wainwright (Oxford: Oxford University Press, 2005), 80–115; Graham Oppy, "The Ontological Argument," in *Philosophy of Religion: Classic and Contemporary Issues*, ed. P. Copan and C. Meister (Oxford: Blackwell, 2007), 112–26; and Robert E. Maydole, "The Ontological Argument," in *The Blackwell Companion to Natural Theology*, ed. W. L. Craig and J. P. Moreland (Oxford: Blackwell, 2009), 553–92.

2. The position expressed by Graham Oppy is exemplary here. Oppy writes that Hegel's lectures "are full of assertions that there is a successful ontological argument," but that ultimately "he gives no argumentative support for those assertions, not any indication of what the premises of the target argument might be." Graham Oppy, "Ontological Arguments," in *The Stanford Encyclopedia of Philosophy*, ed. E. N. Zalta, Spring 2015 ed., http://plato.stanford.edu/archives/spr2015/entries/ontological-arguments/.

3. Cf. Alister E. McGrath, *Science and Religion: An Introduction* (Oxford: Wiley-Blackwell, 1999), 89–91.

4. According to Oppy, this is the conceptual (or hyperintensional) formulation of the ontological argument. See Graham Oppy, *Ontological Arguments and Belief in God* (New York: Cambridge University Press, 1995), 245.

5. "When I turn my mind's eye upon myself, I understand that I am a thing which is incomplete and dependent on another and which aspires without limit to ever greater and better things; but I also understand at the same time that he on whom I depend has within him all those greater things, not just indefinitely and potentially but actually and infinitely." René Descartes, *Meditations on First Philosophy*, trans. and ed. J. Cottingham (Cambridge: Cambridge University Press, 1996), III, 35.

6. Leibniz's argument is included in Gottfried Wilhelm Leibniz, *New Essay Concerning Human Understanding*, trans. A. Langley (1709; New York: Macmillan, 1896). Cf. Oppy, "Ontological Arguments," 24.

7. Kant, *Critique of Pure Reason*, A5991 B627/567.

8. Ibid., A601 B629/568.

9. Paul Redding and I have developed this argument in our joint paper, "Hegel and the Ontological Argument for the Existence of God," 468ff.

10. An exception is represented by the logic advanced by the Stoics—something that was captured by Hegel himself: in the *Lectures on the History of Philosophy*, in fact, he comments that the Stoics had gone beyond the "empirical" approach of Aristotle in that, for the Stoics, "the forms of thought are *set forth as such for themselves*" (GP, 19:243/2:255).

11. In this light, Adams's claim that Hegel "says that Anselm's ontological argument displays a logic in which the Cartesian false opposition between thinking and being is absent" does not seem entirely correct. Adams, *Eclipse of Grace*, 224.

12. Hegel comes back to the "deficiency [*Mangel*] in Anselm's argument" in Rel I, 328/439, in the context of a passage that I will consider at length in the next section.

13. A similar explanation of Hegel's remark in E I, 8:349/268, is provided by Lauer, *Hegel's Concept of God*, 100. Lauer, however, seems more concerned with the "untrue nature" of the finite.

14. In modern philosophy, all that is required for some thing or state of affairs to be considered possible is that its concept be noncontradictory, but in

classic ancient philosophy there is a tendency to identify possibility with that which in some way can be effected by action, and because of this to associate possibility with the *future*, which is seen as open to action in contrast to the fixed necessity of the past. Put differently, for classic ancient philosophy, possibility is thought of in terms of future states of *this world*, not in terms of logically possible *alternative worlds*.

15. On this point, Anderson comments that Kant's criticism "is telling only because he attacks the lesser form of the ontological proof, which conceives of existence as a predicate of God. But, in Hegel's view, existence is the essence of God. Thus conceived, the ontological proof expresses the absolute unity of thinking (subject) and being (predicate), the foundation and coping-stone of true philosophy" (Anderson, *Hegel's Speculative Good Friday*, 25).

16. Hegel usually employs the term *Gegenstand* when he wants to refer to an object conceived "as an object of the mind." The adjective *gegenständlich*, in Hegel's view, suits well an approach that assumes a sharp distinction between being and thought (cf. E I, 8:346/265). About the use of *gegenständlich*, and Hegel's critique of Kant, see also Stephen Houlgate, *Hegel, Nietzsche and the Criticism of Metaphysics* (Cambridge: Cambridge University Press, 1986), 114–15.

17. For a defense of Kant against Hegel's charge of subjectivism, see Alexander Dunlop Lindsay, *Kant* (Westport: Greenwood, 1970), 157.

18. Cf. Lauer, *Hegel's Concept of God*, 194. In the article coauthored with Paul Redding ("Hegel and the Ontological Argument for the Existence of God"), we argue that Hegel's alternative conception of concept was, however, modeled on Kant's transcendental unity of apperceptions (the "I think").

19. "Since Anselm's day," Hegel comments, "we have come no further in any respect" (Rel I, 328/440).

20. See Magee, *The Hegel Dictionary*, 59.

21. Cf. Inwood, *An Hegel Dictionary*, 59–60.

22. Cf. Redding and Bubbio, "Hegel and the Ontological Argument for the Existence of God," 474.

23. Kant, *Critique of Practical Reason*, 122/155.

24. Cf. Patricia Marie Calton, *Hegel's Metaphysics of God: The Ontological Proof as the Development of a Trinitarian Divine Ontology* (Aldershot: Ashgate, 2001), 63.

25. Cf. Hodgson, *Hegel and Christian Theology*, 122.

26. Cf. Inwood, *A Hegel Dictionary*, 60.

27. Redding, *Hegel's Hermeneutics*, 157.

28. Will Dudley, *Hegel, Nietzsche, and Philosophy: Thinking Freedom* (Cambridge: Cambridge University Press, 2002), 92.

29. Pinkard continues: "For Hegel, the justification for the concept of God would come not by showing it to be a condition of the possibility of experience (thus sidestepping Kant's objections), but instead by showing it to be a commitment that becomes explicit once one has made explicit ('posited') the

other commitments inherent in making judgments about the world. The move to 'Objectivity,' therefore, is not a move that posits the existence of anything on the basis of our thoughts about the world (as the ontological argument would have it), but rather one that makes more fully explicit and consistent the various commitments inherent in thinking about the world at all. Thus, it remains internal to the development of thought, not a jumping outside of the realm of 'logic' to 'existence.'" Pinkard, *German Philosophy 1760–1860*, 261.

30. "In achieving thought, 'Knowledge of God' has reached its culmination. The alterity posited between humans and God in earlier stages of knowledge of God has been overcome. In the thinking that characterizes philosophy, spirit becomes transparent to itself such that the absolute is grasped as spirit and thus our own essence. The appearance of independent existence intrinsic to representations of God has been overcome, and human beings have thereby been elevated to the divine." Lewis, *Religion, Modernity, and Politics in Hegel*, 169.

31. Hodgson, *Hegel and Christian Theology*, 264.

## Chapter 5. The Trinity and the "I"

1. Walter Kaufmann, *Hegel: A Reinterpretation* (New York: Anchor Books, 1966), 168.

2. Magee, *The Hegel Dictionary*, 202.

3. As Griffioen comments, "Although prima facie this phrase seems to refer to the birth of Jesus, in fact, as the context makes clear, it speaks about the doctrine of Trinity" (Sander Griffioen, "The Finite Does Not Hinder: Hegel's Philosophy of Christian Religion Placed against the Backdrop of Kant's Theory of the Sublime," in Desmond, Onnasch, and Cruysberghs, eds., *Philosophy and Religion in German Idealism*, 111–12.

4. Cf. Redding, "G. W. F. Hegel," 10.

5. Walter Jaeschke, *Reason in Religion: The Foundations of Hegel's Philosophy of Religion*, ed. J. M. Stewart and P. C. Hodgson (Berkeley: University of California Press, 1990).

6. Hodgson, *Hegel and Christian Theology*.

7. O'Regan, *The Heterodox Hegel*.

8. Calton, *Hegel's Metaphysics of God*.

9. William Desmond, *Hegel's God: A Counterfeit Double?* (Aldershot: Ashgate, 2003).

10. Hodgson, *Hegel and Christian Theology*, 106.

11. Hodgson, *Hegel and Christian Theology*.

12. Wallace, *Hegel's Philosophy of Reality, Freedom, and God*.

13. Martin Wendte, *Gottmenschliche Einheit bei Hegel: Eine logische und theologische Untersuchung* (Berlin and New York: De Gruyter, 2007).

14. Lewis writes: "As important as the doctrine is, to try to further systematize it in non-philosophical terms—to elaborate the doctrines as if they were philosophical concepts rather than representations—is to fail to appreciate the distinction between these two forms of cognition" (Lewis, *Religion, Modernity, and Politics in Hegel*, 212). While I agree with Lewis's broad interpretative account of Hegel and believe his book represents an important contribution to scholarship in this area, I think that a position that categorically excludes the trinitarian doctrine from the realm of the conceptual does not do full justice to the complexity of Hegel's position.

15. Beiser, *German Idealism*.

16. See Stern, *Hegel, Kant, and the Structure of the Object*, 115.

17. The translation is based on Klaus Brinkmann and Daniel O. Dahlstrom's recent version, but it is somewhat modified, as I believe certain terms are better translated by W. Wallace, *Hegel's Logic: Being Part One of the Encyclopaedia of the Philosophical Sciences* (Oxford: Oxford University Press, 2nd ed., 1975), 67–68.

18. Friedrich Daniel Ernst Schleiermacher, *Der christliche Glaube nach den Grundsätzen der evangelischen Kirche im Zusammenhange dargestellt*, 2 vols. (Berlin: G. Reimer, 1821–22); now in F. D. E. Schleiermacher, *Kritische Gesamtausgabe*, Div. 1, vol. 7/1–2, ed. H. Peiter (Berlin and New York: De Gruyter, 1980), §187. See Rel I, 43/127. Cf. Hodgson, Editorial Introduction, 81.

19. Cf. Hodgson, Editorial Introduction, 34–35.

20. Pinkard, in his recent book, *Hegel's Naturalism*, clarifies this point in an endnote: "Hegel's conception of divinity is thus to be distinguished from that of his student, Ludwig Feuerbach, who claimed that 'we' were divine. For Hegel, that would make no sense. 'We' did not create or order the universe, and so forth. On the other hand, 'we' are also not simply projecting ourselves onto some fictional deity. Such a reduction of the religious point of view to the merely anthropological simply could not be satisfactory. There could be no 'religion of humanity,' even if the divine principle of reason is realized only in the activities of human communities reflecting on their highest concerns" (201n52). Pinkard's polemical target here is Henry S. Harris, *Hegel: Phenomenology and System* (Indianapolis: Hackett, 1995), x, as supporter of such a thesis.

21. The German text reads thus: "Wenn in der Tat unter der Religion nur ein Verhältnis von uns aus zu Gott verstanden werden sollte, so würde nicht ein selbständiges Sein Gottes zugelassen; *Gott wäre nur in der Religion*, ein von uns *Gesetztes*, Erzeugtes." Feuerbach's first book, *Gedanken über Tod und Unsterblichkeit* (*Thoughts on Death and Immortality*), was published one year earlier, in 1830. Thus, the possibility that Hegel had Feuerbach in mind must be considered.

22. For this definition of "spirit," I am indebted to Redding, *Continental Idealism*, 143.

23. See Williams, *Recognition*, 222.

24. This dynamic can also by expressed by one of Meister Eckhart's claims that Hegel quotes in the *Lectures on the Philosophy of Religion*: "The eye with which God sees me is the eye with which I see him; my eye and his eye are one and the same. [. . .] If God did not exist nor would I; if I did not exist nor would he" (Rel I, 248/347).

25. Hodgson, Editorial Introduction, 249.

26. Maurizio Pagano argues that only a comprehensive analysis of all Hegel's courses allows an adequate grasp of his agenda. See Maurizio Pagano, "Hegel as an Interpreter of Religious Experience," in *Religion After Kant: God and Culture in the Idealist Era*, ed. Paul Redding and Paolo Diego Bubbio (Cambridge: Cambridge Scholars, 2012), 47–70.

27. Williams, *Recognition*, 222.

28. The definition of the Trinity as "decorative timbering" (*Fachwerk*) is provided by the German theologian Friedrich August Gottreu Tholuck in his *Die Lehre von der Sunde und vom Versohner*, 2nd ed. (Hamburg: Perthes, 1825). According to Hodgson, from the allusion to the "pious theologians" and from the preface to the second edition of the *Encyclopedia* (1827), it can be assumed Hegel was referring to Tholuck here. Hegel responds to this view critically in his letter to Tholuck on July 3, 1826 (B IV, 2, 60–61). See the editorial footnote in Rel I, 68/157n17.

29. To clarify this idea, Hegel uses the example of the definition of someone as a "true friend," signifying that the friend acts in accordance with the concept of friendship. Hegel does not reject the Aristotelian "correspondence theory" of truth, but he locates truth as correctness within a broader ontological theory of truth. This also means that the traditional "correspondence theory" does not exhaust the notion of truth, as "[t]he idea is the truth [*Die Idee ist die Wahrheit*]; for the truth is this, that objectivity corresponds to the concept, not that external things correspond to my representations; these are only correct representations that *I, this person* [*Ich Dieser*], have" (E I, 8:368/283). As Daniel Berthold-Bond, *Hegel's Grand Synthesis: A Study of Being, Thought, and History* (Albany: State University of New York Press, 1989), 29, comments, Hegel's point "is that there is ultimately no such thing as a purely external thing; precisely in being an object of thought, the object cannot be 'external to thought,' if by 'external' we mean wholly alien, unreachable." In other words, as Redding puts it in his discussion of McDowell as an interpreter of Hegel, "the traditional 'correspondence theory' of truth presupposes there is [. . .] a gap between mind and world, asks how that gap is bridged, and answers with the idea of something mental, a 'representation,' corresponding with something worldly, some fact"; but what if there is no gap to be bridged and hence "no need of an intermediary 'representation'"? (Redding, "Idealism: A Love (of Sophia) That Dare Not Speak Its Name," 76–77).

30. The term "personhood" is not used by Hegel in this context but is employed by Hodgson (Editorial Introduction, 28). I believe Hodgson's expression captures well Hegel's emphasis on the unity of the Trinity, of which the three traditional "persons" are its expression.

31. "Although Hegel does not use the term 'Trinity' to refer to the latter [the economic Trinity] and does not employ the language of the classical distinction ('immanent' and 'economic'), the 'economic' Trinity is in fact coterminous with the three 'elements' or 'moments' in the 'development of the idea of God' as described in the later lectures." Hodgson, Rel III, 77, editorial footnote 51.

32. In the light of these remarks, it is hard to understand on what grounds some interpreters—for example, Hugh Ross MacKintosh, *Types of Modern Theology* (London: Nisbet, 1937), 105; Donald G. Bloesh, *God the Almighty: Power, Wisdom, Holiness, Love* (Downers Grove: InterVarsity, 2005), 196—deny the presence of an immanent Trinity in Hegel's philosophical theology. Of course, it is to be understood that Hegel is dealing with the Trinity as a concept and that, therefore, the notion of the immanent and pre-worldly Trinity is meant to capture the relationality of God as existing independently of the knowledge of the socially recognizing community.

33. See Hodgson, *Hegel and Christian Theology*, 130.

34. Cf. Hodgson, Editorial Introduction, 16.

35. See the 1831 Excerpts, Rel III, 280–81/362; cf. also editorial note 8 on the same page.

36. Cf. Hodgson, *Hegel and Christian Theology*, 130.

37. Ibid.

38. Cf. Redding, "The Relevance of Hegel's 'Absolute Spirit' to Social Normativity," 237–38.

39. Cf. ibid., 227.

40. Redding, "Hegel, Idealism and God," 30.

41. The claim here is that the notion of the "God's-eye view" is incoherent. The idea of a "point of view" is used to characterize the knowledge possessed by *finite* subjects; thus, the very idea of a God's-eye point of view is a contradictory anthropomorphization from the start.

42. "Had the hidden God, who is one unified essence and will, not projected himself into divisibility of will, and had God not injected this divisibility into enclosedness or identity (return in the relation to self) so that this divisibility would not stand in conflict [with it]—how should God's will be manifest to him? How might there be a cognition in one unified will?" Böhme, quoted in VGP, 84/3:126.

43. Cf. Miklós Vassányi, *Anima Mundi: The Rise of the World Soul Theory in Modern German Philosophy* (Dordrecht: Springer, 2011), 130.

44. VGP, 84/3:126. Cf. Redding, "Some Metaphysical Implications of Hegel's Theology," 148.

45. Cf. Hodgson, *Hegel and Christian Theology*, 133; Redding, "G. W. F. Hegel," 14.

46. "Love is therefore the most immense contradiction; the understanding cannot resolve it, because there is nothing more intractable than this punctiliousness [*Punktualität*] of the self-consciousness which is negated and which I ought nevertheless to possess as affirmative. Love is both the production and the resolution of this contradiction." R, 7:308/199.

47. Cf. Fred R. Dallmayr, *G. W. F. Hegel: Modernity and Politics* (Lanham: AltaMira, 2000), 119.

48. Hodgson, *Hegel and Christian Theology*, 31.

49. Burbidge, "The Relevance of Hegel's Logic," 217.

50. O'Regan, *The Heterodox Hegel*, 360.

51. The premises for such an argument are already present, in my view, in Redding, *Continental Idealism*, 135–54.

52. Hodgson, *Hegel and Christian Theology*, 198.

53. VGP, 9:84–87/3:126–30. Cf. Redding, "Some Metaphysical Implications of Hegel's Theology," 147.

54. Jaeschke, *Reason in Religion*, 311.

55. Williams, *Recognition*, 224.

56. Cf. Wendte, *Gottmenschliche Einheit bei Hegel*, and Desmond, *Hegel's God*.

57. Williams, *Recognition*, 239.

58. Ibid., 224.

59. To this brief survey of previous works addressing the relationship between the idea of God and the idea of the self in Hegel's philosophy, Wendte's *Gottmenschliche Einheit bei Hegel* must be added. Wendte, however, does not emphasize the Trinity and confines it to the background.

60. Although an analysis of Hegel's critique of Fichte cannot be pursued here, that critique can be considered an area of speculation where the entire Hegelian conception is at stake. In fact, the theory of recognition is not intended to deny independence to "metaphysical objects." Indeed, the opposite is true: only through recognition can an object of reason achieve independence from an individual self-consciousness—that is, from the "I."

61. Clearly, there is more involved in Fichte's account of the "I"; here I am just providing a brief sketch of Hegel's reading of the Fichtean "I."

62. Redding, "Hegel, Idealism and God," 27.

63. Building on Hegel's philosophy, Jonael Angelus Schickler, *Metaphysics as Christology: An Odyssey of the Self from Kant and Hegel to Steiner* (Aldershot: Ashgate, 2005), argues that Christ's appearance determines a development in human consciousness to restore humanity's relationship to the world; however, Schickler also considers Hegel as unable to solve the problem of the ground of our sensory impression and ends up by appealing to Rudolf Steiner (the founder of anthroposophy) as effectively able to solve that problem. In my view, Schickler's

noteworthy book is nonetheless trapped in that traditional interpretation that considers Hegel's idealism as a peculiar type of "spiritual realism."
    64. Cf. Hodgson, Editorial Introduction, 16.
    65. Redding, *Continental Idealism*, 148.
    66. Hodgson, *Hegel and Christian Theology*, 137.
    67. Griffioen, "The Finite Does Not Hinder," 120.
    68. Hodgson, Editorial Introduction, 40.

## Chapter 6. The Death of God and Recognition of the Self

    1. "God is dead! God remains dead! And we have killed him!" Friedrich Nietzsche, *The Gay Science*, ed. B. Williams, trans. J. Nauckhoff (Cambridge: Cambridge University Press 2001), sec. 125, p. 120.

    2. Nietzsche's reading of the "death of God" is, of course, more profound and tragic than the simplistic account presented here, which as such does not do justice to his thought; here I am merely pointing out Nietzsche's endorsement of a reading that sees "God" as the highest expression of those religious and metaphysical values that he regards as disappearing.

    3. This is, for instance, the position of Frederick Copleston, *A History of Philosophy*, vol. 7, part 1 (New York: Image Books, 1965). Cf. Williamson, *Introduction to Hegel's Philosophy of Religion*, 299.

    4. "Since the beginning of the European intellectual tradition, it has been the thought of God which has served as the concept which preserved the entire coherent context in general. In God, thought had a guarantor not only for the context of all things but also for the coherent context of thinking and being." Eberhard Jüngel, *God as the Mystery of the World*, trans. D. L. Guder (Grand Rapids: Eerdmans, 1983), 105.

    5. As pointed out by Beatrice Longuenesse, "Kant shares Descartes' conviction of the foundational role of the proposition 'I think' on the one hand, of the concept of God on the other hand, in framing all cognitive use of reason." Beatrice Longuenesse, "Kant's 'I Think' versus Descartes' 'I Am a Thing That Thinks,'" in *Kant and the Early Moderns*, ed. D. Garber and B. Longuenesse (Princeton: Princeton University Press, 2008), 10.

    6. Cf., for instance, Williams: "What dies is not the divine being per se, but its abstraction, i.e., abstract transcendence, the infinite that, since it is opposed to the finite, is itself finite" (Williams, *Recognition*, 233). Cf. also Ken S. R. Foldes, *Hegel and the Solution to Our Postmodern World Crisis: From Nihilism to Kingdom Come; Essays* (Philadelphia: Xlibris, 2003), 305, and Giacomo Rinaldi, *Ragione e verità: Filosofia della religione e metafisica dell'essere* (Rome: Aracne, 2010), 496.

    7. Cf. Deland Anderson, "The Death of God and Hegel's System of Philosophy," *Sophia* 35, no. 1 (1996): 37.

8. Jaeschke, "Philosophical Theology and Philosophy of Religion," 2. Cf. Martin J. De Nys, "Philosophical Thinking and the Claims of Religion, in Kolb, ed., *New Perspectives on Hegel's Philosophy of Religion*, 19: "Hegel affirms the Enlightenment position regarding the self-determining character of reason. At the same time he criticizes the Enlightenment insofar as it terminates in a philosophy of reflection and a one-sided subjectivity whose consequence is the position that God is unknown and unknowable, a philosophical 'death of God.'"

9. Williams, "The Inseparability of Love and Anguish," 135.

10. Cf. von der Luft, "Sources of Nietzsche's 'God is dead!,'" 266.

11. "This Idea came into the world through Christianity, according to which the individual as such has an infinite value since it is the object and aim of God's love, destined to stand in its absolute relationship with God as mind, and to have this mind dwelling in himself, i.e. man in himself is destined to supreme freedom." E III, 10:301/215.

12. John Burbidge, "Man, God, and Death in Hegel's *Phenomenology*," *Philosophy and Phenomenological Research* 42, no. 2 (1981): 194–95. To the best of my knowledge, this is a thought that no other Hegel commentator has subsequently worked upon.

13. Jaeschke, "Philosophical Theology and Philosophy of Religion," 3.

14. Ibid. Cf. also Hans Küng, *The Incarnation of God: An Introduction to Hegel's Theological Thought as Prolegomena to a Future Christology*, trans. R. Stephens (New York: Crossroad, 1987), 168: "there is no going back on the Enlightenment. [. . .] the old naïve immediacy of faith has been a thing of the past."

15. Cf. Anderson and Bell, *Kant and Theology*, 33. For an in-depth analysis of the question of the divinity of Christ in Kant's religion, see Palmquist, "Could Kant's Jesus Be God?"

16. Miller translates *Gegenständlichkeit* as "objective existence." Here I follow Pinkard's new translation of the *Phenomenology of Spirit*, available at http://terrypinkard.weebly.com/phenomenology-of-spirit-page.html.

17. Jaeschke, "Philosophical Theology and Philosophy of Religion," 16.

18. Cf. Anderson, *Hegel's Speculative Good Friday*, 21.

19. John Burbidge, "Is Hegel a Christian?," in Kolb, ed., *New Perspectives on Hegel's Philosophy of Religion*, 95.

20. Ibid.

21. Cf. Lauer, *Hegel's Concept of God*, 319. My interpretation is similar to Lauer's on this point, with the difference being that I see a causal connection between the two main issues that clearly constitute the backbone of Hegel's account of the death of God in the *Phenomenology*—that is, the overcoming of abstraction is possible *because* it is the death of the mediator.

22. Jaeschke translates *Vorstellung* as "picture." I have altered the translation for the sake of consistency with my translation of *Vorstellung* in the passages from the *Phenomenology*.

23. "Love entails a supreme surrender of oneself in the other, and the death of God in the death of Christ is the highest expression of divine love." Hodgson, *Hegel and Christian Theology*, 171.

24. The hymn in question is "Ein trauriger Grabgesang." See von der Luft, "Sources of Nietzsche's 'God is dead!,'" 263–64.

25. Williams, "Theology and Tragedy," 51.

26. Hodgson, *Hegel and Christian Theology*, 173.

27. Williams, "Theology and Tragedy," 50.

28. Cf. William Franke, "The Deaths of God in Hegel and Nietzsche and the Crisis of Values in Secular Modernity and Post-secular Postmodernity," *Religion and the Arts* 11 (2007): 217.

29. Jena aphorism, quoted in Friedhelm Nicolin, "Unbekannte Aphorismen Hegels aus der Jenaer Period," *Hegel-Studien* 4 (1967): 16.

30. Küng, *The Incarnation of God*, 168.

31. O'Regan continues: "The double divestment of death concerns at one and the same time: (1) the divestment of finitude; (2) the divestment of the eternally complete, invulnerable, apathetic divine" (O'Regan, *The Heterodox Hegel*, 205).

32. Hodgson, *Hegel and Christian Theology*, 255.

33. Williams, "Theology and Tragedy," 53. On the gratuitousness of the kenotic act, see also Paolo Diego Bubbio, "Sacrifice in Hegel's *Phenomenology of Spirit*," *British Journal for the History of Philosophy* 20, no. 4 (2012): 797–815.

34. Williams, *Recognition*, 233.

35. Williams, "The Inseparability of Love and Anguish," 137.

36. Ibid., 138.

37. Helmut Thielicke, *The Evangelical Faith*, trans. G. W. Bromiley (Grand Rapids: Eerdmans, 1974), vol. I, 259–64. Anderson also agrees that "[w]hen taken as a formal proposition, this sentence expresses a contradiction," but he adds that "if taken speculatively, it bespeaks a basic truth of reason. For, as a speculative sentence, the words, God is dead, transcend and cancel the simple A = A of traditional understanding, and they do so in such a way as to call most urgently for further explication of the subject-predicate identity" (Anderson, *Hegel's Speculative Good Friday*, 25).

38. Beiser, *Hegel*, 138.

39. Ibid. Inwood also defines Hegel's use of the death of God as "metaphorical," but he suggests that it represents the *Aufhebung* of our "immediate consciousness," which is "in part effected by the prospect of actual death," thus suggesting a slightly stronger metaphorical reading than the one suggested by Beiser. Inwood, *A Hegel Dictionary*, 72.

40. Pinkard, *Hegel: A Biography*, 591.

41. Ibid., 219. Redding agrees with Pinkard that the death of God is the death of the old metaphysical God (Redding, "Some Metaphysical Implications of Hegel's Theology," 149). Jaeschke also seems to express a similar opinion, when

he interprets the death of God as "the death of the personal God of traditional philosophical theology." Walter Jaeschke, "Philosophy of Religion after the Death of God," in Desmond, Onnasch, and Cruysberghs, eds., *Philosophy and Religion in German Idealism*, 18.

42. Redding, "Some Metaphysical Implications of Hegel's Theology."

43. Williams, "The Inseparability of Love and Anguish," 140. A similar "semi-realist" position is held by Anderson, *Hegel's Speculative Good Friday*, xiii. A less sophisticated position along the same lines is that of Hodgson, who claims that "[d]eath is as real for God as it is for finite creatures; but it is not the final or most powerful reality" (Hodgson, *Hegel and Christian Theology*, 175).

44. Thomas J. J. Altizer, *The Gospel of Christian Atheism* (London: Collins, 1967), 55–75.

45. "There can be no reconciliation without prior disunion and disruption and the most agonizing 'disruption' is the death of God." Williams, "The Inseparability of Love and Anguish," 134.

46. Here I am not suggesting that Pinkard's interpretation of Hegel's philosophy of religion is "anthropological"; actually, I think that Pinkard is moving away from a standard anthropological reading of Hegel, especially with his most recent book, *Hegel's Naturalism*.

47. "[. . .] what dies is the abstraction of the divine being that is devoid of self or subject. God is not the abstract immutable of the unhappy consciousness. For Hegel, God's self-divestment means that God freely renounces abstract, exclusive *forsichsein* and enters into relation and community. Hegel departs from the traditional monarchial metaphor and the impassible divine that exclude divine community and suffering. [. . .] In that dissolution, the subject discovers itself, and this is the transition from substance to subject." Williams, "The Inseparability of Love and Anguish," 139.

48. Cf. Magee, *The Hegel Dictionary*, 239.

49. Williams, "Theology and Tragedy," 49.

50. Ibid., 52. Cf. also Williams, *Recognition*, 234.

51. Williams, "Theology and Tragedy," 53.

52. English translation by Quentin Lauer, who comments: "Only if man seeks to achieve in himself the image of the triune God can 'reconciliation' have any 'objective' meaning whatever" (Lauer, *Hegel's Concept of God*, 319).

53. Williams, "The Inseparability of Love and Anguish," 137. Cf. also Williams, *Recognition*, 232; and Williams, *Tragedy, Recognition, and the Death of God*, 237.

54. Jüngel addresses the problem of the separation of Christianity and metaphysics, although he seems dubious about Hegel actually performing that separation. See Jüngel, *God as the Mystery of the World*, 47.

55. This expression has been used by Deranty to refer to Redding's interpretation of Hegel. See Deranty, "Hegel's Metaphysics as Hermeneutics," 80–83.

56. Jüngel, *God as the Mystery of the World*, 74.

57. Williams, "The Inseparability of Love and Anguish," 140.
58. Ibid.
59. Redding, *Continental Idealism*, 148.
60. The speech act of mutual forgiveness, says Hegel, "is God manifested in the midst of those who know themselves in the form of pure knowledge" (PG, 3:494/409). Cf. Redding and Bubbio, "Hegel and the Ontological Argument for the Existence of God," 18.
61. Cf. Franke, "The Deaths of God in Hegel and Nietzsche."

## Chapter 7. Beyond Subjectivism

1. Jeff Malpas, *Heidegger's Topology: Being, Place, World* (Cambridge: MIT Press, 2006), 356.
2. Longuenesse, "Kant's 'I Think' versus Descartes' 'I Am a Thing That Thinks,'" 10.
3. Magee, *The Hegel Dictionary*, 90.
4. Redding, *Continental Idealism*, 109.
5. Cf. Janet Radcliffe Richards, *Human Nature after Darwin: A Philosophical Introduction* (London and New York: Routledge, 2000).
6. I borrow this expression from Michelle Kosch, who uses it, in the context of her discussion of Kant's and Kierkegaard's philosophical agenda, not in relation to the conception of the "I" but more broadly in relation to "our metaphysical views (including our conception of the divine and its relation to the human)." See Kosch, *Freedom and Reason in Kant, Schelling, and Kierkegaard*, 140.
7. Cf. Inwood, *A Hegel Dictionary*, 121.
8. Kant, *Critique of Pure Reason*, Bxvi/110.
9. The translation is based, as always in this book, on Brinkmann and Dahlstrom's 2010 version, but it is somewhat modified, as I believe certain terms are better translated in the Wallace version (Oxford: Oxford University Press, 2nd ed., 1975), 67–68.
10. Cf. Lee Braver, *A Thing of This World: A History of Continental Anti-Realism* (Evanston: Northwestern University Press, 2007), 83. Cf. also Mark C. Taylor, *Journeys to Selfhood: Hegel and Kierkegaard* (New York: Fordham University Press, 2000), 44. Taylor comments: "If subject and object remain antithetical, the object becomes an unknowable other, and the subject 'a noumenal monad,' a 'fixed noumenal unit conditioned by infinite opposition.'"
11. Stern, *Hegel, Kant, and the Structure of the Object*, 115.
12. Paul Guyer, "Absolute Idealism and the Rejection of Kantian Dualism," in *The Cambridge Companion to German Idealism*, ed. K. Ameriks (Cambridge: Cambridge University Press, 2000), 37.
13. Inwood, *A Hegel Dictionary*, 205.

14. This has been suggested by Mark C. Taylor: "From Hegel's point of view, Kant's failure to unite subject and object leads to a subjectivism that makes knowledge, *sensu eminentiori*, impossible. [. . .] If subject and object remain antithetical, the object becomes an unknowable other" (Taylor, *Journeys to Selfhood*, 44).

15. I have slightly modified the Harris-Cerf translation. The emphasis is mine.

16. Johann Gottlieb Fichte, *The Science of Knowledge*, ed. and trans. P. Heath and J. Lachs (Cambridge: Cambridge University Press, 1982), 8–9 (I/426). Cf. di Giovanni, Introduction, xxxix.

17. Inwood, *A Hegel Dictionary*, 121.

18. Ibid., 122.

19. "Abstract" and "immediate" may appear to be contradictory terms, but in Hegel's view, they are not. As di Giovanni explains, "On Hegel's analysis of both Kant and Fichte, the problem is that the 'I' that figures so prominently in their theories is too abstract a product of conceptualization. It means to say much but in fact says nothing" (di Giovanni, Introduction, xxxiv). Fichte then takes this product of conceptualized abstraction and presents it as "immediate"—and it is supposed to be immediate because it is prior to any conceptualization. But even the "I = I" requires explanatory mediation or, if taken as immediate, it is equivalent to pure being. See E I, 8:182ff./136ff. See also Inwood, *A Hegel Dictionary*, 122.

20. Magee, *The Hegel Dictionary*, 215.

21. Ibid.

22. See ibid.

23. Inwood, *A Hegel Dictionary*, 122.

24. Dennis Schmidt, *The Ubiquity of the Finite: Hegel, Heidegger, and the Entitlements of Philosophy* (Cambridge, MA, and London: MIT Press, 1988), 50.

25. Inwood, *A Hegel Dictionary*, 122.

26. This conception is illustrated by di Giovanni by using the (Fichtean) notion of facticity: "This is not to say that Hegel does not recognize that facticity is an irreducible element of experience. This is the lesson that he had indeed learned from Fichte. Hegel's canonical term for it [. . .] is 'immediacy.' But the point is that such a facticity, this immediacy of experience, ought to be absorbed conceptually even as facticity. It has to be comprehended positively. To avoid Fichte's inevitable slide from logic into rhetoric, one needs a kind of conceptualization that permeates that facticity" (di Giovanni, Introduction, xxxiv–xxxv).

27. See for instance Kant, *Critique of Pure Reason*, xxvii–xxviii.

28. Cf. Bubbio and Redding, "Hegel and the Ontological Argument for the Existence of God," 471ff.

29. Cf. Inwood, *A Hegel Dictionary*, 123.

30. Ibid.

31. Brandom appears to suggest such an instrumentalist view when he insists that "[f]or Hegel all transcendental constitution is social institution" (Brandom, *Tales of the Mighty Dead*, 216).

32. Heidegger perfectly captures Hegel's position on this issue by commenting: "The subject has its essence in a representational relation to the object." Martin Heidegger, *Off the Beaten Track*, ed. and trans. J. Young and K. Haynes (Cambridge: Cambridge University Press, 2002), 99.

33. As Gadamer observes, it was the dialectic that enabled Hegel "to go beyond the subjectivity of the subject and to think mind as objective." Hans-Georg Gadamer, "*Destruktion* and Deconstruction," in *Heidegger Reexamined: Language and the Critique of Subjectivity*, ed. H. Dreyfus and M. Wrathall (London and New York: Routledge, 2002), 78.

34. Ibid., 104.

## Chapter 8. The Relevance of Hegel's Philosophy of Religion Today

1. Ameriks, *Kant and the Historical Turn*, 242.

2. I borrow this expression from Hodgson, who writes: "Hegel's God is not the wholly other but the whole of wholes, the universal that embraces all otherness and difference. As spirit God is both substance and subject, power and person, life and mind, essence and existence" (Hodgson, *Hegel and Christian Theology*, 264).

3. Thomas Dixon, "Scientific Atheism as a Faith Tradition," *Studies in History and Philosophy of Biological and Biomedical Sciences* 33 (2002): 337–59.

4. Tom Sorrell, *Scientism: Philosophy and the Infatuation with Science* (London and New York: Routledge, 1991), 1, quoted in Dixon, "Scientific Atheism as a Faith Tradition," 342.

5. Dixon, "Scientific Atheism as a Faith Tradition," 342. As Dixon stresses, "This corresponds roughly to the fifth of Stenmark's five sorts of scientism, which he calls 'redemptive scientism,' that is, 'the view that science alone is sufficient for dealing with our existential questions or for creating a world view by which he could live." Cf. Mikael Stenmark, "What Is Scientism?," *Religious Studies* 33, no. 1 (1997): 31.

6. David William Bebbington, *Evangelicalism in Modern Britain: A History from the 1730s to the 1980s* (London: Unwin Hyman, 1989).

7. "Top Questions—1. What Is the Theory of Intelligent Design?," Discovery Institute, http://www.discovery.org/csc/topQuestions.php, accessed May 29, 2015. The Discovery Institute's Center for Science and Culture is the hub of the intelligent design movement. Thinkers such as William Lane Craig and Robert Koons seem to be committed to this notion (the center's website lists both Craig and Koons as fellows).

8. Naturalists tend to maintain that methodological naturalism does not necessarily entail metaphysical naturalism. Cf. Barbara Forrest, "Methodological

Naturalism and Philosophical Naturalism: Clarifying the Connection," *Philo* 3, no. 2 (2000): 7–29. Forrest examines the question of whether methodological naturalism entails philosophical (ontological or metaphysical) naturalism. She concludes that the relationship between methodological and philosophical naturalism, while not one of logical entailment, is the only reasonable metaphysical conclusion.

9. Quentin Smith, "The Metaphilosophy of Naturalism," *Philo* 4, no. 2 (2001): 195–215.

10. Ibid., 207.

11. Jaeschke, "Philosophical Theology and Philosophy of Religion," 17.

12. Cf. Ludwig Heyde, "The Unsatisfied Enlightenment: Faith and Pure Insight in Hegel's *Phenomenology of Spirit*," in Desmond, Onnasch, and Cruysberghs, eds., *Philosophy and Religion in German Idealism*, 71ff. Heyde argues quite convincingly that, for Hegel, the conception of God possessed by faith hardly differs from the deism of the Enlightenment.

13. Jaeschke, "Philosophy of Religion after the Death of God," 15ff.

14. I am not the first interpreter to attribute to Hegel a hermeneutic or quasi-hermeneutic philosophical style. Cf. Redding, *Hegel's Hermeneutics*; and Maurizio Pagano, *Hegel: La religione e l'ermeneutica del concetto* (Naples: ESI, 1992), which convincingly argues for a hermeneutic approach to Hegel's account of religion.

15. Paul Ricoeur, "Phenomenology and Hermeneutics," in *From Text to Action: Essays in Hermeneutics II*, trans. K. Blarney and John B. Thompson (Evanston: Northwestern University Press, 1991), 30.

16. Ibid.

17. I am grateful to Paul Redding for suggesting this example.

# Bibliography

Adams, Nicholas. *Eclipse of Grace: Divine and Human Action in Hegel.* Malden: Wiley-Blackwell, 2013.
Altizer, Thomas J. J. *The Gospel of Christian Atheism.* London: Collins, 1967.
Ameriks, Karl. *Kant and the Historical Turn: Philosophy as Critical Interpretation.* Oxford: Oxford University Press, 2006.
Anderson, Deland S. "The Death of God and Hegel's System of Philosophy." *Sophia* 35, no. 1 (1996): 35–61.
———. *Hegel's Speculative Good Friday: The Death of God in Philosophical Perspective.* Atlanta: Scholars Press, 1996.
Anderson, Pamela Sue, and Jordan Bell. *Kant and Theology.* London and New York: Continuum, 2010.
Auerbach, Erich. *Mimesis: The Representation of Reality in Western Literature.* Trans. Willard R. Trask. Princeton: Princeton University Press. 2003. First published 1953.
———. *Scenes from the Drama of European Literature.* Minneapolis: University of Minnesota Press, 1984.
Banham, Gary. *Kant's Practical Philosophy: From Critique to Doctrine.* Houndmills: Palgrave, 2003.
Bebbington, David William. *Evangelicalism in Modern Britain: A History from the 1730s to the 1980s.* London: Unwin Hyman, 1989.
Beiser, Frederick C. "Dark Days: Anglophone Scholarship since the 1960s." In *German Idealism: Contemporary Perspectives*, ed. Espen Hammer, 15–29. London and New York: Routledge, 2007.
———. *German Idealism. The Struggle against Subjectivism, 1781–1801.* Cambridge: Harvard University Press, 2002.
———. *Hegel.* New York and London: Routledge, 2005.
———. "Moral Faith and the Highest Good." In *The Cambridge Companion to Kant and Modern Philosophy*, ed. Paul Guyer, 588–629. Cambridge: Cambridge University Press, 2007.
Berthold-Bond, Daniel. *Hegel's Grand Synthesis. A Study of Being, Thought, and History.* Albany: State University of New York Press, 1989.

Bird, Graham. *The Revolutionary Kant: A Commentary on the Critique of Pure Reason*. Chicago and La Salle: Open Court, 2006.

Bloesh, Donald G. *God the Almighty: Power, Wisdom, Holiness, Love*. Downers Grove: InterVarsity Press, 2005.

Brandom, Robert. *Tales of the Mighty Dead: Historical Essays in the Metaphysics of Intentionality*. Cambridge: Harvard University Press, 2002.

Braver, Lee. *A Thing of This World: A History of Continental Anti-Realism*. Evanston: Northwestern University Press, 2007.

Bubbio, Paolo Diego. "Sacrifice in Hegel's *Phenomenology of Spirit*." *British Journal for the History of Philosophy* 20, no. 4 (2012): 797–815.

———. *Sacrifice in the Post-Kantian Tradition: Perspectivism, Intersubjectivity, and Recognition*. Albany: State University of New York Press, 2014.

Burbidge, John. *Hegel on Logic and Religion: The Reasonableness of Christianity*. Albany: State University of New York Press, 1992.

———. "Is Hegel a Christian?" In *New Perspectives on Hegel's Philosophy of Religion*, ed. David Kolb, 93–108. Albany: State University of New York Press, 1992.

———. "Man, God, and Death in Hegel's Phenomenology." *Philosophy and Phenomenological Research* 42, no. 2 (1981): 183–96.

———. "The Relevance of Hegel's Logic." *Cosmos and History: The Journal of Natural and Social Philosophy* 3, no. 2–3 (2007): 211–21.

Buterin, Damion. "Hegel, Recognition, and Religion." *Review of Metaphysics* 64, no. 4 (2011): 789–821.

Byrne, Peter. *Kant on God*. Aldershot: Ashgate, 2007.

Calton, Patricia Marie. *Hegel's Metaphysics of God: The Ontological Proof as the Development of a Trinitarian Divine Ontology*. Aldershot: Ashgate, 2001.

Caygill, Howard. *A Kant Dictionary*. London: Blackwell, 2000.

Charity, Alan C. *Events and Their Afterlife: The Dialectics of Christian Typology in the Bible and Dante*. Cambridge: Cambridge University Press, 1966.

Cicovacki, Predrag. *Between Truth and Illusion: Kant at the Crossroads of Modernity*. Lanham: Rowman & Littlefield, 2002.

Copleston, Frederick. *A History of Philosophy*. New York: Image Books, 1965.

Dallmayr, Fred R. *G. W. F. Hegel: Modernity and Politics*. Lanham: AltaMira, 2000.

De Benedictis, Raffaele. "Dante's *Epistola a Can Grande*: Allegory, Discourse, and Their Semiotic Implications." *Quaderni d'italianistica* 31, no. 1 (2010): 3–42.

de Boer, Karin. "Hegel's Account of Contradiction in the *Science of Logic* Reconsidered." *Journal of the History of Philosophy* 48, no. 3 (2010): 345–73.

De Nys, Martin J. "Philosophical Thinking and the Claims of Religion." In *New Perspectives on Hegel's Philosophy of Religion*, ed. David Kolb, 19–26. Albany: State University of New York Press, 1992.

Deranty, Jean-Paul. "Hegel's Metaphysics as Hermeneutics." *Parrhesia* 11 (2011). Accessed May 1, 2015. http://parrhesiajournal.org/parrhesia11/parrhesia11_deranty.pdf.

Descartes, René. *Meditations on First Philosophy*. Trans. and ed. John Cottingham. Cambridge: Cambridge University Press, 1996.

Desmond, William. "Evil and Dialectic." In *New Perspectives on Hegel's Philosophy of Religion*, ed. David Kolb, 159–82. Albany: State University of New York Press, 1992.

———. *Hegel's God: A Counterfeit Double?* Aldershot: Ashgate, 2003.

———. "Religion and the Poverty of Philosophy." In *Philosophy and Religion in German Idealism*, ed. William Desmond, Ernst-Otto Onnasch, and Paul Cruysberghs, 105–33. New York: Kluwer Academic, 2004.

Dews, Peter. *The Idea of Evil*. Malden: Blackwell, 2008.

di Giovanni, George. *Freedom and Religion in Kant and His Immediate Successors: The Vocation of Humankind, 1774–1800*. Cambridge: Cambridge University Press, 2005.

———. Introduction to G. W. F. Hegel, *The Science of Logic*. Cambridge: Cambridge University Press, 2010.

Dixon, Thomas. "Scientific Atheism as a Faith Tradition." *Studies in History and Philosophy of Biological and Biomedical Sciences* 33 (2002): 337–59.

Dowson, John David. *Christian Figural Reading and the Fashioning of Identity*. Berkeley: University of California Press, 2001.

Dudley, Will. *Hegel, Nietzsche, and Philosophy: Thinking Freedom*. Cambridge: Cambridge University Press, 2002.

Fackenheim, Emil. "Kant and Radical Evil." *University of Toronto Quarterly* 23 (1954): 339–53.

Fichte, Johann Gottlieb. *The Science of Knowledge*. Ed. and trans. Peter Heath and John Lachs. Cambridge: Cambridge University Press, 1982.

Firestone, Chris L., and Nathan Jacobs. *In Defense of Kant's Religion*. Bloomington: Indiana University Press, 2008.

Foldes, Ken S. R. *Hegel and the Solution to Our Postmodern World Crisis: From Nihilism to Kingdom Come; Essays*. Philadelphia: Xlibris, 2003.

Forrest, Barbara. "Methodological Naturalism and Philosophical Naturalism: Clarifying the Connection." *Philo* 3, no. 2 (2000): 7–29.

Foucault, Michel. "The Discourse on Language." Appendix to *The Archeology of Knowledge*. Trans. A. M. Sheridan Smith. New York: Pantheon Books, 1972.

Franke, William. "The Deaths of God in Hegel and Nietzsche and the Crisis of Values in Secular Modernity and Post-secular Postmodernity." *Religion and the Arts* 11 (2007): 214–41.

Frierson, Patrick R. *Freedom and Anthropology in Kant's Moral Philosophy*. Cambridge: Cambridge University Press, 2003.

Gadamer, Hans-Georg. "*Destruktion* and Deconstruction." In *Heidegger Reexamined: Language and the Critique of Subjectivity*, ed. Hubert Dreyfus and Mark Wrathall, 72–83. London and New York: Routledge, 2002.

———. *Philosophical Hermeneutics*. Trans. and ed. D. E. Linge. Berkeley: University of California Press, 1976.

———. *Truth and Method*. Trans. J. Weinsheimer and D. G. Marshall. New York: Continuum, 1997.

Geuss, Raymond. *Outside Ethics*. Princeton: Princeton University Press, 2005.

Gjesdal, Kristin. *Gadamer and the Legacy of German Idealism*. Cambridge: Cambridge University Press, 2009.

Grenberg, Jeanine. *Kant and the Ethics of Humility. A Story of Dependence, Corruption, and Virtue*. Cambridge: Cambridge University Press, 2005.

Griffioen, Sander. "The Finite Does Not Hinder: Hegel's Philosophy of Christian Religion Placed against the Backdrop of Kant's Theory of the Sublime." In *Philosophy and Religion in German Idealism*, ed. William Desmond, Ernst-Otto Onnasch, and Paul Cruysberghs, 111–24. New York: Kluwer Academic, 2004.

Guyer, Paul. "Absolute Idealism and the Rejection of Kantian Dualism." In *The Cambridge Companion to German Idealism*, ed. Karl Ameriks, 37–56. Cambridge: Cambridge University Press, 2000.

Hammer, Espen. Introduction. In *German Idealism: Contemporary Perspectives*, ed. Espen Hammer, 1–15. London and New York: Routledge, 2007.

Hanna, Robert. *Kant, Science, and Human Nature*. Oxford: Oxford University Press, 2006.

Hare, John E. *The Moral Gap: Kantian Ethics, Human Limits, and God's Assistance*. Oxford: Oxford University Press, 1966.

Harris, Henry S. *Hegel: Phenomenology and System*. Indianapolis: Hackett, 1995.

———. *Hegel's Ladder*. Indianapolis: Hackett, 1997.

———. "The Young Hegel and the Postulates of Practical Reason." In *Hegel and the Philosophy of Religion: The Wofford Symposium*, ed. Darrel E. Christensen, 61–68. The Hague: Nijhoff, 1970.

Hartmann, Klaus. "Hegel: A Non-Metaphysical View." In *Hegel: A Collection of Critical Essays*, ed. Alasdair MacIntyre, 101–24. Notre Dame: University of Notre Dame Press, 1976.

Heidegger, Martin. *Off the Beaten Track*. Ed. and trans. J. Young and K. Haynes. Cambridge: Cambridge University Press, 2002.

Henrich, Dieter. "Some Historical Presuppositions of Hegel's System." In *Hegel and the Philosophy of Religion: The Wofford Symposium*, ed. Darrel E. Christensen, 25–44. The Hague: Nijhoff, 1970.

Heyde, Ludwig. "The Unsatisfied Enlightenment: Faith and Pure Insight in Hegel's *Phenomenology of Spirit*." In *Philosophy and Religion in German Idealism*, ed. William Desmond, Ernst-Otto Onnasch, and Paul Cruysberghs, 71–80. New York: Kluwer Academic, 2004.

Hodgson, Peter C. Editorial Introduction to G. W. F. Hegel, *Lectures on the Philosophy of Religion*, vol. 3, 1–57. Berkeley and Los Angeles: University of California Press, 1985.

———. *Hegel and Christian Theology: A Reading of the Lectures on the Philosophy of Religion.* Oxford and New York: Oxford University Press, 2005.
Horstmann, Rolf-Peter. *Wahrheit aus dem Begriff: Eine Einführung in Hegel.* Frankfurt am Main: Hain, 1990.
Houlgate, Stephen. *Hegel, Nietzsche and the Critique of Metaphysics.* Cambridge: Cambridge University Press, 1986.
———. "Religion, Morality and Forgiveness in Hegel's Philosophy." In *Philosophy and Religion in German Idealism,* ed. William Desmond, Ernst-Otto Onnasch, and Paul Cruysberghs, 81–110. New York: Kluwer Academic, 2004.
Inwood, Michael. *A Hegel Dictionary.* Oxford: Blackwell, 1992.
Jaeschke, Walter. "Philosophical Theology and Philosophy of Religion." In *New Perspectives on Hegel's Philosophy of Religion,* ed. David Kolb, 1–18. Albany: State University of New York Press, 1992.
———. "Philosophy of Religion after the Death of God." In *Philosophy and Religion in German Idealism,* ed. William Desmond, Ernst-Otto Onnasch, and Paul Cruysberghs, 1–20. New York: Kluwer Academic, 2004.
———. *Reason in Religion: The Foundations of Hegel's Philosophy of Religion.* Ed. J. M. Stewart and P. C. Hodgson. Berkeley: University of California Press, 1990.
Jüngel, Eberhard. *God as the Mystery of the World.* Trans. Darrell L. Guder. Grand Rapids: Eerdmans, 1983.
Kant, Immanuel. *Anthropologie in pragmatischer Hinsicht.* Trans. R. B. Louden, ed. M. Kuehn, *Anthropology from a Pragmatic Point of View.* Cambridge: Cambridge University Press, 2006.
———. *Grundlegung zur Metaphysik der Sitten.* Trans. M. Gregor, *Groundwork of the Metaphysic of Morals.* Cambridge: Cambridge University Press, 1997.
———. *Handschriftlicher Nachlaß.* Trans. C. Bowman, P. Guyer, and F. Rauscher, ed. P. Guyer, *Notes and Fragments.* Cambridge: Cambridge University Press, 2005.
———. *Kritik der praktischen Vernunft.* Trans. M. J. Gregor, *Critique of Practical Reason.* New York: Macmillan, 1996.
———. *Kritik der reinen Vernunft.* Trans. and ed. P. Guyer and A. W. Wood, *Critique of Pure Reason.* Cambridge: Cambridge University Press, 1998.
———. *Kritik der Urteilskraft.* Trans. W. S. Pluhar, *Critique of Judgment.* Indianapolis: Hackett, 1987.
———. *Logik.* Trans. and ed. J. Michael Young, *Lectures on Logic.* Cambridge: Cambridge University Press, 1992.
———. *Metaphysik der Sitten.* Trans. M. Gregor, *The Metaphysics of Morals.* Cambridge: Cambridge University Press, 1991.
———. *Metaphysik.* Trans. and ed. Karl Ameriks and Steve Naragon, *Lectures on Metaphysics.* Cambridge: Cambridge University Press, 1997.
———. *Der Streit der Fakultäten.* Trans. and ed. A. W. Wood and G. di Giovanni, *The Conflict of the Faculties,* in *Religion and Natural Theology.* Cambridge: Cambridge University Press, 1996.

———. *Die Religion innerhalb der Grenzen der bloßen Vernunft*. Trans. W. S. Pluhar, ed. S. Palmquist, *Religion within the Bounds of Bare Reason*. Indianapolis: Hackett, 2009.

———. *Über das Mißlingen aller Philosophischen Versuche in der Theodicee*. Trans. George di Giovanni, *On the Miscarriage of All Philosophical Trials in Theodicy*, in *Religion and Rational Theology*. Cambridge: Cambridge University Press, 1996.

———. *Über ein vermeintes Recht aus Menschenliebe zu lügen*. Trans. and ed. Mary J. Gregor, *On a Supposed Right to Lie from Philanthropy*, in *Practical Philosophy*. Cambridge: Cambridge University Press, 1996.

Kaufmann, Walter. *Hegel: A Reinterpretation*. New York: Anchor Books, 1966.

Kosch, Michelle. *Freedom and Reason in Kant, Schelling, and Kierkegaard*. Oxford: Oxford University Press, 2006.

Kreines, James. "Between the Bounds of Experience and Divine Intellect: Kant's Epistemic Limits and Hegel's Ambitions." *Inquiry* 50, no. 3 (2007): 306–34.

———. "Hegel: Metaphysics without Pre-Critical Monism." *Bulletin of the Hegel Society of Great Britain* 57/58 (2008): 48–70.

———. "Hegel's Metaphysics: Changing the Debate." *Philosophy Compass* 1.5 (2006): 466–80.

Küng, Hans. *The Incarnation of God: An Introduction to Hegel's Theological Thought as Prolegomena to a Future Christology*. Trans. R. Stephens. New York: Crossroad, 1987.

Larrimore, Mark. "Autonomy and the Invention of Theodicy." In *New Essays on the History of Autonomy*, ed. Natalie Brender and Larry Krasnoff, 61–91. Cambridge: Cambridge University Press, 2004.

Lauer, Quentin. *Hegel's Concept of God*. Albany: State University of New York Press, 1982.

Leftow, Brian. "The Ontological Argument." In *The Oxford Handbook of Philosophy of Religion*, ed. William J. Wainwright, 80–115. Oxford: Oxford University Press, 2005.

Leibniz, Gottfried Wilhelm. *New Essay Concerning Human Understanding*. Trans. A. Langley. New York: Macmillan, 1896.

Lewis, Thomas A. "Beyond the Totalitarian: Ethics and the Philosophy of Religion in Recent Hegel Scholarship." *Religion Compass* 2 (4/2008): 556–74.

———. *Religion, Modernity, and Politics in Hegel*. Oxford: Oxford University Press, 2011.

Lindsay, Alexander Dunlop. *Kant*. Westport: Greenwood Press, 1970.

Longuenesse, Beatrice. *Hegel's Critique of Metaphysics*. Cambridge: Cambridge University Press, 2007.

———. "Kant's 'I Think' versus Descartes' 'I Am a Thing That Thinks.'" In *Kant and the Early Moderns*, ed. Daniel Garber and Beatrice Longuenesse, 9–31. Princeton: Princeton University Press, 2008.

Louden, Robert B. "Making the Law Visible: The Role of Examples in Kant's Ethics." In *Kant's Groundwork of the Metaphysics of Morals: A Critical Guide*, ed. Jens Timmermann. Cambridge: Cambridge University Press, 2009.

MacKintosh, Hugh Ross. *Types of Modern Theology*. London: Nisbet, 1937.

Magee, Glenn Alexander. *The Hegel Dictionary*. London: Continuum, 2010.

Malpas, Jeff. *Heidegger's Topology: Being, Place, World*. Cambridge: MIT Press, 2006.

Matthews, Gareth B. "The Ontological Argument." In *The Blackwell Guide to the Philosophy of Religion*, ed. William E. Mann, 81–102. Oxford: Blackwell, 2005.

Maydole, Robert E. "The Ontological Argument." In *The Blackwell Companion to Natural Theology*, ed. William Lane Craig and James P. Moreland, 553–92. Oxford: Blackwell, 2009.

McCammon, Christopher. "Overcoming Deism: Hope Incarnate in Kant's Rational Religion." In *Kant and the New Philosophy of Religion*, ed. Chris L. Firestone and Stephen R. Palmquist. Bloomington and Indianapolis: Indiana University Press, 2006.

McGrath, Alister E. *Science and Religion: An Introduction*. Oxford: Wiley-Blackwell, 1999.

Michalson, Gordon E., Jr. *Fallen Freedom: Kant on Radical Evil and Moral Regeneration*. Cambridge: Cambridge University Press, 1990.

———. "Kant, the Bible, and the Recovery from Radical Evil." In *Kant's Anatomy of Evil*, ed. Sharon Anderson-Gold and Pablo Muchnik. Cambridge: Cambridge University Press, 2009.

Moggach, Douglas. *The New Hegelians: Politics and Philosophy in the Hegelian School*. Cambridge: Cambridge University Press, 2006.

Moors, Martin. "Kant on Religion in the Role of Moral Schematism." In *Philosophy and Religion in German Idealism*, ed. William Desmond, Ernst-Otto Onnasch, and Paul Cruysberghs, 21–33. New York: Kluwer Academic, 2005.

Nicolin, Friedhelm. "Unbekannte Aphorismen Hegels aus der Jenaer Period." *Hegel-Studien* 4 (1967): 9–19.

Nietzsche, Friedrich. *The Gay Science*. Ed. Bernard Williams, trans. Josefine Nauckhoff. Cambridge: Cambridge University Press 2001.

Nuzzo, Angelica. *Ideal Embodiment: Kant's Theory of Sensibility*. Bloomington: Indiana University Press, 2008.

———. *Memory, History, Justice in Hegel*. Basingstoke: Palgrave Macmillan, 2012.

O'Regan, Cyril. *The Heterodox Hegel*. Albany: State University of New York Press, 1994.

Oppy, Graham. *Ontological Arguments and Belief in God*. New York: Cambridge University Press, 1995.

———. "Ontological Arguments." In *The Stanford Encyclopedia of Philosophy* (Spring 2015 Edition), ed. Edward N. Zalta. http://plato.stanford.edu/archives/spr2015/entries/ontological-arguments/.

———. "The Ontological Argument." In *Philosophy of Religion: Classic and Contemporary Issues*, ed. Paul Copan and Chad Meister, 112–126. Oxford: Blackwell, 2007.

Origen. *De Principiis*. Trans. Frederick Crombie, in *Ante-Nicene Fathers*, vol. 4, ed. Alexander Roberts, James Donaldson, and A. Cleveland Coxe. Buffalo: Christian Literature, 1885.

Pagano, Maurizio. *Hegel: La religione e l'ermeneutica del concetto*. Naples: ESI, 1992.

———. "Hegel as an Interpreter of Religious Experience." In *Religion After Kant: God and Culture in the Idealist Era*, ed. by Paul Redding and Paolo Diego Bubbio, 47–70. Cambridge: Cambridge Scholars, 2012.

Palmquist, Stephen R. *Comprehensive Commentary on Kant's Religion within the Bounds of Bare Reason*. Chichester: Wiley-Blackwell, 2015.

———. "Could Kant's Jesus Be God?" *International Philosophical Quarterly* 52, no. 4 (2012): 421–37.

———. Introduction to Immanuel Kant, *Die Religion innerhalb der Grenzen der bloßen Vernunft*. Trans. Werner S. Pluhar, ed. Stephen Palmquist, *Religion within the Bounds of Bare Reason*. Indianapolis: Hackett, 2009.

———. *Kant's Critical Religion*. Aldershot: Ashgate, 2000.

———. "Kant's Ethics of Grace." *The Journal of Religion* 90 (4/2010): 530–53.

Peters, Curtis H. *Kant's Philosophy of Hope*. New York: Peter Lang, 1993.

Pinkard, Terry. *German Philosophy 1760–1860: The Legacy of Idealism*. Cambridge: Cambridge University Press, 2002.

———. *Hegel: A Biography*. Cambridge: Cambridge University Press, 2000.

———. *Hegel's Naturalism: Mind, Nature, and the Final Ends of Life*. Oxford: Oxford University Press, 2011.

———. *Hegel's Phenomenology: The Sociality of Reason*. Cambridge: Cambridge University Press, 1994.

Pippin, Robert B. *Hegel's Idealism: The Satisfaction of Self-Consciousness*. Cambridge: Cambridge University Press, 1989.

———. *Hegel's Practical Philosophy: Rational Agency as Ethical Life*. Cambridge: Cambridge University Press, 2008.

———. *Idealism as Modernism: Hegelian Variations*. Cambridge: Cambridge University Press, 1997.

———. *Modernism as a Philosophical Problem*. Cambridge: Cambridge University Press, 1991; 2nd ed. 1999.

Quinn, Philip L. "Christian Atonement and Kantian Justification." *Faith and Philosophy* 3 (4/1986): 440–62.

Railton, Peter G., and Gideon Rosen. "Realism." In *A Companion to Metaphysics*, ed. J. Kim and E. Sosa, 533–537. Oxford: Blackwell, 1995.

Reardon, Bernard M. G. *Kant as Philosophical Theologian*. Totowa: Barnes and Noble Books, 1988.

Redding, Paul. *Analytic Philosophy and the Return of Hegelian Thought*. Cambridge: Cambridge University Press, 2007.

———. *Continental Idealism: Leibniz to Nietzsche*. London and New York: Routledge, 2009.

———. "G. W. F. Hegel." In *The History of Western Philosophy of Religion*, ed. Graham Oppy and N. N. Trakakis, vol. 4, *Nineteenth-Century Philosophy of Religion*, 49–60. Oxford: Oxford University Press, 2009.

———. "Georg Wilhelm Friedrich Hegel." In *The Stanford Encyclopedia of Philosophy* (Spring 2014 Edition), ed. Edward N. Zalta. http://plato.stanford.edu/archives/spr2014/entries/hegel/.

———. "Hegel, Fichte and the Pragmatic Contexts of Moral Judgment." In *German Idealism. Contemporary Perspectives*, edited by Espen Hammer, 225–242. London and New York: Routledge, 2007.

———. "Hegel, Idealism and God: Philosophy as the Self-Correcting Appropriation of the Norms of Life and Thought." *Cosmos and History: The Journal of Natural and Social Philosophy* 3, no. 2–3 (2007): 16–31.

———. *Hegel's Hermeneutics*. Ithaca: Cornell University Press, 1996.

———. "Idealism: A Love (of Sophia) That Dare Not Speak Its Name." *Arts: The Journal of the Sydney University Arts Association* 29 (2007): 71–94.

———. "Kantian Origins: One Possible Path from Transcendental Idealism to a Post-Kantian Theology." In *Religion After Kant: God and Culture in the Idealist Era*, ed. Paolo Diego Bubbio and Paul Redding, 1–21. Cambridge: Cambridge Scholars, 2012.

———. "Mind of God, Point of View of Man, or Spirit of the World? Platonism and Organicism in the Thought of Kant and Hegel." Conference paper, Von Kant bis Hegel IV: Naturalism and Naturphilosophie, Concordia University, Montreal, October 11–12, 2008. http://www-personal.usyd.edu.au/~pred9095/Redding_Platonism-Organicism-Kant-Hegel.pdf. Accessed May 8, 2015.

———. "Some Metaphysical Implications of Hegel's Theology." *European Journal for Philosophy of Religion* 4, no. 1 (2012): 129–50.

———. "The Metaphysical and Theological Commitments of Idealism: Kant, Hegel, Hegelianism." In *Politics, Religion, and Art: Hegelian Debates*, ed. Douglas Moggach, 47–65. Evanston: Northwestern University Press, 2011.

———. "The Relevance of Hegel's 'Absolute Spirit' to Social Normativity." In *Recognition and Social Ontology*, ed. Heikki Ikäheimo and Arto Laitinen, 211–30. Leiden and Boston: Brill, 2011.

Redding, Paul, and Paolo Diego Bubbio. "Hegel and the Ontological Argument for the Existence of God." *Religious Studies* 50, no. 4 (2014): 465–86.

Reid, Jeffrey. "Objective Language and Scientific Truth in Hegel." In *Hegel and Language*, ed. J. O. Surber, 95–110. Albany: State University of New York Press, 2006.

Richards, Janet Radcliffe. *Human Nature after Darwin. A Philosophical Introduction*. London and New York: Routledge, 2000.
Ricoeur, Paul. "Phenomenology and Hermeneutics." In *From Text to Action: Essays in Hermeneutics II*, trans. Kathleen Blarney and John B. Thompson, 25–52. Evanston: Northwestern University Press, 1991.
Rinaldi, Giacomo. *Ragione e verità: Filosofia della religione e metafisica dell'essere*. Rome: Aracne, 2010.
Rockmore, Tom. "Hegel on Reason, Faith and Knowledge." In *Philosophy and Religion in German Idealism*, ed. William Desmond, Ernst-Otto Onnasch, and Paul Cruysberghs, 125–38. New York: Kluwer Academic, 2004.
Schickler, Jonael Angelus. *Metaphysics as Christology. An Odyssey of the Self from Kant and Hegel to Steiner*. Aldershot: Ashgate 2005.
Schleiermacher, Friedrich Daniel Ernst. *Der christliche Glaube nach den Grundsätzen der evangelischen Kirche im Zusammenhange dargestellt*, 1st ed., 2 vols. (Berlin: 1821–1822). Now in F. D. E. Schleiermacher, *Kritische Gesamtausgabe*, div. 1, vol. 7/1–2, ed. H. Peiter. Berlin and New York: De Gruyter, 1980.
Schmidt, Dennis. *The Ubiquity of the Finite: Hegel, Heidegger, and the Entitlements of Philosophy*. Cambridge, MA, and London: MIT Press, 1988.
Seung, T. K. *Kant: A Guide for the Perplexed*. Continuum 2007.
Siep, Ludwig. *Anerkennung als Prinzip der praktischen Philosophie*. Munich: Alber, 1979.
Singleton, Charles S. *"Commedia": Elements of Structure*. Cambridge: Harvard University Press, 1954.
Smith, Quentin. "The Metaphilosophy of Naturalism." *Philo* 4, no. 2 (2001): 195–215.
Sorrell, Tom. *Scientism: Philosophy and the Infatuation with Science*. London and New York: Routledge, 1991.
Speight, Allen. *Hegel, Literature and the Problem of Agency*. Cambridge: Cambridge University Press, 2001.
Stenmark, Mikael. "What Is Scientism?" *Religious Studies* 33, no. 1 (1997): 15–32.
Stern, Robert. "Freedom, Self-Legislation and Morality in Kant and Hegel: Constructivist vs. Realist Accounts." In *German Idealism: Contemporary Perspectives*, ed. Espen Hammer. London and New York: Routledge, 2007.
———. *Hegel, Kant, and the Structure of the Object*. London: Routledge: 1990.
———. *Hegelian Metaphysics*. Oxford: Oxford University Press, 2009.
———. *Routledge Philosophy Guidebook to Hegel and the Phenomenology of Spirit*. London: Routledge, 2002.
Storr, Gottlob Christian. *Annotationes quaedam theologicae ad philosophicam Kantii de religione doctrinam* (Tübingen: 1793); German translation *Bemerkungen über Kant's philosophische Religionslehre*, trans. Friedrich Gottlieb Süskind. Tübingen: J. G. Cotta, 1794; Reprint: Brussels: Culture et civilisation, 1968.
Surber, Jere O'Neill. Introduction. In *Hegel and Language*, ed. J. O. Surber. Albany: State University of New York Press, 2006.

Sussman, David. "'Unforgivable Sins': Revolution and Reconciliation in Kant." In *Kant's Anatomy of Evil*, ed. Sharon Anderson-Gold and Pablo Muchnik. Cambridge: Cambridge University Press, 2009.

Taylor, Charles. *Hegel*. Cambridge: Cambridge University Press, 1975.

Taylor, Mark C. *Journeys to Selfhood: Hegel and Kierkegaard*. New York: Fordham University Press, 2000.

Thielicke, Helmuth. *The Evangelical Faith*. Trans. Geoffrey W. Bromiley. Grand Rapids: Eerdmans, 1974.

Tholuck, August Gottreu. *Die Lehre von der Sunde und vom Versohner*, 2nd ed. Hamburg: Perthes, 1825.

Vassányi, Miklós. *Anima Mundi: The Rise of the World Soul Theory in Modern German Philosophy*. Dordrecht: Springer, 2011.

Vater, Michael. "Religion, Worldliness, and *Sittlichkeit*." In *New Perspectives on Hegel's Philosophy of Religion*, ed. David Kolb, 201–16. Albany: State University of New York Press, 1992.

von der Luft, Eric. "Sources of Nietzsche's 'God is dead!' and Its Meaning for Heidegger." *Journal of the History of Ideas* 45, no. 2 (1984): 263–276.

Wallace, Robert M. *Hegel's Philosophy of Reality, Freedom, and God*. Cambridge: Cambridge University Press, 2005.

Walsh, David. *The Modern Philosophical Revolution: The Luminosity of Existence*. Cambridge: Cambridge University Press, 2008.

Webb, Clement C. J. *Kant's Philosophy of Religion*. Oxford: Oxford University Press, 1926.

Wendte, Martin. *Gottmenschliche Einheit bei Hegel: Eine logische und theologische Untersuchung*. Berlin and New York: De Gruyter, 2007.

Westphal, Kenneth. *Hegel's Epistemology: A Philosophical Introduction to the "Phenomenology of Spirit."* Indianapolis: Hackett, 2003.

Wildt, Andreas. *Autonomie und Anerkennung: Hegels Moralitdtskritik im Lichte seiner Fichte-Rezeption*. Stuttgart: Klett-Cotta, 1982.

William of Ockham. *Philosophical Writings: A Selection*. Trans. Philotheus Boehner. Indianapolis: Bobbs-Merrill, 1964.

Williams, Robert R. *Hegel's Ethics of Recognition*. Berkeley: University of California Press, 1997.

———. "The Inseparability of Love and Anguish: Hegel's Theological Critique of Modernity." In *Hegel on Religion and Politics*, ed. Angelica Nuzzo, 133–156. Albany: State University of New York Press, 2013.

———. *Recognition: Fichte and Hegel on the Other*. Albany: State University of New York Press, 1992.

———. "Theology and Tragedy." In *New Perspectives on Hegel's Philosophy of Religion*, ed. David Kolb, 39–58. Albany: State University of New York Press, 1992.

———. *Tragedy, Recognition, and the Death of God: Studies in Hegel and Nietzsche.* Oxford: Oxford University Press, 2012.

Williamson, Raymond Keith. *Introduction to Hegel's Philosophy of Religion.* Albany: State University of New York Press, 1984.

Wood, Allen W. "Kant's Life and Works." In *A Companion to Kant*, ed. Graham Bird, 10–29. London: Blackwell, 2006.

———. *Kant's Moral Religion.* Ithaca and London: Cornell University Press, 1970.

Zupančič, Alenka. *Ethics of the Real: Kant, Lacan.* London and New York: Verso, 2000.

# Index

Aquinas, Thomas, 70
Alighieri, Dante, 68, 69–70
Altizer, Thomas, 137–138
Ameriks, Karl, 42
Anselm of Canterbury, 85–90, 95, 98
archetype (*Urbild*), 17–20, 22–25, 28–30, 39–40, 74, 144, 161 182n44
Aristotle, 41, 51, 61, 70, 88–89, 140
Auerbach, Erich, 69–73, 74, 77

Bebbington, David, 165
Beiser, Frederick, 2, 4, 5, 32, 41–42, 56, 58, 107, 137–138
Berkeley, George, Bishop of Cloyne, 42, 64
Böhme, Jacob, 50, 62, 115–117, 119, 153, 189n52, 193n30, 202n42
Brandom, Robert, 4
Burbidge, John, 129, 131–132

Calton, Patricia, 106
Charity, Alan C., 69
Christ, 13, 17–20, 21–25, 28–30, 47, 49–50, 51, 69, 72, 74–75, 81, 113–115, 128–129, 134, 182n44
Christianity, 61–62, 67, 75, 83, 95, 101, 105, 112, 129, 138–139, 158, 163
Concept (*Begriff*), 9, 10–11, 39, 42, 60, 62, 64, 73, 78–84, 89, 91–98, 100, 102, 108, 110, 116–119, 123–124, 140, 154–157, 162–163, 167–168, 191n4, 192n23, 196n76
conceptual realist interpretation, 5, 56–60, 108, 126, 151

*Darstellung*, 7, 13, 48, 107, 123–124, 192n26
Dawkins, Richard, 165
Descartes, René, 41, 70, 85, 86–87, 89–90, 98–99, 107, 123, 126, 147, 148–149, 164, 197n5, 204n5
Desmond, William, 5, 106, 120
di Giovanni, George, 38, 184n74, 209n26
Diez, Immanuel Carl, 34
Divestment (*Entäußerung*), 38, 49–51, 61–62, 102, 132–136, 140, 164, 207n47. *See also* kenosis
Duns Scotus, 70

Eckhart, Meister, 62, 193n30, 201n24

Feuerbach, Ludwig, 56, 80, 110, 119, 125, 129, 136–137, 140, 143, 157, 200n21
Fichte, Johann Gottlieb, 10, 34–35, 39, 108, 109, 119, 120–121, 145, 148, 152–156, 186n6, 188n35, 203n60–61, 209n16, 209n19, 209n26

figural interpretation/reading, 10, 68–78, 84, 142, 158, 195n65.
Firestone, Chris L., 29
Flatt, Johann Friedrich, 33
forgiveness, 14, 23–28, 29, 33, 45–50, 51–52, 121–122, 144, 161, 184n76, 189n40
Foucault, Michel, 12
Frierson, Patrick R., 15, 23
Fries, Jakob Friedrich, 84, 102, 109

Gadamer, Hans-Georg, 3, 158, 177n10
Goethe, Johann Wolfgang von, 32
Goeze, Johann Melchior, 31–32
grace, 9, 13–14, 17, 25, 28, 32, 40, 47, 161, 164, 180n2, 184n74
Guyer, Paul, 151

Hanna, Robert, 27
Hartmann, Klaus, 5, 178n23
Harris, Henry S., 47
Harris, Sam, 165
Hegel, Georg Wilhelm Friedrich, works
 *The Difference between Fichte's and Schelling's Systems of Philosophy*, 36, 151
 *Elements of the Philosophy of Right*, 39, 116
 *Encyclopedia of the Philosophical Sciences*, 38–39, 48, 78, 92, 97, 98, 105, 150, 153, 169
 *Faith and Knowledge*, 36, 39, 94, 127, 170
 *Lectures on the History of Philosophy*, 74–75, 115
 *Phenomenology of Spirit*, 2, 11, 36, 37, 45, 46, 48, 49, 50, 64, 73, 75, 122, 128, 130, 132–133, 140
 *Lectures on the Philosophy of Religion*, 35, 49, 61, 68, 71–72, 74, 82, 91, 94, 96, 106, 109, 111–112, 133, 134–135

 *Lectures on the Philosophy of Spirit*, 51
 *The Positivity of Christian Religion*, 35
 *Science of Logic*, 9, 37–38, 93, 106, 123, 140
Hammer, Espen, 57
Hare, John E., 16, 22, 30
Heidegger, Martin, 170
Hodgson, Peter C., 8, 102, 105, 106, 119, 135–136
Hölderlin, Friedrich, 34, 35
Horstmanm, Rolf-Peter, 4
Houlgate, Stephen, 72, 190n2
Hume, David, 41, 148

I (the), 10–11, 95–97, 105–124 *passim*, 144–145, 147–159 *passim*, 171, 174, 183n66
Idea (*Idee*), 10, 56, 78–84, 92, 102, 127, 133, 150, 151–152
image (*Bild*), 10, 71–73, 75, 80, 196n76

Jacobi, Friedrich Heinrich, 39, 84, 102, 109
Jacobs, Nathan, 29
Jaeschke, Walter, 105, 120, 128, 129, 168
Job, 26–28, 46, 167
Jüngel, Eberhard, 143

Kant, Immanuel, 5–6, 9, 13–30 *passim*, 39–44, 45–48, 56–57, 60, 63, 65–67, 76, 83, 85–92, 94, 102, 108, 117, 123, 126, 127–129, 138, 140, 142, 144, 147–148, 150–152, 156, 161–162, 171, 182n44
 *Anthropology from a Pragmatic Point of View*, 14–16
 *The Conflict of the Faculties*, 22, 28–29
 *Critique of Practical Reason*, 17–18, 19, 34, 130, 149–150

*Critique of Pure Reason*, 18, 33, 86, 87–88
*Groundwork of The Metaphysics of Morals*, 19
*The Metaphysics of Morals*, 17
*On the Miscarriage of All Philosophical Trials in Theodicy*, 26
*On a Supposed Right to Lie Because of Philanthropic Concerns*, 26–27
*Religion within the Boundaries of Bare Reason*, 13, 14–16, 18, 19, 20–23, 27, 31, 32–34, 39–40, 130
Kaufmann, Walter, 105
*kenosis*, 9, 45–52, 76, 135–136, 141, 143–144
kenotic sacrifice. *See* kenosis
Kreines, James, 56, 59
Kristeller, Paul, 3
Küng, Hans, 135

Lauer, Quentin, 205n21
left Hegelians, 10, 56, 80, 110, 119, 125, 144, 145, 157
Leibniz, Gottfried Wilhelm, 85, 87, 90, 98
Lessing, Gotthold, 31, 187n
Lewis, Thomas A., 106, 200n14
Locke, John, 60, 148
Longuenesse, Béatrice, 6, 57–58, 63, 147
Luther, Martin, 73

Magee, Glenn Alexander, 60
Malpas, Jeff, 147
Marx, Karl, 125
mediated objectivity, 6, 10, 48, 60, 63–68, 71–73, 75–78, 84, 96, 99–100, 102, 109–110, 123, 154–155, 157 162–164, 167, 170–171, 174–175, 179n27
Michalson, Gordon E. 24, 181n35
Mozart, Wolfgang Amadeus, 73

Munchausen, Baron, 64

Nietzsche, Friedrich, 9, 125, 144, 147, 204n2
Nuzzo, Angelica, 73, 195n65

Ockham, William of, 70
O'Regan, Cyril, 2, 62, 105, 117, 136
Origen, 69, 72
Orwell, George, 68

Palmquist, Stephen R., 25
perspectivism, 7, 15, 22, 45–50, 51–52, 66, 100–102, 163, 181n35, 183n67
Plato, 93
Pinkard, Terry, 4, 8, 45, 49, 51–52, 57, 137–138
Pippin, Robert B., 3, 4, 5–6, 51, 52, 57, 58, 138
post-Kantian interpretation. *See* revisionist interpretation
prototype (*Vorbild*), 18, 35, 39, 45, 117, 130, 144, 161, 181n35, 182n44, 184n76

qualified revisionist interpretation, 6–8, 57–60, 63, 68, 76, 79

Reardon, Bernard, 29, 183n67
recognition, 7, 37, 46, 48–51, 57, 59–60, 64–65, 76–77, 80, 83, 93, 101–102, 107–109, 111, 116, 118–123, 125–145 *passim*, 154–158, 163–164, 176
Redding, Paul, 4–6, 7–8, 43, 52–53, 57, 59–60, 63, 64, 79, 99–100, 115, 137, 144, 191n7, 191n12, 192n23, 203n60
representation (*Vorstellung*), 8, 9, 37–38, 60–61, 67, 71, 73, 78, 91–92, 103, 108, 110, 116–117,

representation *(continued)*
  122–123, 130–131, 133, 139, 144, 157, 192n26
revisionist interpretation, 4–6, 8–9, 52, 56–60, 66, 106, 108, 126, 191n7
Ricoeur, Paul, 171, 172
right Hegelians, 56, 80, 125, 144, 157
Rist, Johann, 134

sacrifice, 13–14, 20–25, 28, 29–30, 37, 46, 48–50, 75, 127, 133, 135, 144, 162, 183n65, 184n74. *See also* kenosis
Sartre, Jean-Paul, 144
Schelling, Friedrich Wilhelm Joseph, 34, 35, 120–121
Schickler, Jonael Angelus, 203–204n
Schleiermacher, Friedrich, 40, 84, 102, 109, 112
Schmidt, Dennis, 154
Semler, Johann Salomo, 31, 32
Singleton, Charles, 69, 70
Smith, Quentin, 165, 166–167, 168
Spinoza, Baruch, 61, 140
Stern, Robert, 56, 188n36
Storr, Gottlob Christian, 32–35

Strauss, David, 56, 110, 119, 157
subjectivism, 7, 10–11, 39–45, 47, 52–53, 63, 65, 67, 78, 84, 91, 102, 107–112, 118–124, 145, 147–159 *passim*, 162, 164, 174

Taylor, Charles, 4
Tertullian, 69, 72, 73
Thielicke, Helmuth, 137–138
trinity, 10, 38, 55, 58, 76–78, 84, 95, 105–124 *passim*, 132–133, 141–142, 144, 164, 167, 190n67, 201n28, 202n31

*vorstellung*. *See* representation

Wallace, Robert M., 106
Wendte, Martin, 106, 120
Wildt, Andreas, 191n7
Williams, Robert, 2–3, 5, 8, 50, 58, 60, 62, 111–112, 120, 126, 134, 136, 137–138, 140–141, 143
Wood, Allen W., 24, 30

Zupančič, Alenka 26
Zwingli, Huldrych, 73

www.ingramcontent.com/pod-product-compliance
Ingram Content Group UK Ltd.
Pitfield, Milton Keynes, MK11 3LW, UK
UKHW041917140426
5217IPUK00013B/202